TALES FROM

HARROW

◆ LOST ONES ◆

COUNTY™

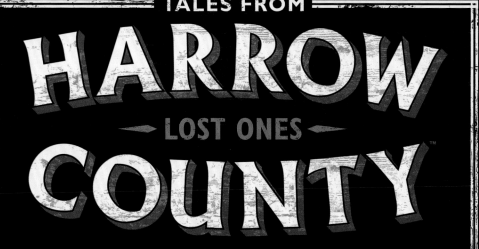

TALES FROM
HARROW
◄ LOST ONES ►
COUNTY

Created by
CULLEN BUNN
TYLER CROOK

Script
CULLEN BUNN

Art
EMILY SCHNALL

Lettering
TYLER CROOK

Cover and Chapter Breaks
EMILY SCHNALL

President and Publisher
MIKE RICHARDSON

Editor
DANIEL CHABON

Assistant Editor
CHUCK HOWITT-LEASE

Assistant Editor
MISHA GEHR

Designer
KEITH WOOD

Digital Art Technician
JOSIE CHRISTENSEN

NEIL HANKERSON Executive Vice President · **TOM WEDDLE** Chief Financial Officer · **DALE LaFOUNTAIN** Chief Information Officer
TIM WIESCH Vice President of Licensing · **MATT PARKINSON** Vice President of Marketing
VANESSA TODD-HOLMES Vice President of Production and Scheduling · **MARK BERNARDI** Vice President of Book Trade and Digital Sales
RANDY LAHRMAN Vice President of Product Development and Sales · **KEN LIZZI** General Counsel · **DAVE MARSHALL** Editor in Chief
DAVEY ESTRADA Editorial Director · **CHRIS WARNER** Senior Books Editor · **CARA O'NEIL** Senior Director of Marketing
CARY GRAZZINI Director of Specialty Projects · **LIA RIBACCHI** Art Director · **MICHAEL GOMBOS** Senior Director of Licensed Publications
KARI YADRO Director of Custom Programs · **KARI TORSON** Director of International Licensing · **CHRISTINA NIECE** Director of Scheduling

Published by Dark Horse Books
A division of Dark Horse Comics LLC
10956 SE Main Street
Milwaukie, OR 97222

First edition: January 2023
Ebook ISBN 978-1-50672-996-1
Trade Paperback ISBN 978-1-50672-995-4

Comic Shop Locator Service: comicshoplocator.com

Tales from Harrow County Volume 3: Lost Ones

This volume collects Tales from Harrow County: Lost Ones #1–#4.

10 9 8 7 6 5 4 3 2 1
Printed in China

DarkHorse.com

MIX
Paper from
responsible sources
FSC® C169962

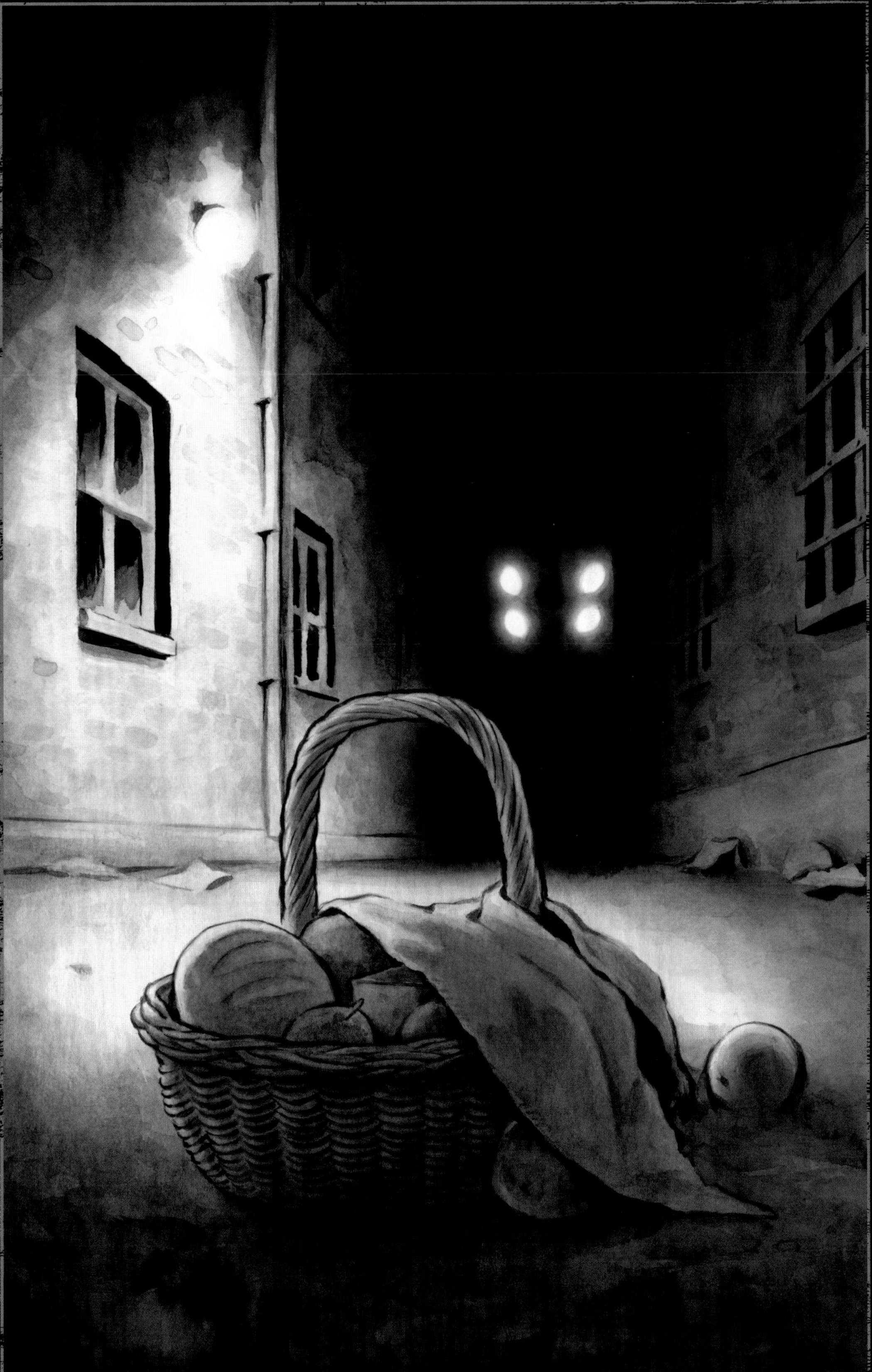

ONE

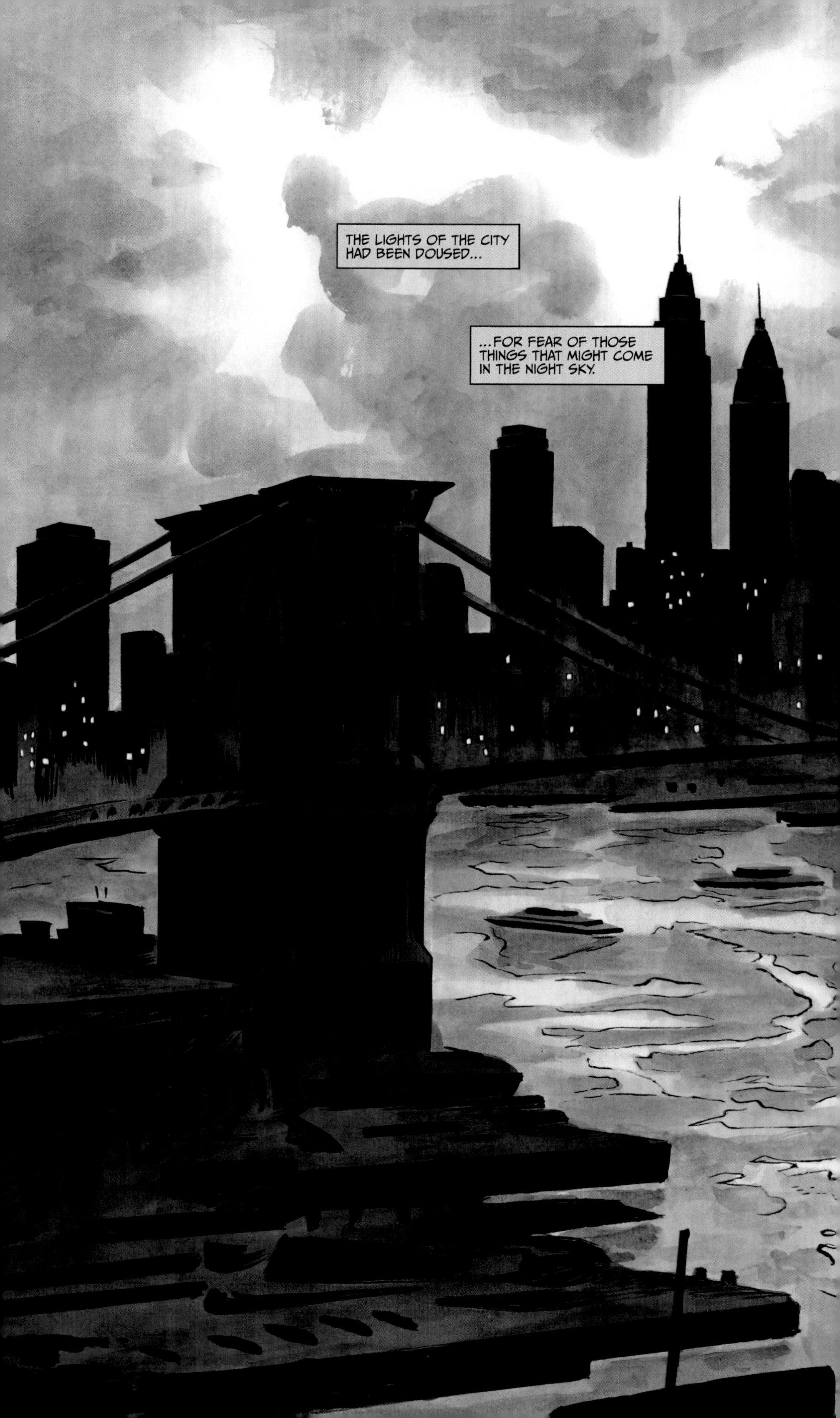
THE LIGHTS OF THE CITY HAD BEEN DOUSED...
...FOR FEAR OF THOSE THINGS THAT MIGHT COME IN THE NIGHT SKY.

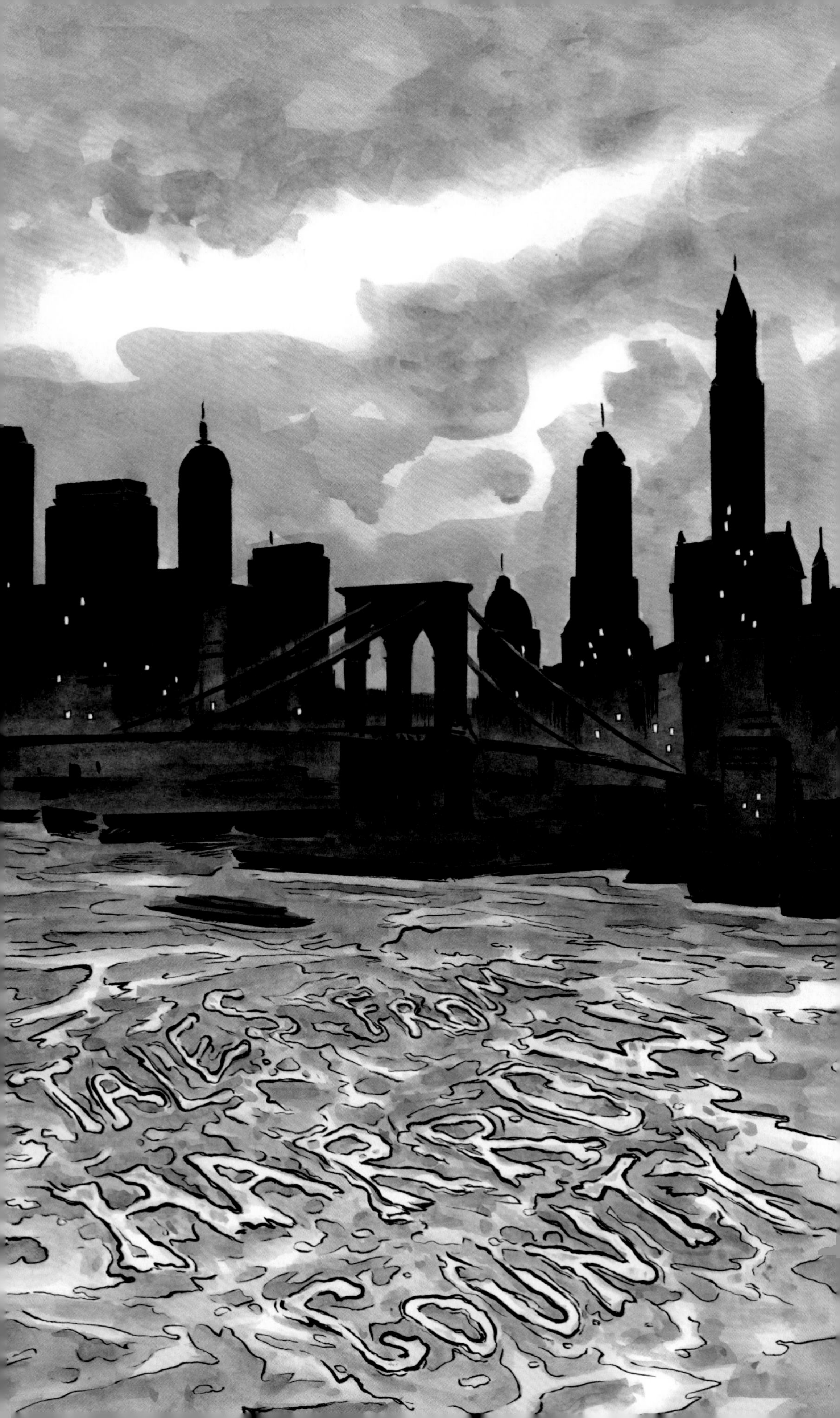
TALES FROM
HARROW
COUNTY

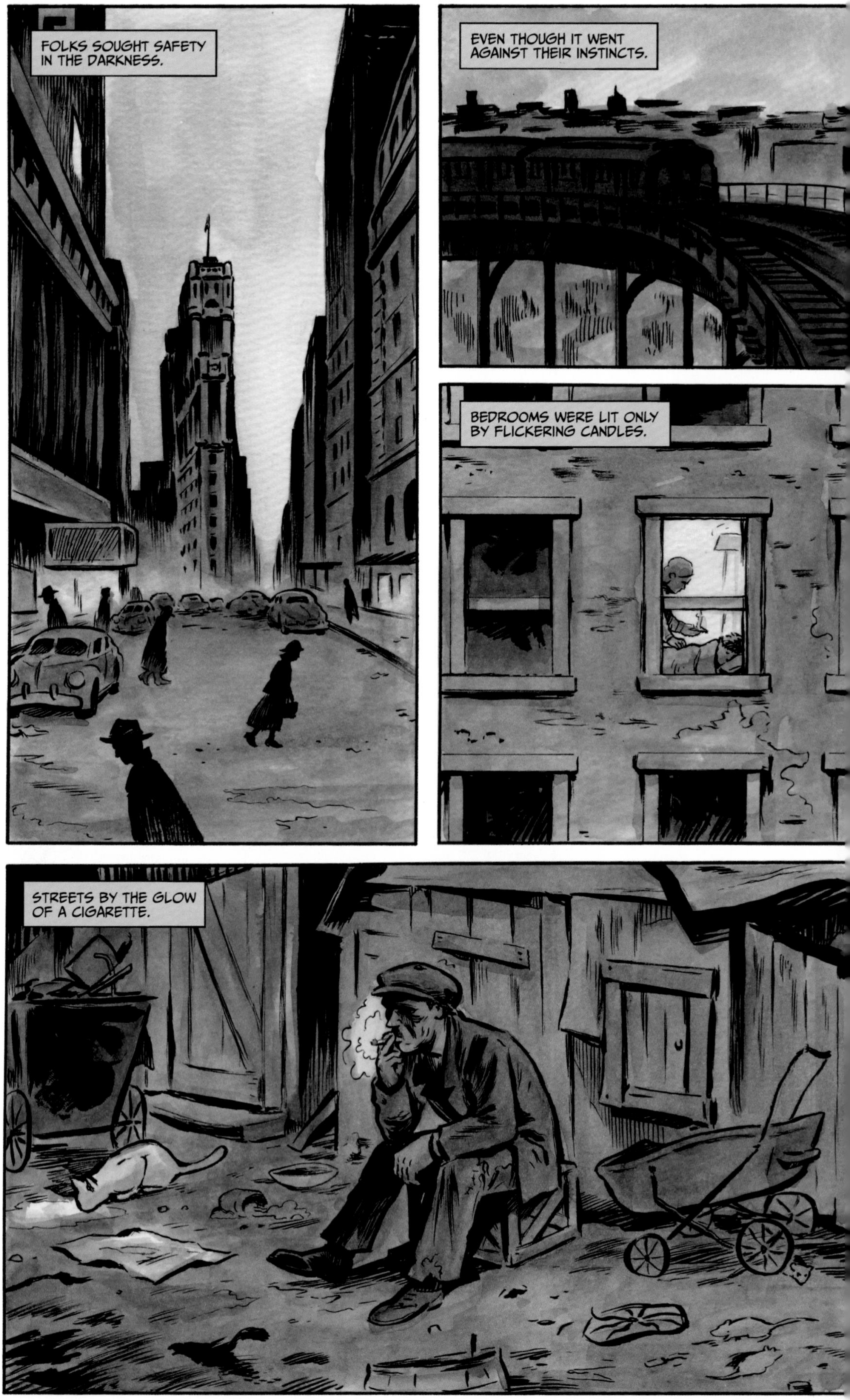
FOLKS SOUGHT SAFETY IN THE DARKNESS.
EVEN THOUGH IT WENT AGAINST THEIR INSTINCTS.
BEDROOMS WERE LIT ONLY BY FLICKERING CANDLES.
STREETS BY THE GLOW OF A CIGARETTE.

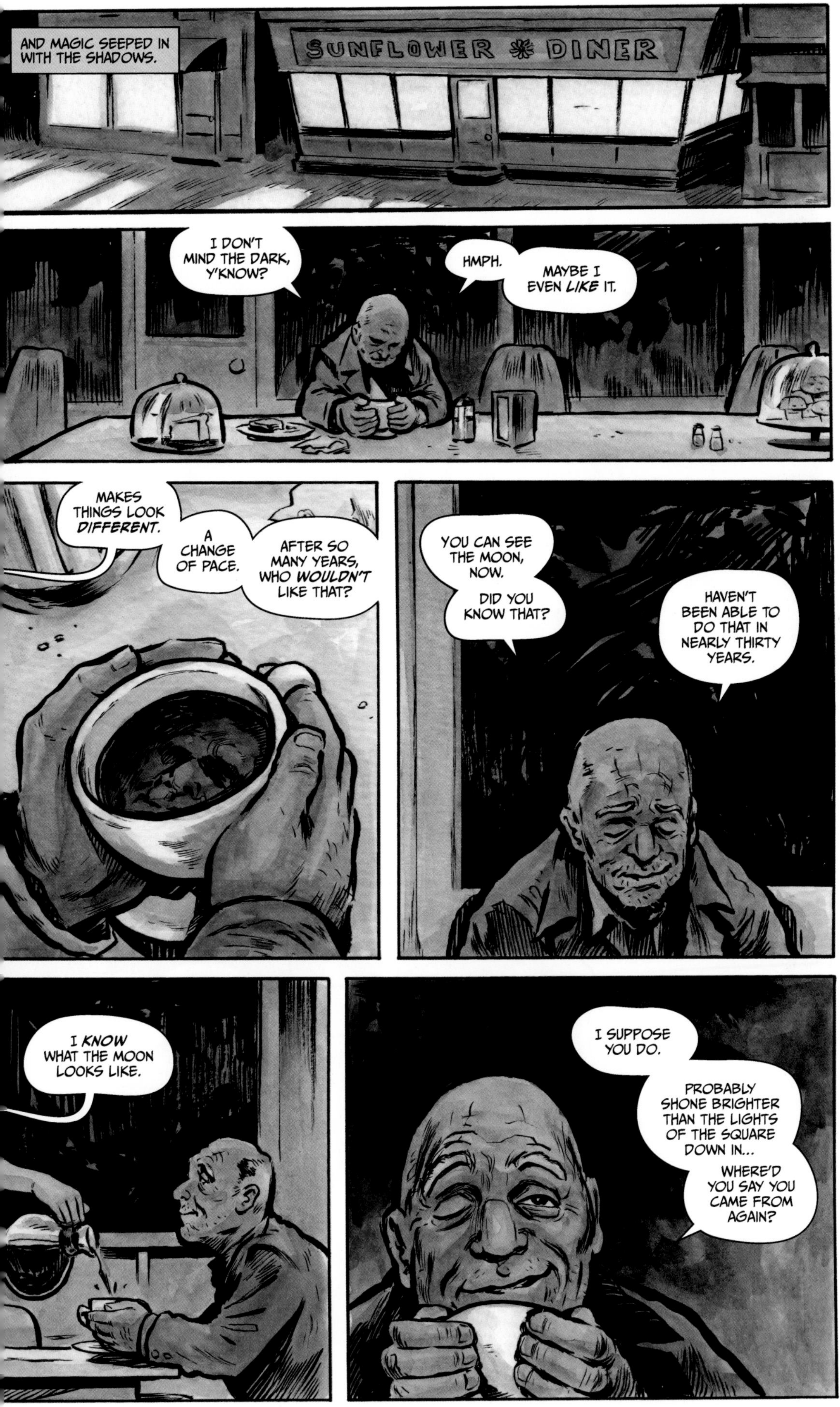
AND MAGIC SEEPED IN WITH THE SHADOWS.
SUNFLOWER DINER
I DON'T MIND THE DARK, Y'KNOW?
HMPH.
MAYBE I EVEN *LIKE* IT.
MAKES THINGS LOOK *DIFFERENT.*
A CHANGE OF PACE.
AFTER SO MANY YEARS, WHO *WOULDN'T* LIKE THAT?
YOU CAN SEE THE MOON, NOW.
DID YOU KNOW THAT?
HAVEN'T BEEN ABLE TO DO THAT IN NEARLY THIRTY YEARS.
I *KNOW* WHAT THE MOON LOOKS LIKE.
I SUPPOSE YOU DO.
PROBABLY SHONE BRIGHTER THAN THE LIGHTS OF THE SQUARE DOWN IN...
WHERE'D YOU SAY YOU CAME FROM AGAIN?

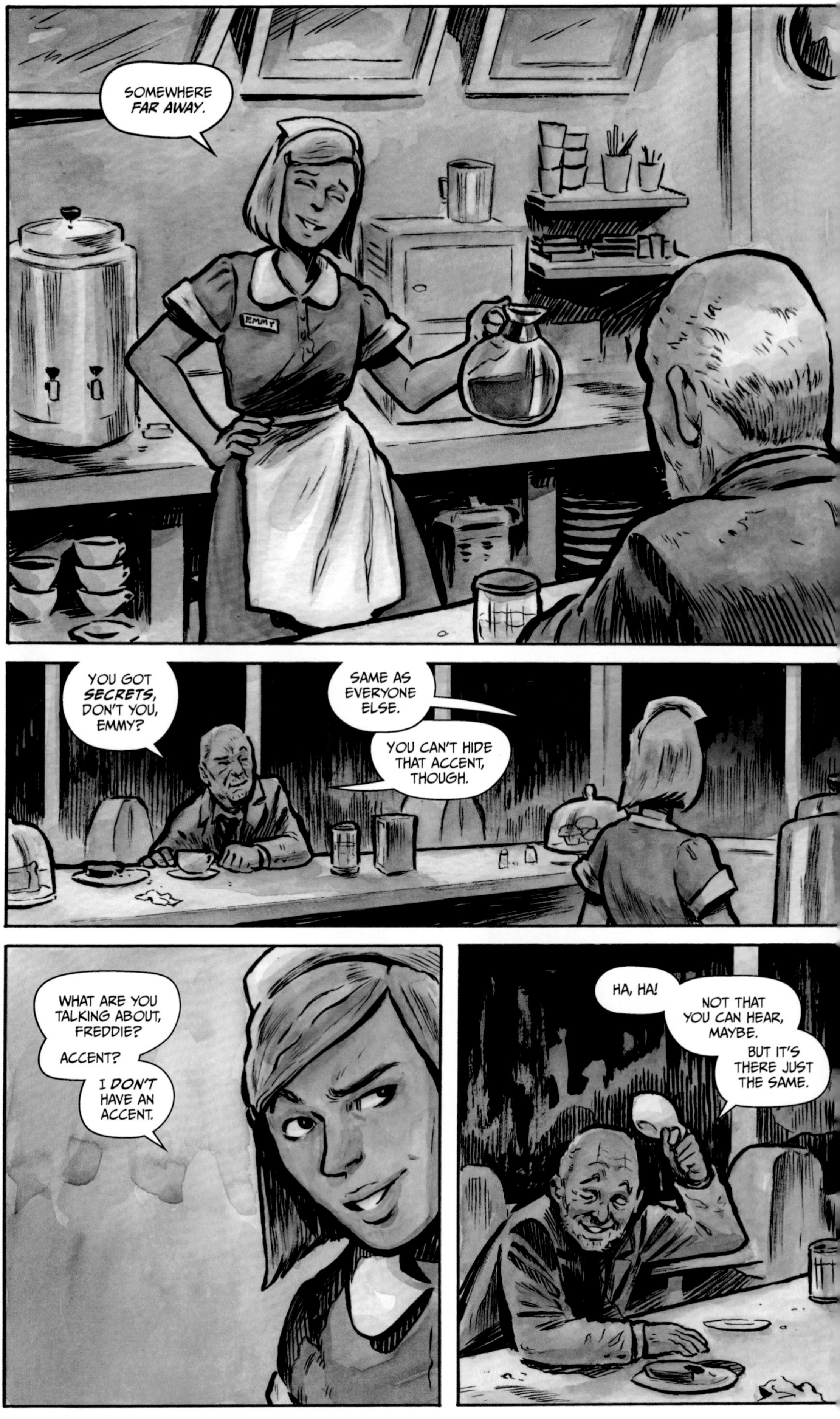
SOMEWHERE *FAR AWAY.*
YOU GOT ***SECRETS***, DON'T YOU, EMMY?
SAME AS EVERYONE ELSE.
YOU CAN'T HIDE THAT ACCENT, THOUGH.
WHAT ARE YOU TALKING ABOUT, FREDDIE?
ACCENT?
I ***DON'T*** HAVE AN ACCENT.
HA, HA!
NOT THAT YOU CAN HEAR, MAYBE.
BUT IT'S THERE JUST THE SAME.

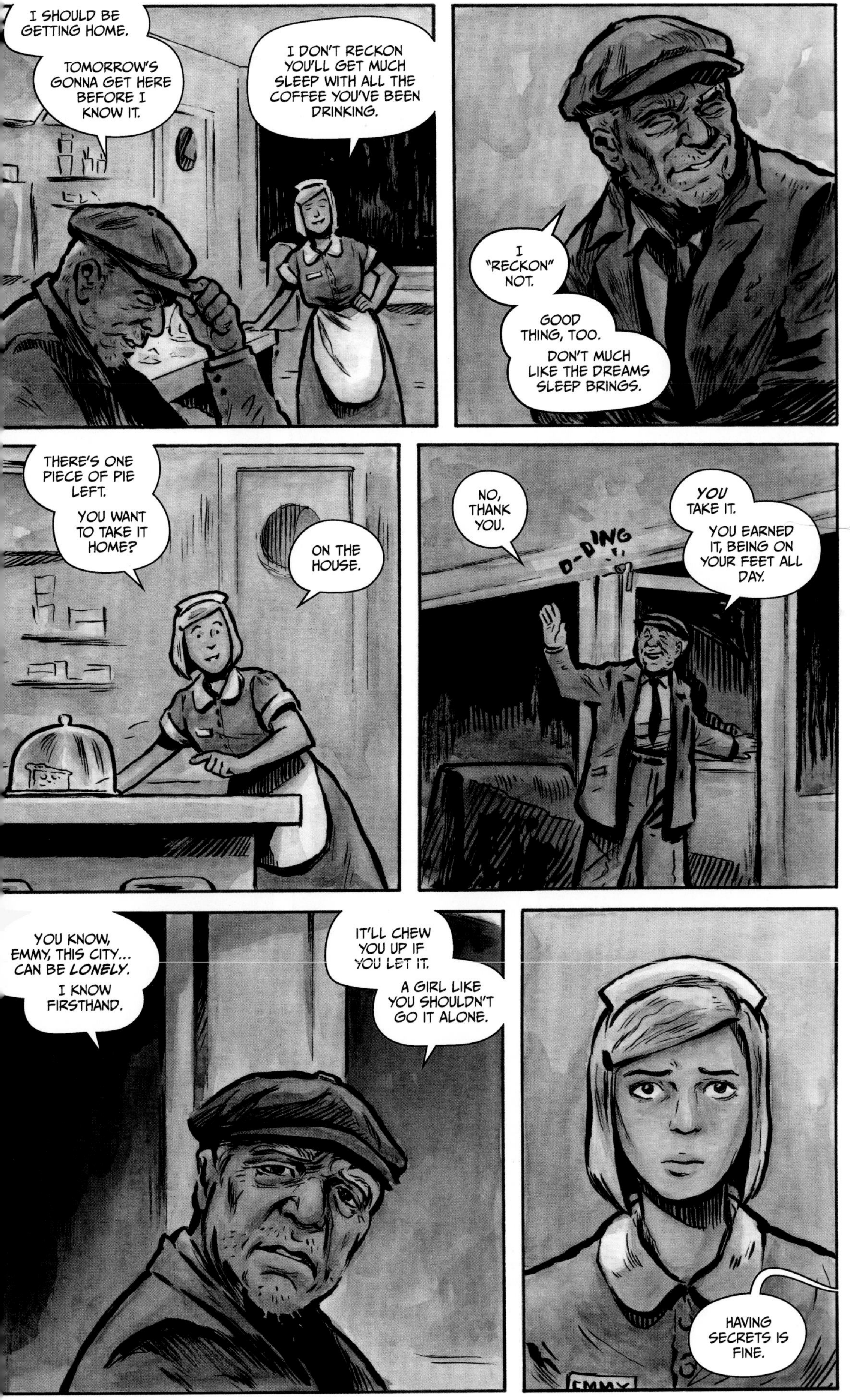
I SHOULD BE GETTING HOME.
TOMORROW'S GONNA GET HERE BEFORE I KNOW IT.
I DON'T RECKON YOU'LL GET MUCH SLEEP WITH ALL THE COFFEE YOU'VE BEEN DRINKING.
I "RECKON" NOT.
GOOD THING, TOO.
DON'T MUCH LIKE THE DREAMS SLEEP BRINGS.
THERE'S ONE PIECE OF PIE LEFT.
YOU WANT TO TAKE IT HOME?
ON THE HOUSE.
NO, THANK YOU.
D-DING
YOU TAKE IT.
YOU EARNED IT, BEING ON YOUR FEET ALL DAY.
YOU KNOW, EMMY, THIS CITY... CAN BE *LONELY*.
I KNOW FIRSTHAND.
IT'LL CHEW YOU UP IF YOU LET IT.
A GIRL LIKE YOU SHOULDN'T GO IT ALONE.
HAVING SECRETS IS FINE.

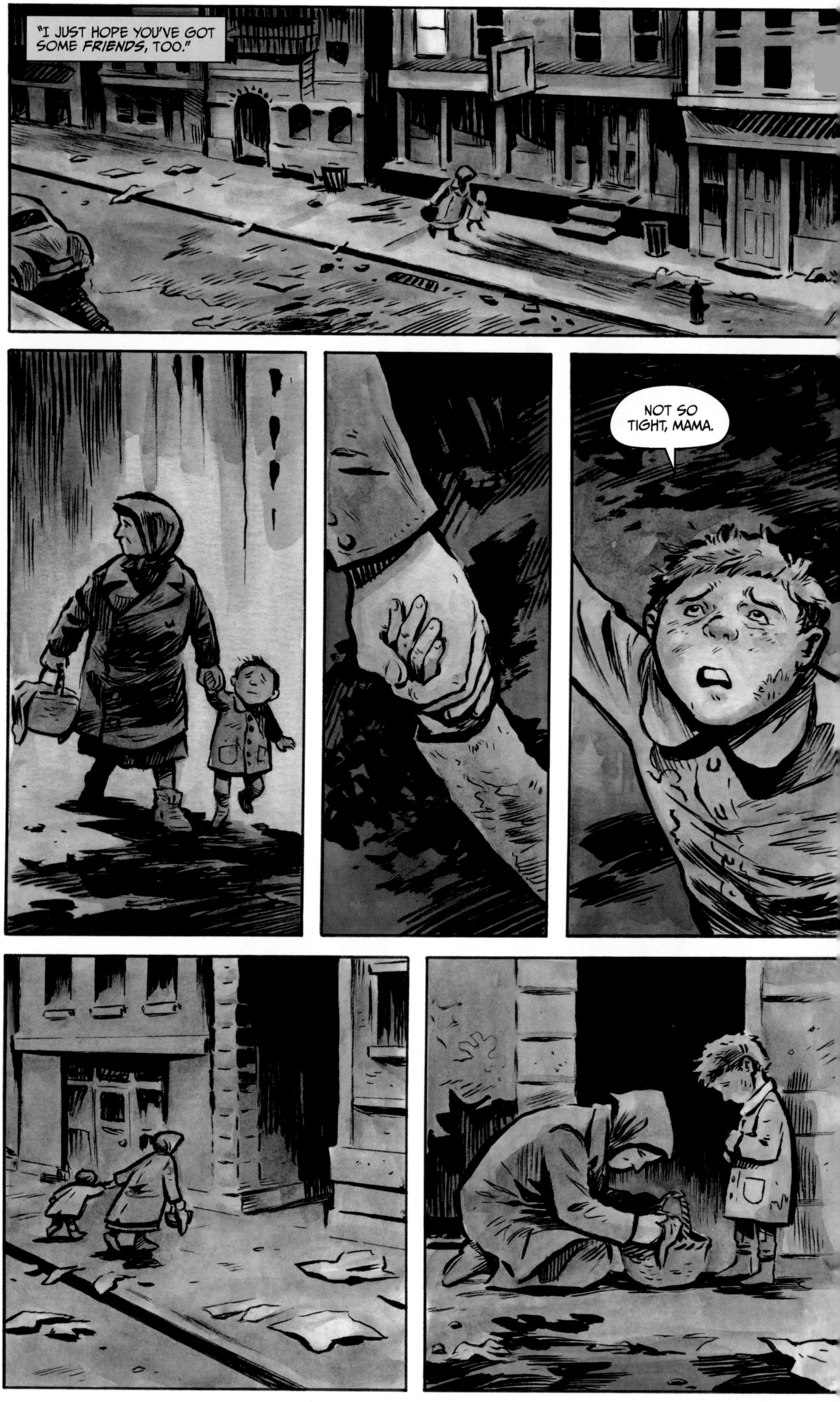
"I JUST HOPE YOU'VE GOT SOME *FRIENDS*, TOO."
NOT SO TIGHT, MAMA.

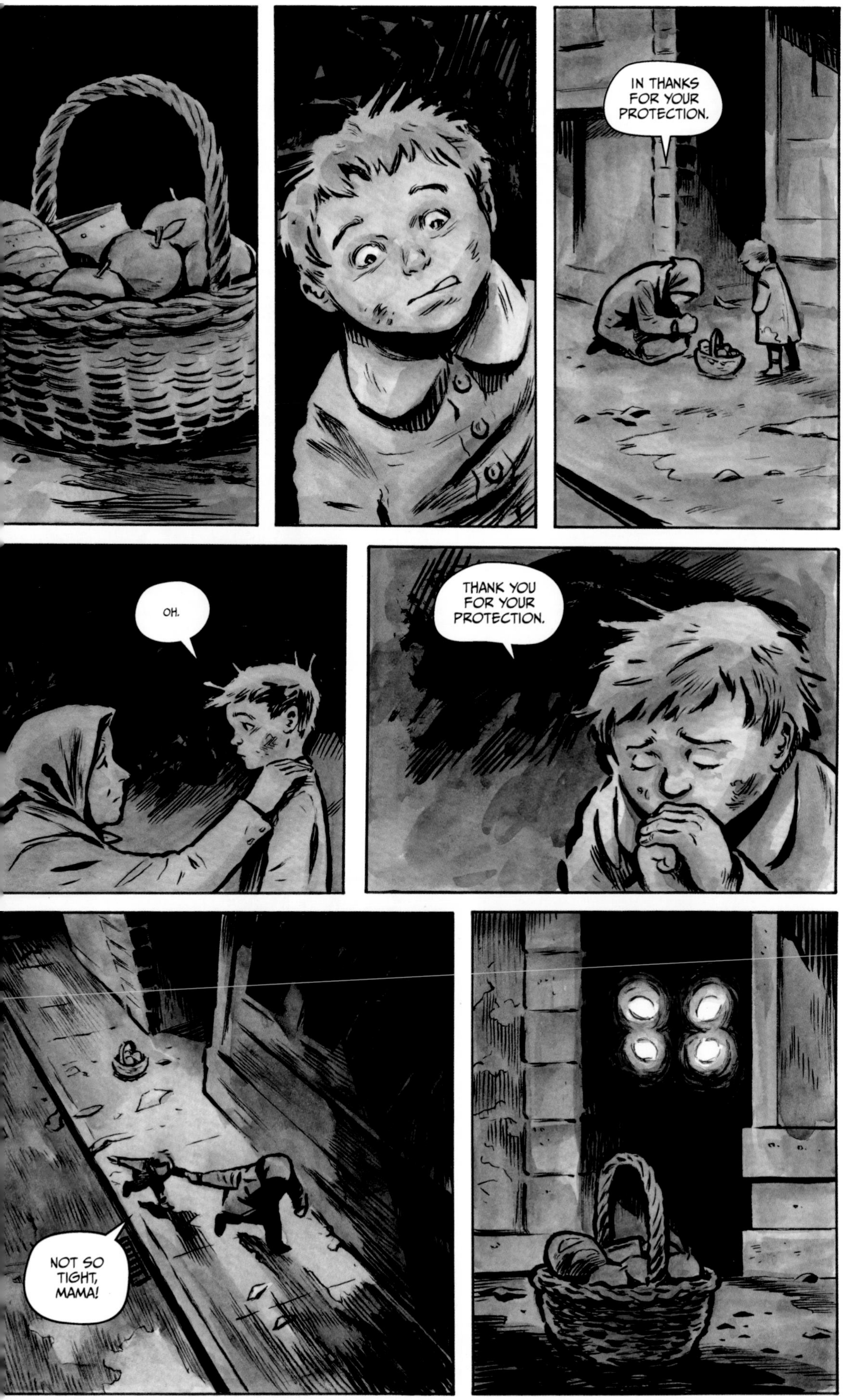
IN THANKS FOR YOUR PROTECTION.
OH.
THANK YOU FOR YOUR PROTECTION.
NOT SO TIGHT, MAMA!

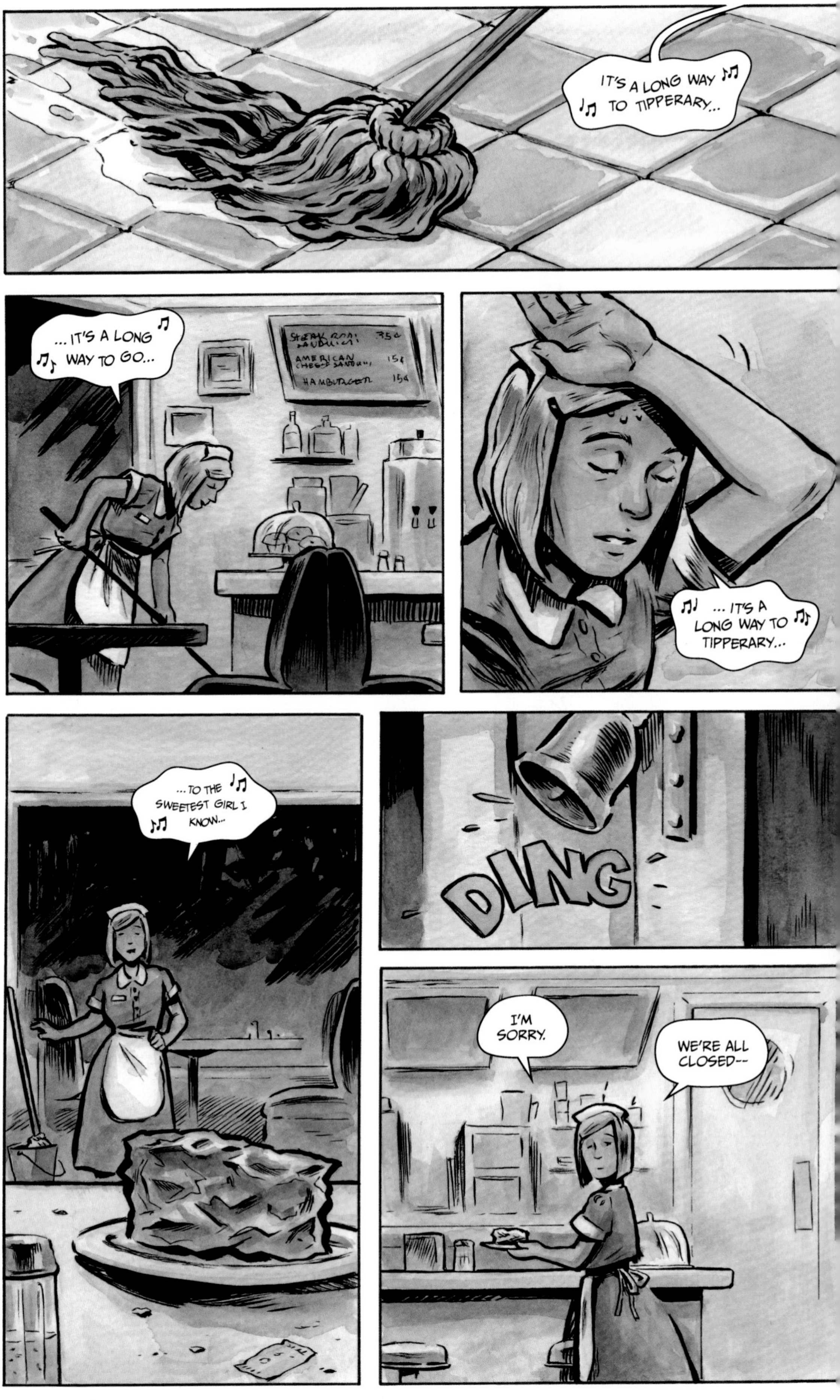

IT'S A LONG WAY ♪♫ ♩♫ TO TIPPERARY...
... IT'S A LONG ♫ ♫♪ WAY TO GO...
AMERICAN 15¢
HAMBURGER 15¢
♫♩ ... IT'S A LONG WAY TO ♫♪ TIPPERARY...
...TO THE ♩♫ SWEETEST GIRL I ♪♫ KNOW...
DING
I'M SORRY.
WE'RE ALL CLOSED--

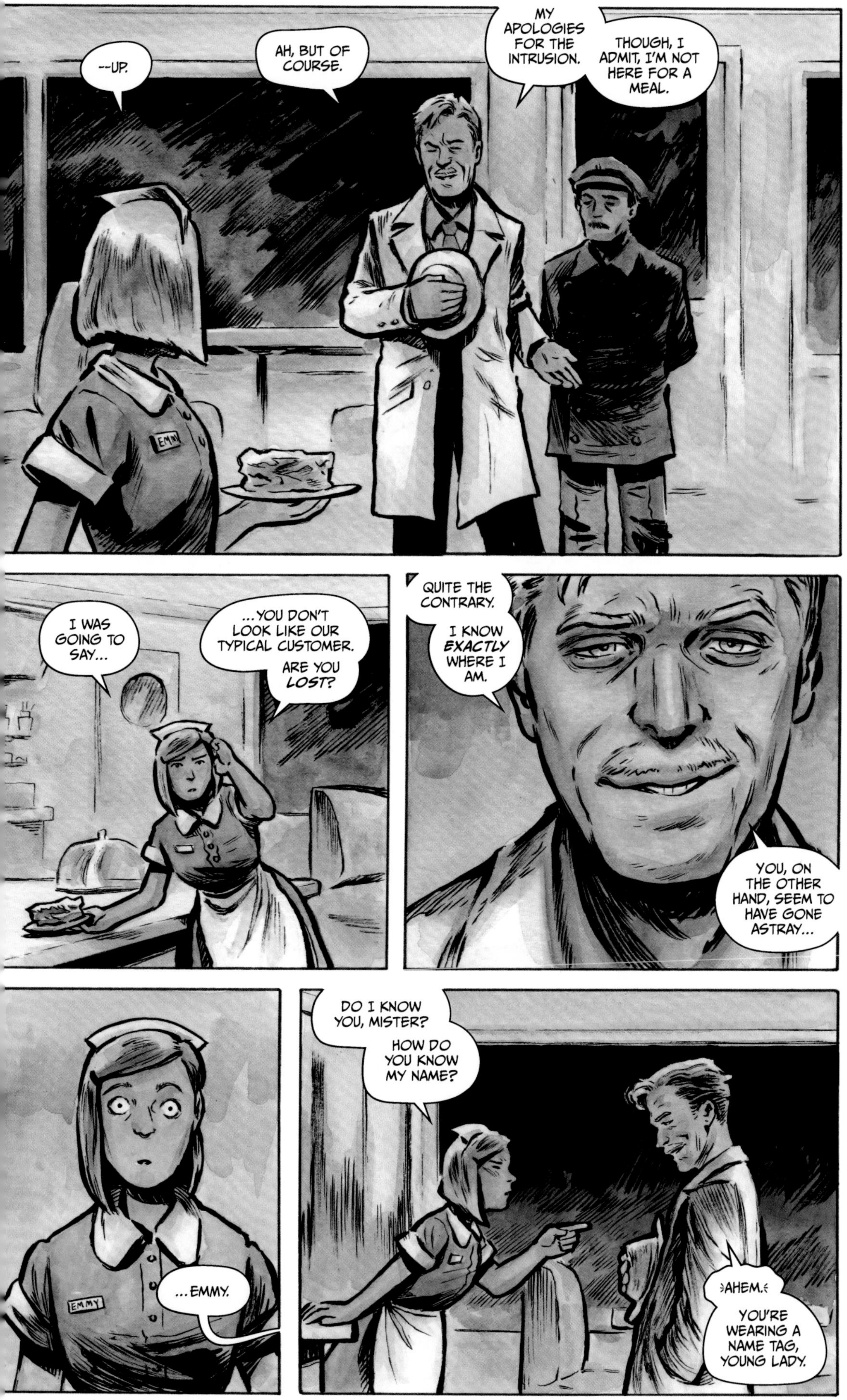
--UP.
AH, BUT OF COURSE.
MY APOLOGIES FOR THE INTRUSION.
THOUGH, I ADMIT, I'M NOT HERE FOR A MEAL.
EMM
I WAS GOING TO SAY...
...YOU DON'T LOOK LIKE OUR TYPICAL CUSTOMER.
ARE YOU *LOST*?
QUITE THE CONTRARY.
I KNOW *EXACTLY* WHERE I AM.
YOU, ON THE OTHER HAND, SEEM TO HAVE GONE ASTRAY...
EMMY
...EMMY.
DO I KNOW YOU, MISTER?
HOW DO YOU KNOW MY NAME?
AHEM.
YOU'RE WEARING A NAME TAG, YOUNG LADY.

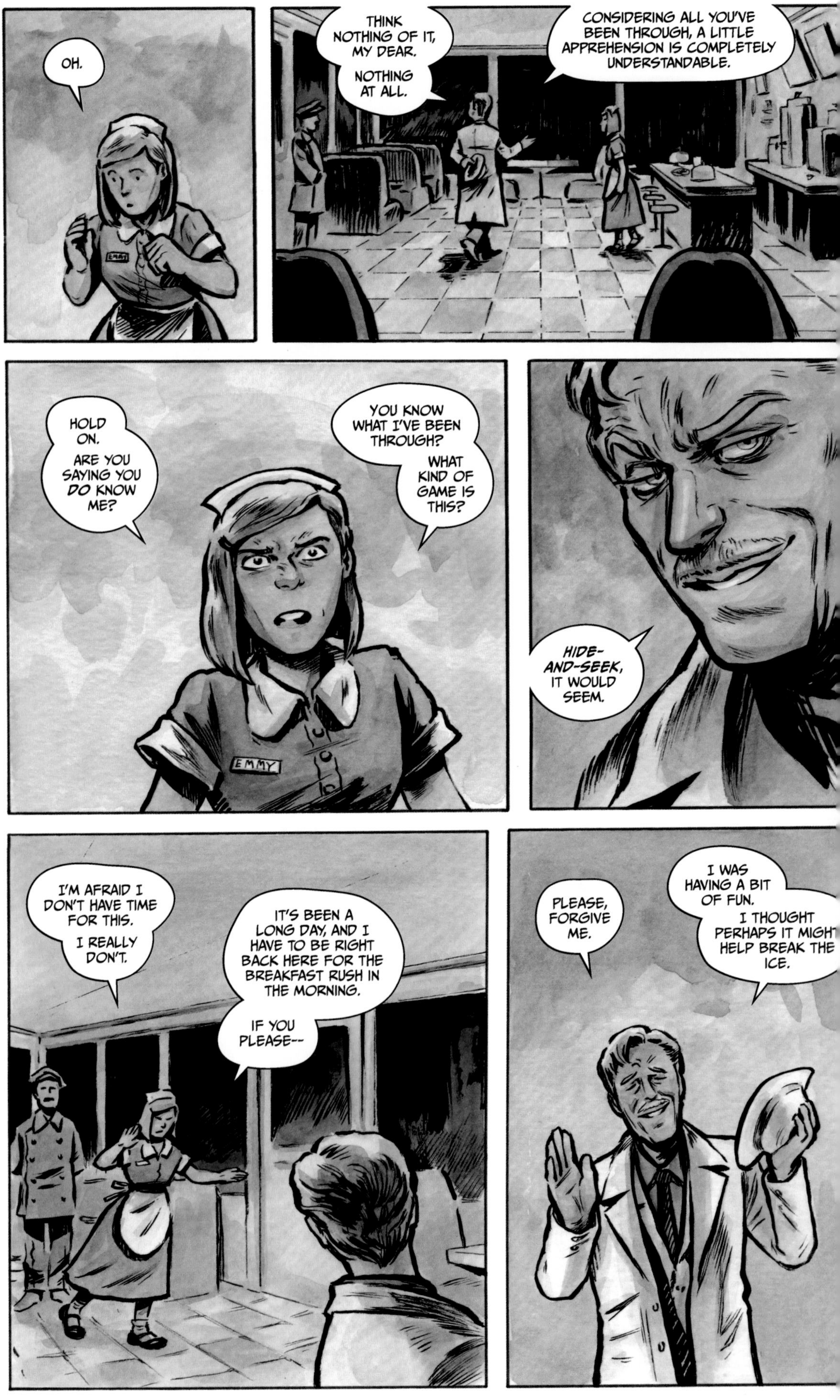

OH.
THINK NOTHING OF IT, MY DEAR.
NOTHING AT ALL.
CONSIDERING ALL YOU'VE BEEN THROUGH, A LITTLE APPREHENSION IS COMPLETELY UNDERSTANDABLE.
EMMY
HOLD ON.
ARE YOU SAYING YOU *DO* KNOW ME?
YOU KNOW WHAT I'VE BEEN THROUGH?
WHAT KIND OF GAME IS THIS?
EMMY
HIDE-AND-SEEK, IT WOULD SEEM.
I'M AFRAID I DON'T HAVE TIME FOR THIS.
I REALLY DON'T.
IT'S BEEN A LONG DAY, AND I HAVE TO BE RIGHT BACK HERE FOR THE BREAKFAST RUSH IN THE MORNING.
IF YOU PLEASE--
PLEASE, FORGIVE ME.
I WAS HAVING A BIT OF FUN.
I THOUGHT PERHAPS IT MIGHT HELP BREAK THE ICE.

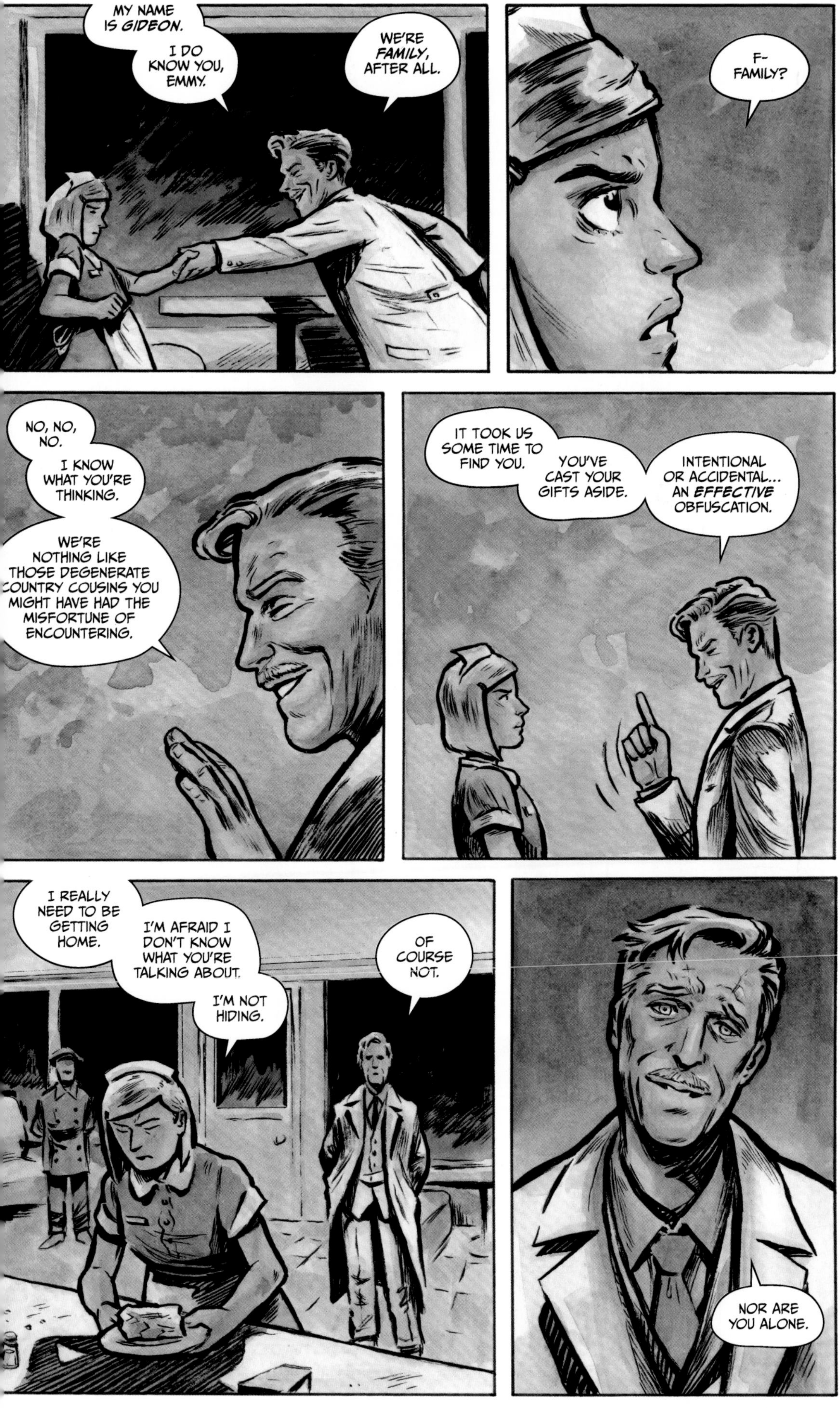
MY NAME IS GIDEON.
I DO KNOW YOU, EMMY.
WE'RE FAMILY, AFTER ALL.
F-FAMILY?
NO, NO, NO.
I KNOW WHAT YOU'RE THINKING.
WE'RE NOTHING LIKE THOSE DEGENERATE COUNTRY COUSINS YOU MIGHT HAVE HAD THE MISFORTUNE OF ENCOUNTERING.
IT TOOK US SOME TIME TO FIND YOU.
YOU'VE CAST YOUR GIFTS ASIDE.
INTENTIONAL OR ACCIDENTAL... AN EFFECTIVE OBFUSCATION.
I REALLY NEED TO BE GETTING HOME.
I'M AFRAID I DON'T KNOW WHAT YOU'RE TALKING ABOUT.
I'M NOT HIDING.
OF COURSE NOT.
NOR ARE YOU ALONE.

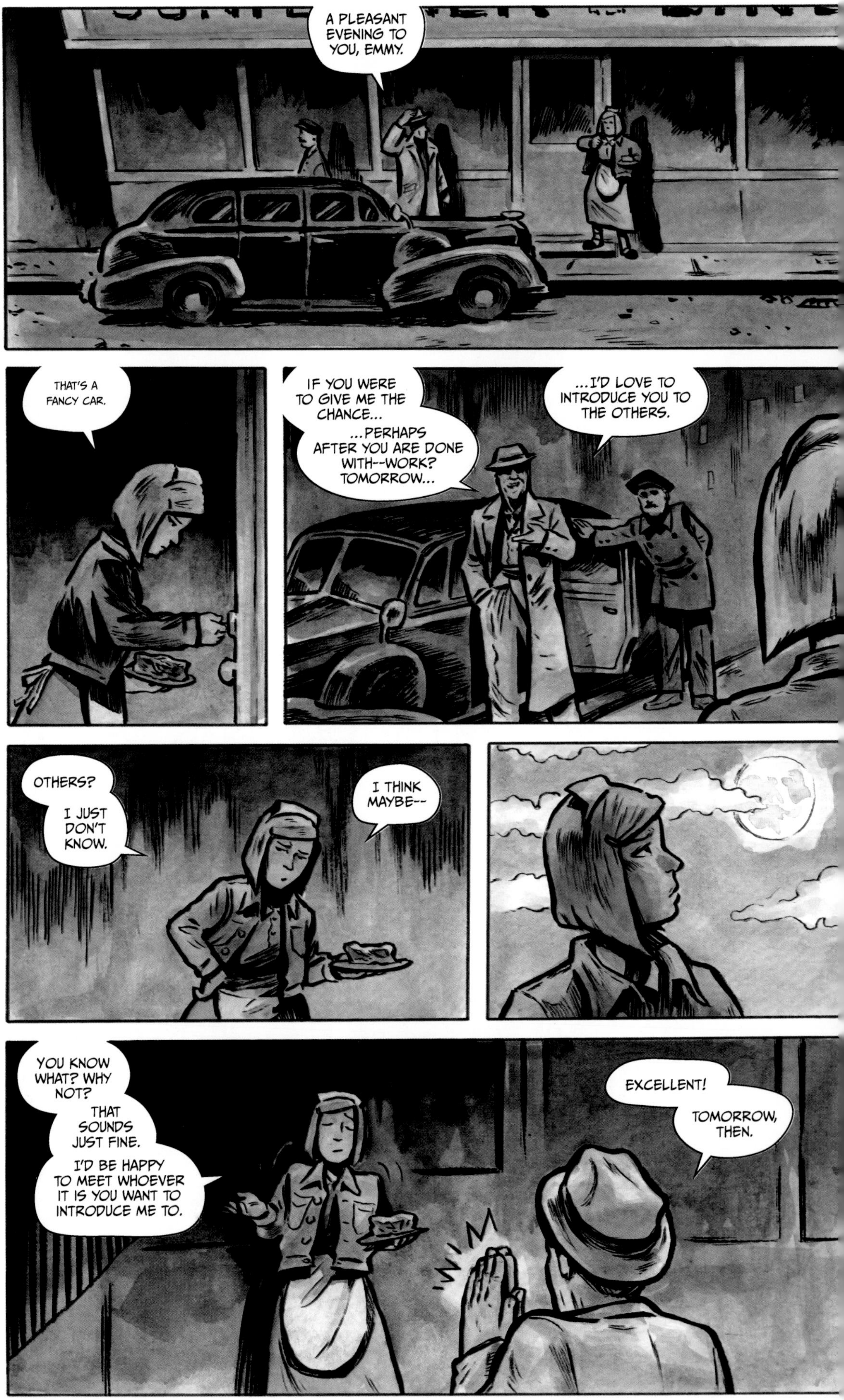
A PLEASANT EVENING TO YOU, EMMY.
THAT'S A FANCY CAR.
IF YOU WERE TO GIVE ME THE CHANCE...
...PERHAPS AFTER YOU ARE DONE WITH--WORK? TOMORROW...
...I'D LOVE TO INTRODUCE YOU TO THE OTHERS.
OTHERS?
I JUST DON'T KNOW.
I THINK MAYBE--
YOU KNOW WHAT? WHY NOT?
THAT SOUNDS JUST FINE.
I'D BE HAPPY TO MEET WHOEVER IT IS YOU WANT TO INTRODUCE ME TO.
EXCELLENT!
TOMORROW, THEN.

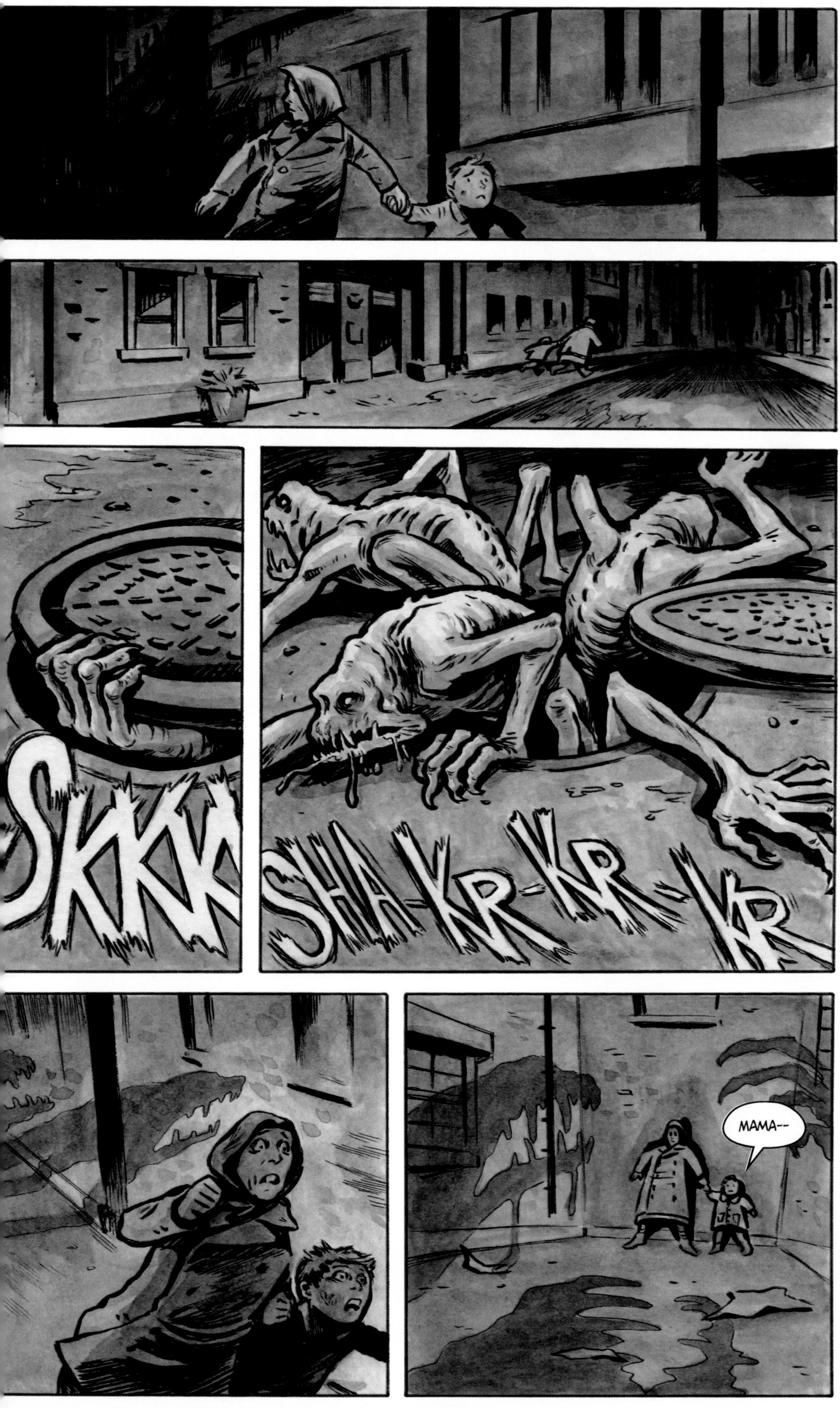
SKKK
SHA-KR-KR-KR
MAMA--

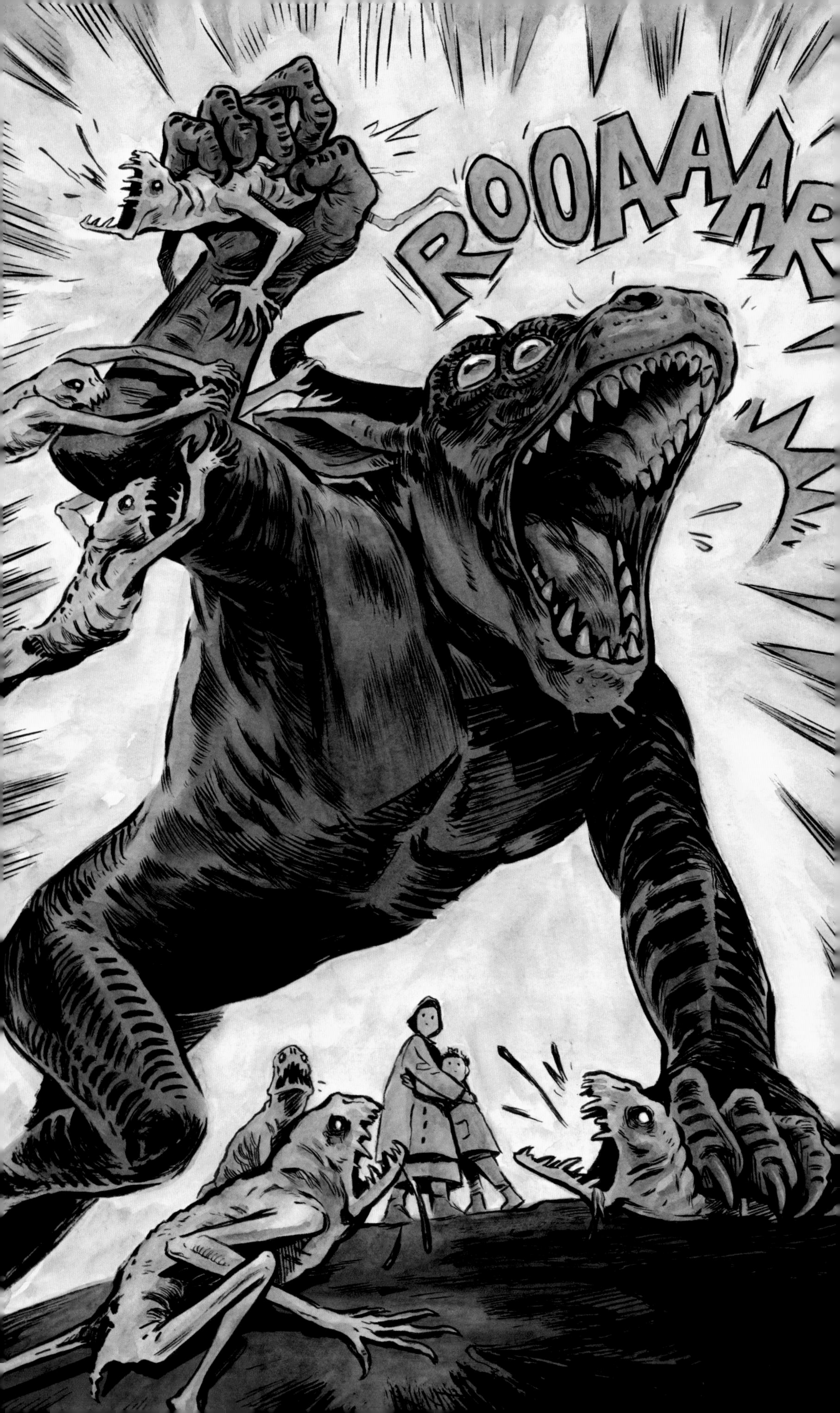
ROOAAAR

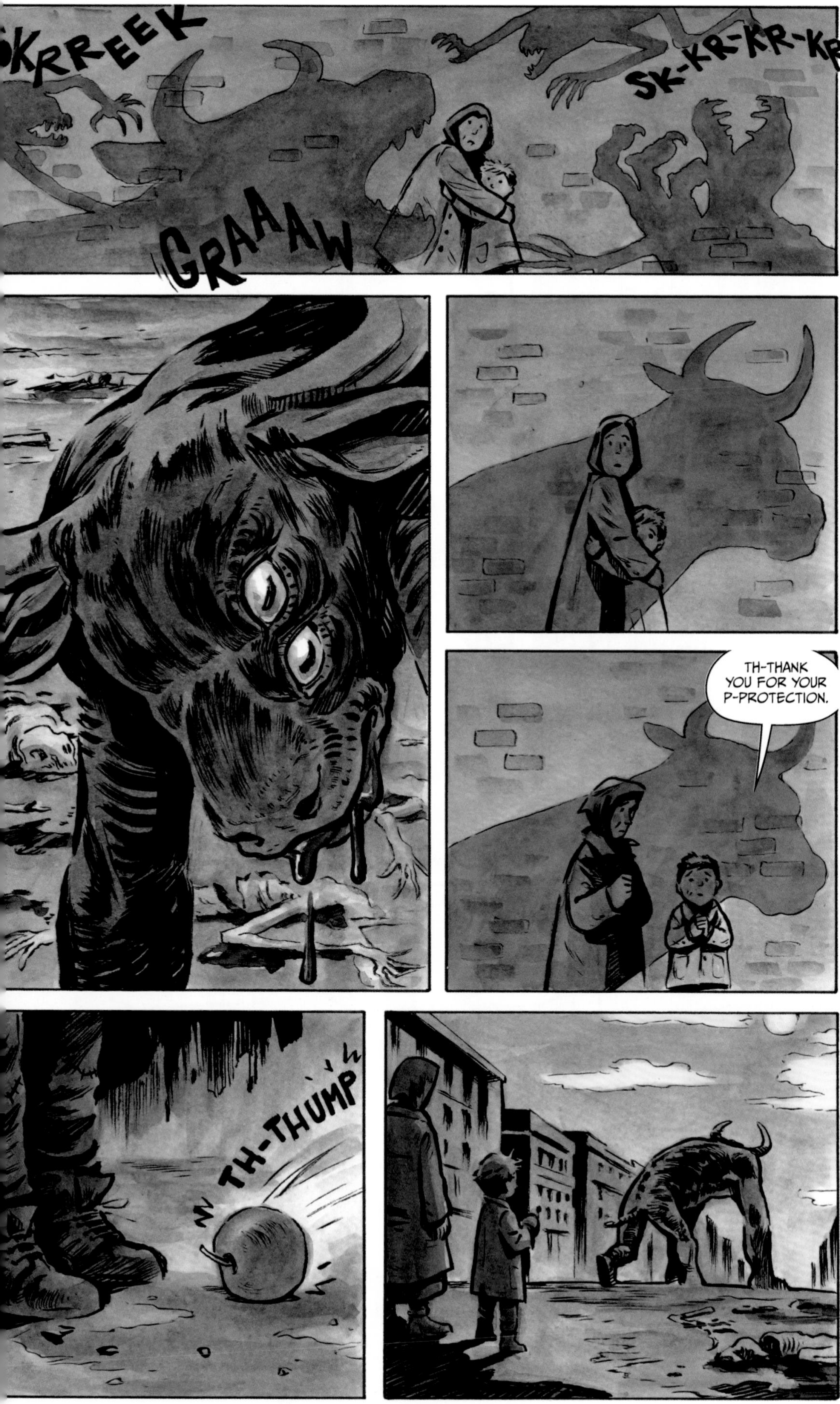
SKRREEK
SK-KR-KR-KR
GRAAAAW
TH-THANK YOU FOR YOUR P-PROTECTION.
TH-THUMP

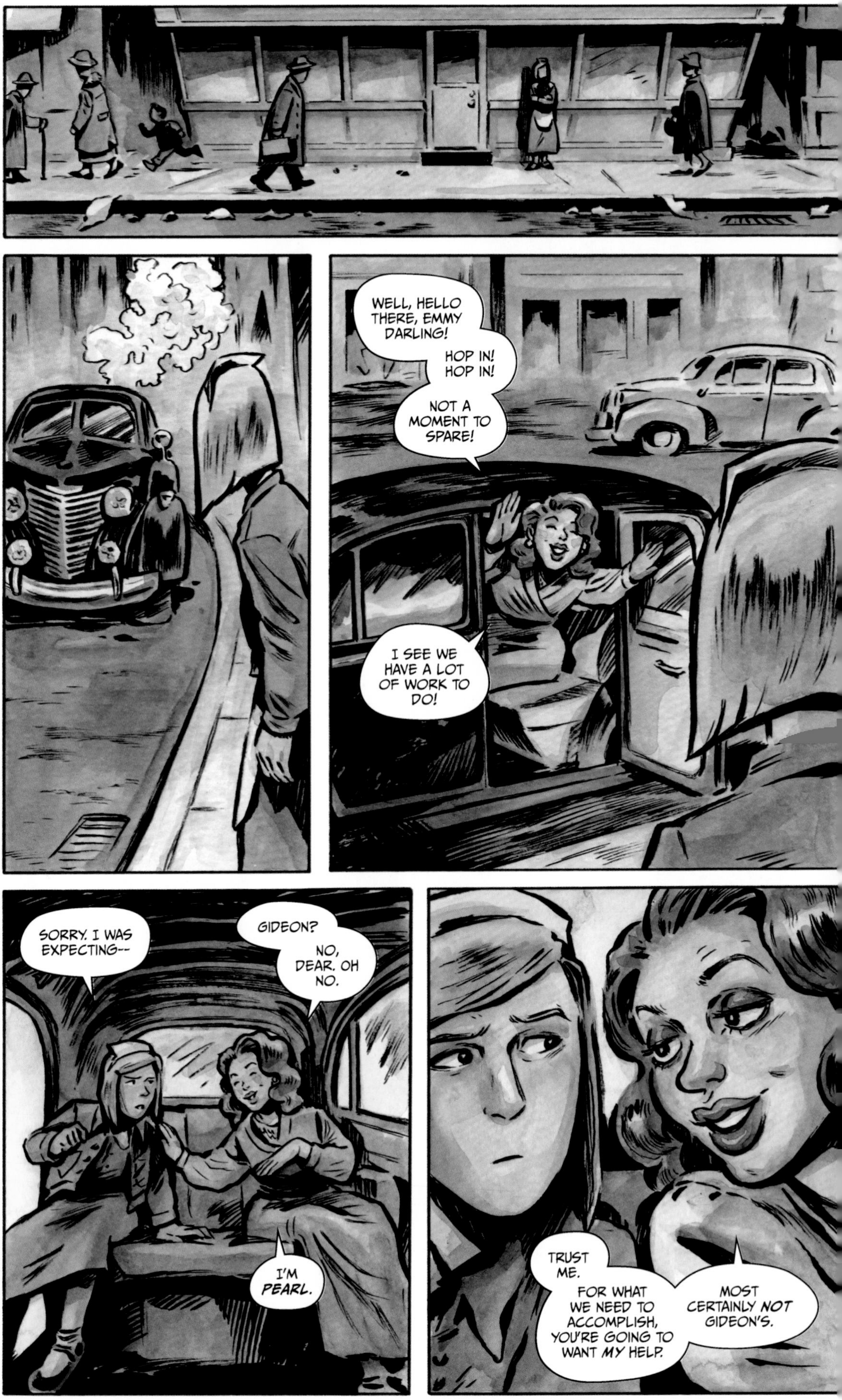
WELL, HELLO THERE, EMMY DARLING!
HOP IN! HOP IN!
NOT A MOMENT TO SPARE!
I SEE WE HAVE A LOT OF WORK TO DO!
SORRY. I WAS EXPECTING--
GIDEON?
NO, DEAR. OH NO.
I'M *PEARL*.
TRUST ME.
FOR WHAT WE NEED TO ACCOMPLISH, YOU'RE GOING TO WANT *MY* HELP.
MOST CERTAINLY *NOT* GIDEON'S.

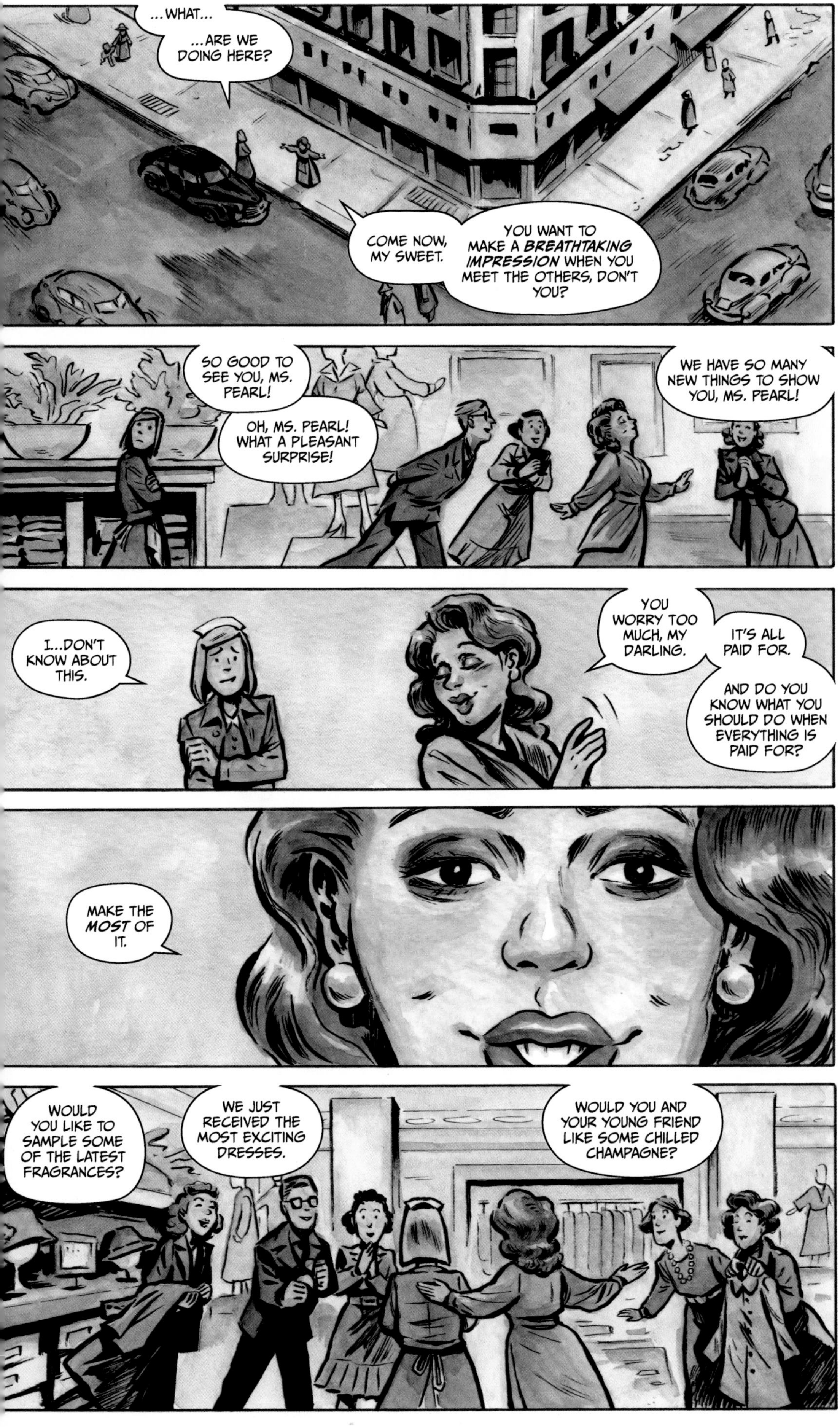
...WHAT...
...ARE WE DOING HERE?
COME NOW, MY SWEET.
YOU WANT TO MAKE A *BREATHTAKING IMPRESSION* WHEN YOU MEET THE OTHERS, DON'T YOU?
SO GOOD TO SEE YOU, MS. PEARL!
OH, MS. PEARL! WHAT A PLEASANT SURPRISE!
WE HAVE SO MANY NEW THINGS TO SHOW YOU, MS. PEARL!
I...DON'T KNOW ABOUT THIS.
YOU WORRY TOO MUCH, MY DARLING.
IT'S ALL PAID FOR.
AND DO YOU KNOW WHAT YOU SHOULD DO WHEN EVERYTHING IS PAID FOR?
MAKE THE *MOST* OF IT.
WOULD YOU LIKE TO SAMPLE SOME OF THE LATEST FRAGRANCES?
WE JUST RECEIVED THE MOST EXCITING DRESSES.
WOULD YOU AND YOUR YOUNG FRIEND LIKE SOME CHILLED CHAMPAGNE?

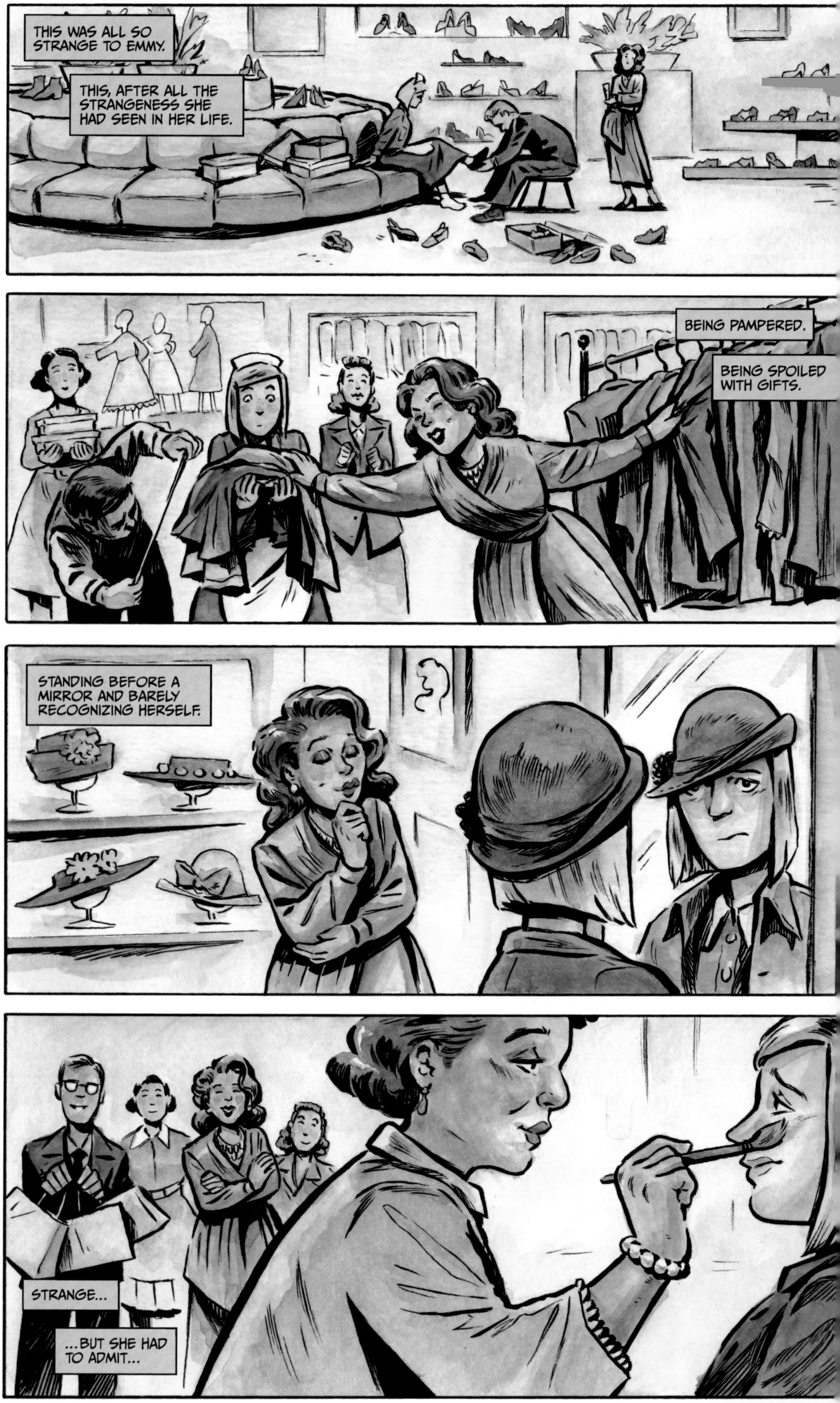
THIS WAS ALL SO STRANGE TO EMMY.
THIS, AFTER ALL THE STRANGENESS SHE HAD SEEN IN HER LIFE.
BEING PAMPERED.
BEING SPOILED WITH GIFTS.
STANDING BEFORE A MIRROR AND BARELY RECOGNIZING HERSELF.
STRANGE...
...BUT SHE HAD TO ADMIT...

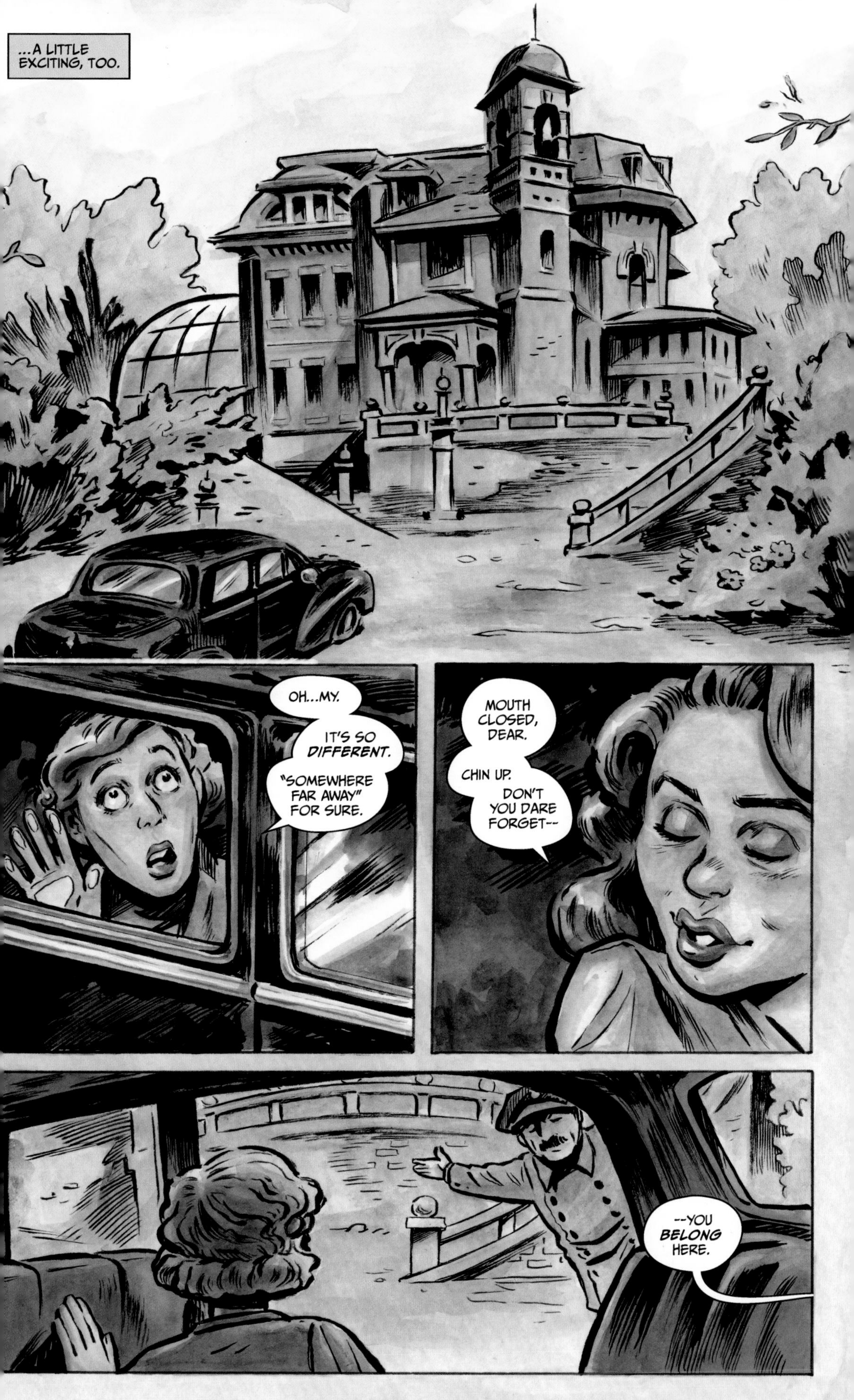
...A LITTLE EXCITING, TOO.
OH...MY.
IT'S SO DIFFERENT.
"SOMEWHERE FAR AWAY" FOR SURE.
MOUTH CLOSED, DEAR.
CHIN UP.
DON'T YOU DARE FORGET--
--YOU BELONG HERE.

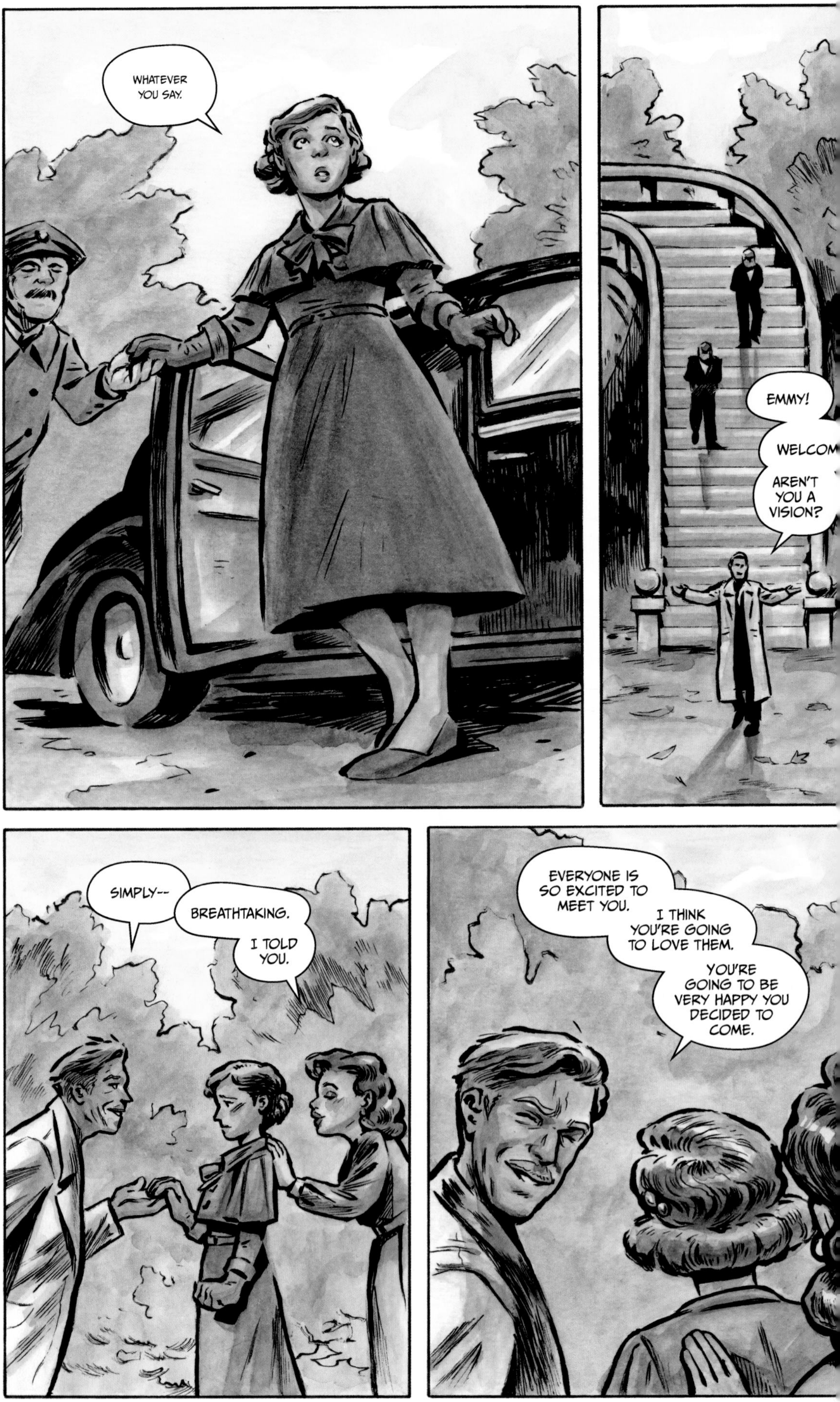
WHATEVER YOU SAY.
EMMY!
WELCOM
AREN'T YOU A VISION?
SIMPLY--
BREATHTAKING.
I TOLD YOU.
EVERYONE IS SO EXCITED TO MEET YOU.
I THINK YOU'RE GOING TO LOVE THEM.
YOU'RE GOING TO BE VERY HAPPY YOU DECIDED TO COME.

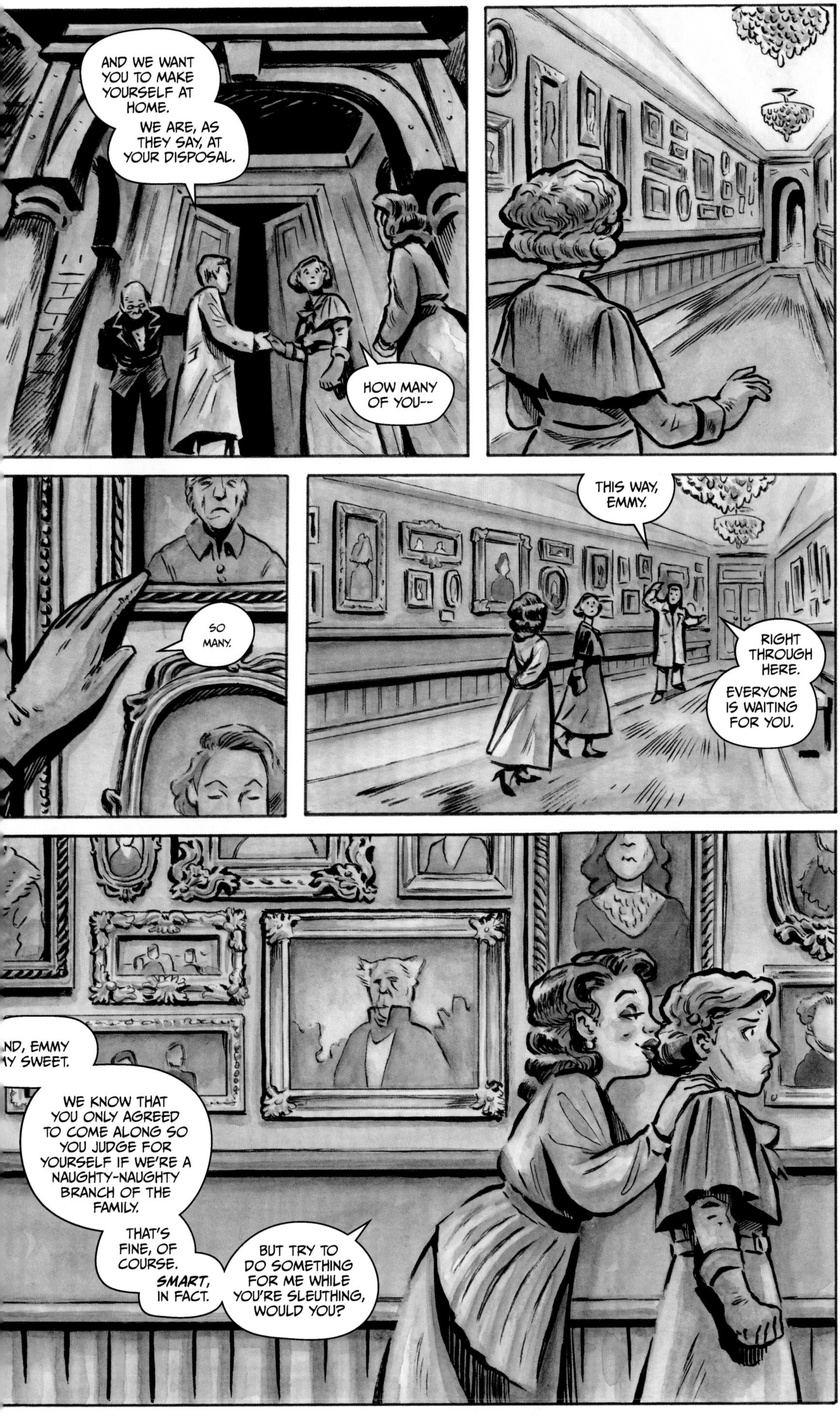
AND WE WANT YOU TO MAKE YOURSELF AT HOME.
WE ARE, AS THEY SAY, AT YOUR DISPOSAL.
HOW MANY OF YOU--
SO MANY.
THIS WAY, EMMY.
RIGHT THROUGH HERE.
EVERYONE IS WAITING FOR YOU.
ND, EMMY MY SWEET.
WE KNOW THAT YOU ONLY AGREED TO COME ALONG SO YOU JUDGE FOR YOURSELF IF WE'RE A NAUGHTY-NAUGHTY BRANCH OF THE FAMILY.
THAT'S FINE, OF COURSE. SMART, IN FACT.
BUT TRY TO DO SOMETHING FOR ME WHILE YOU'RE SLEUTHING, WOULD YOU?

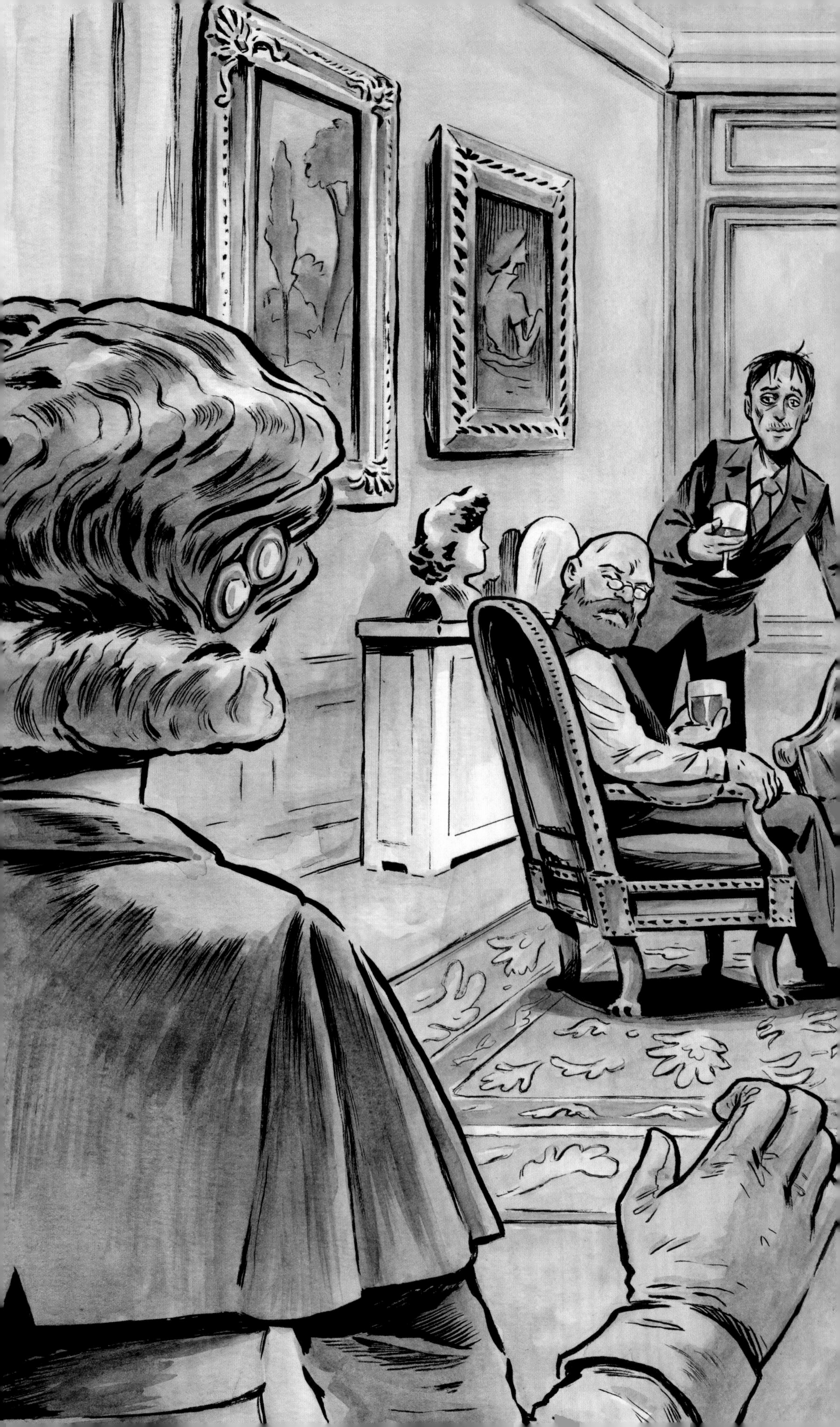

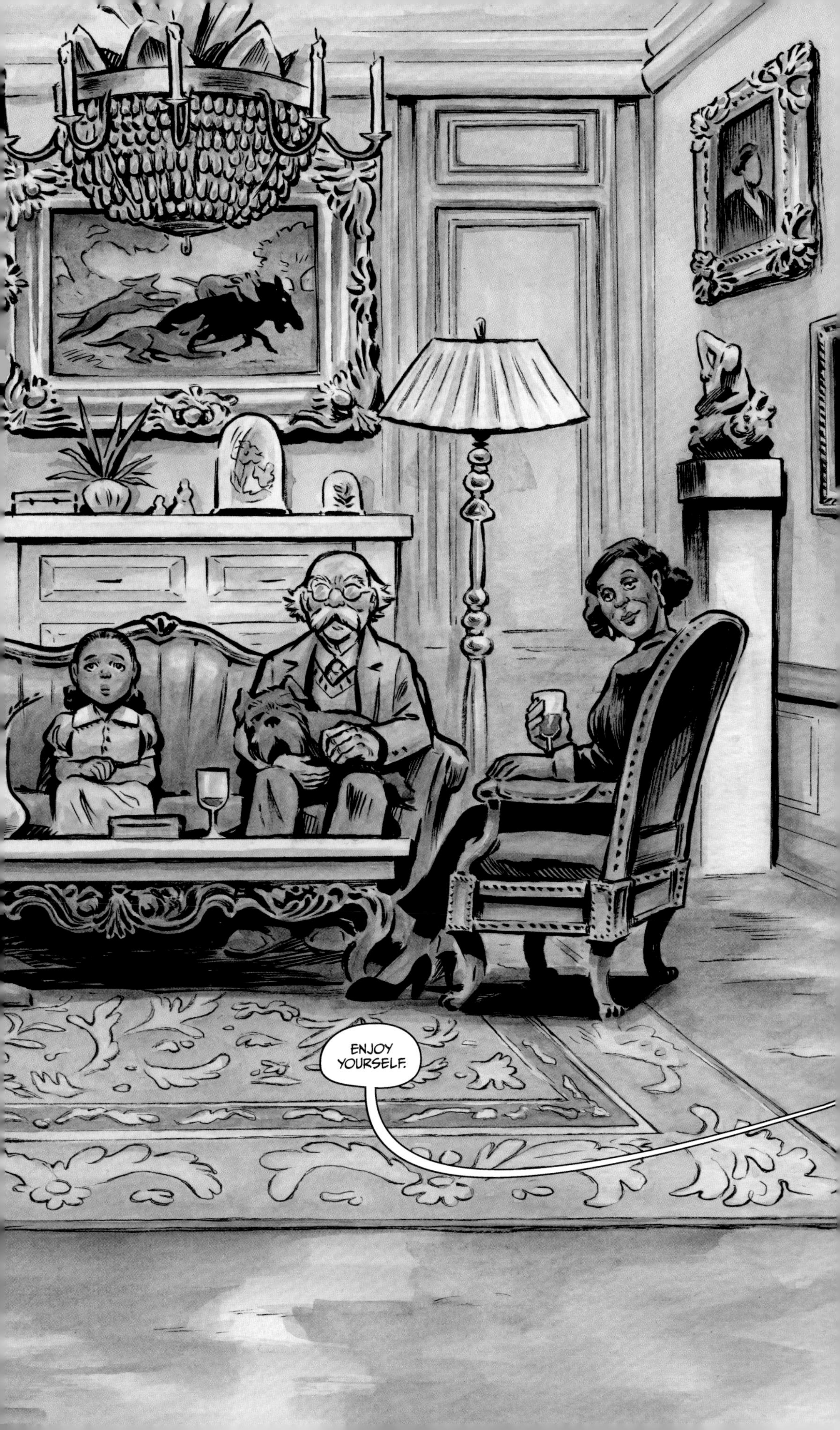
ENJOY YOURSELF.

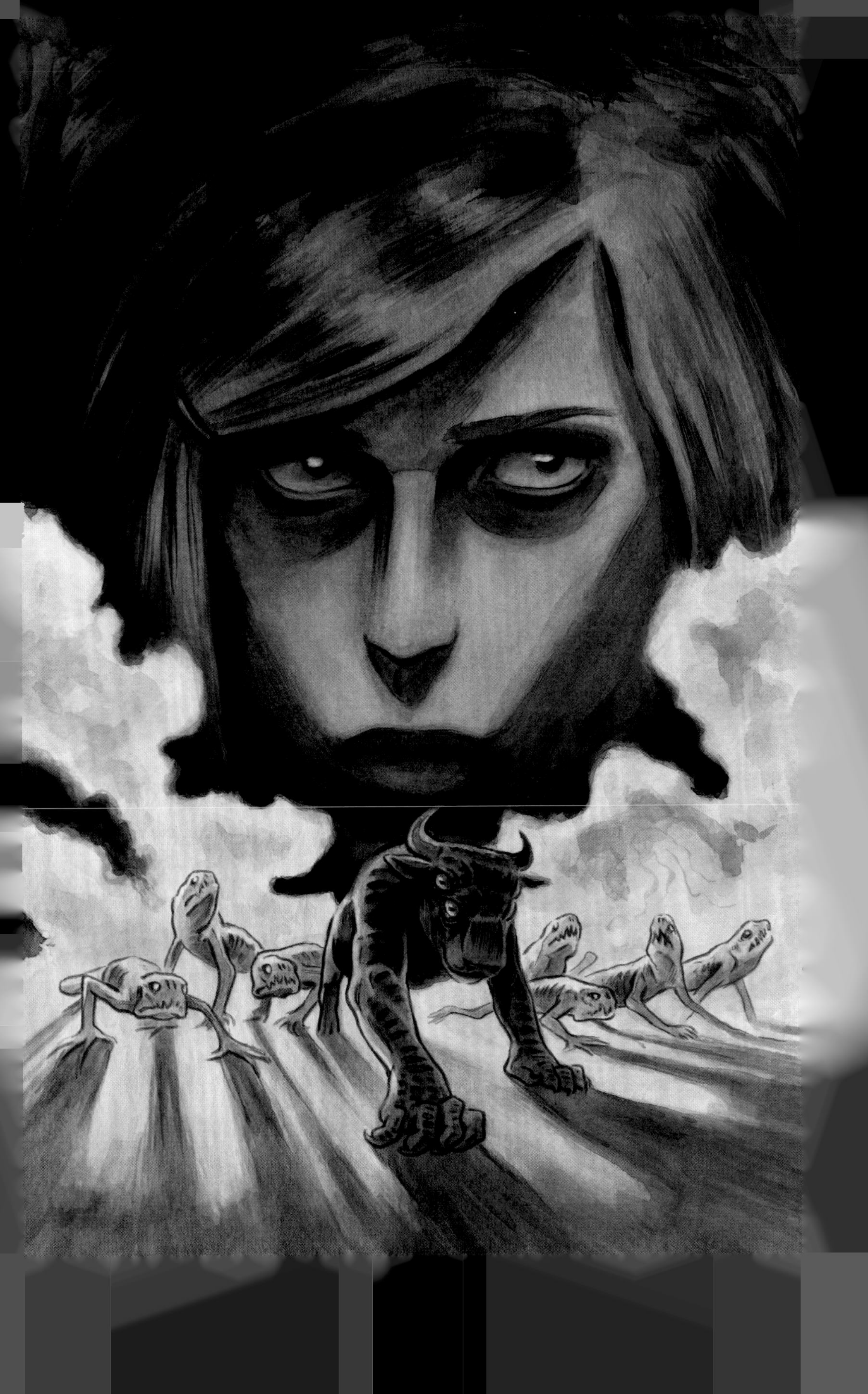

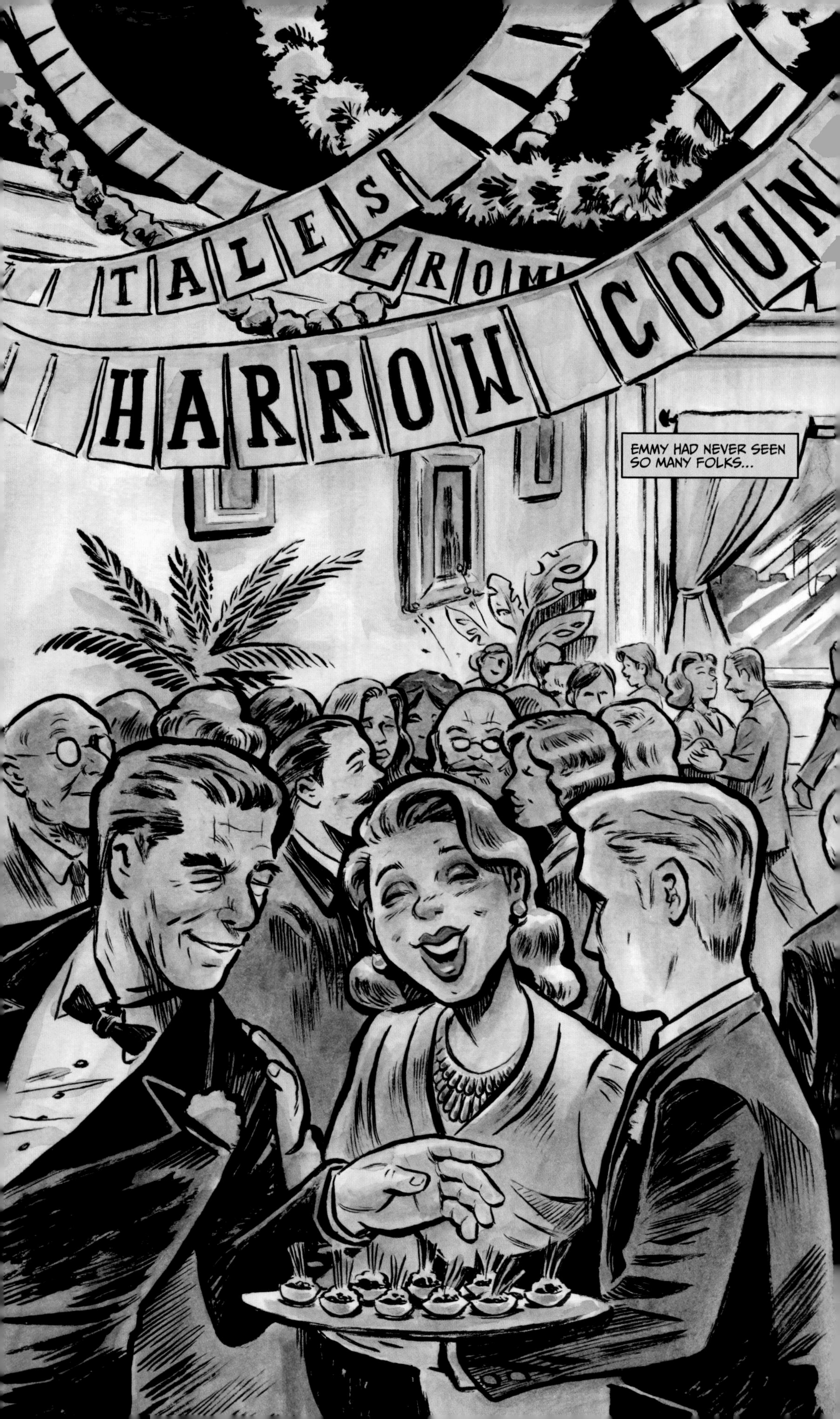
TALES FROM
HARROW COUN
EMMY HAD NEVER SEEN SO MANY FOLKS...

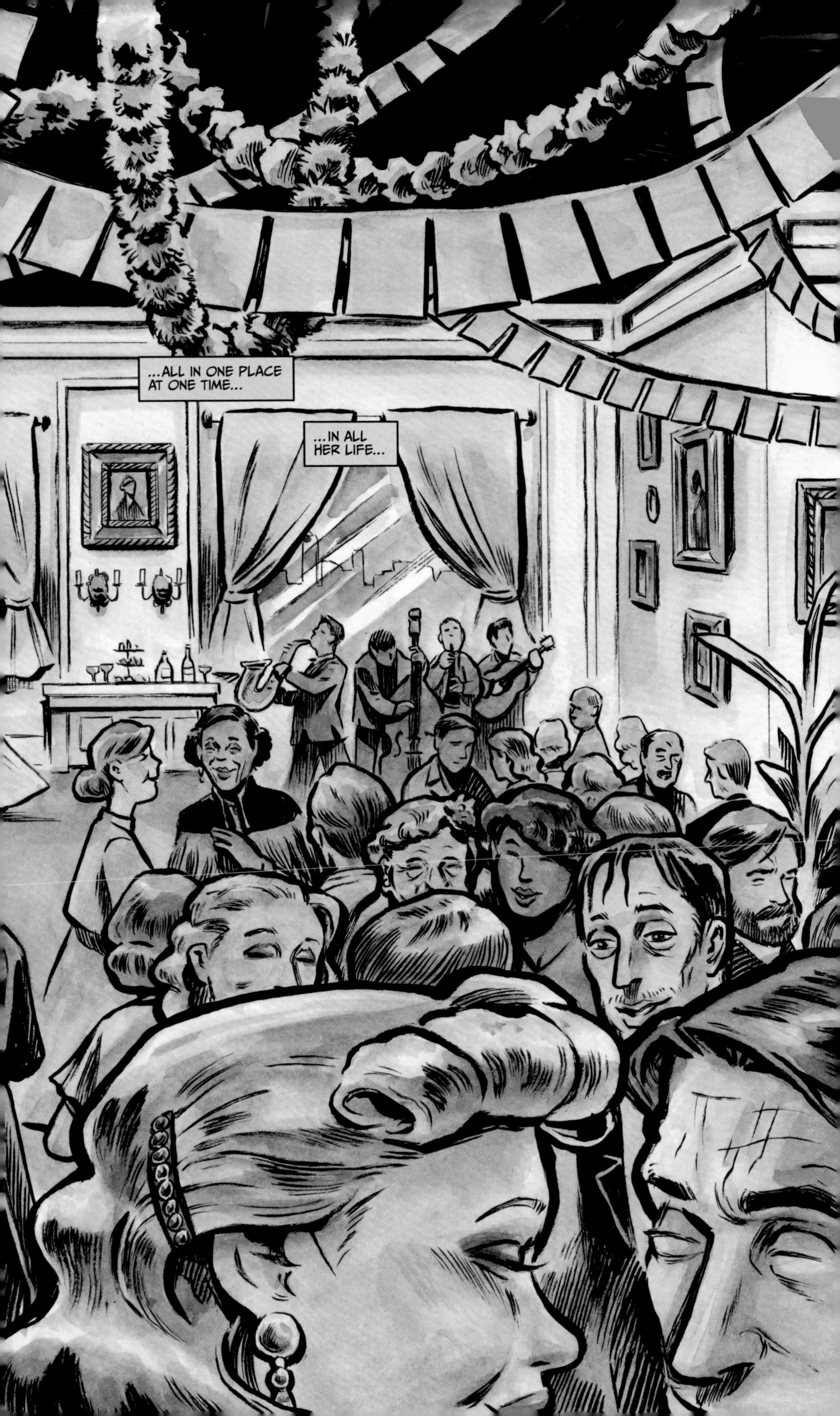
...ALL IN ONE PLACE
AT ONE TIME...
...IN ALL
HER LIFE...

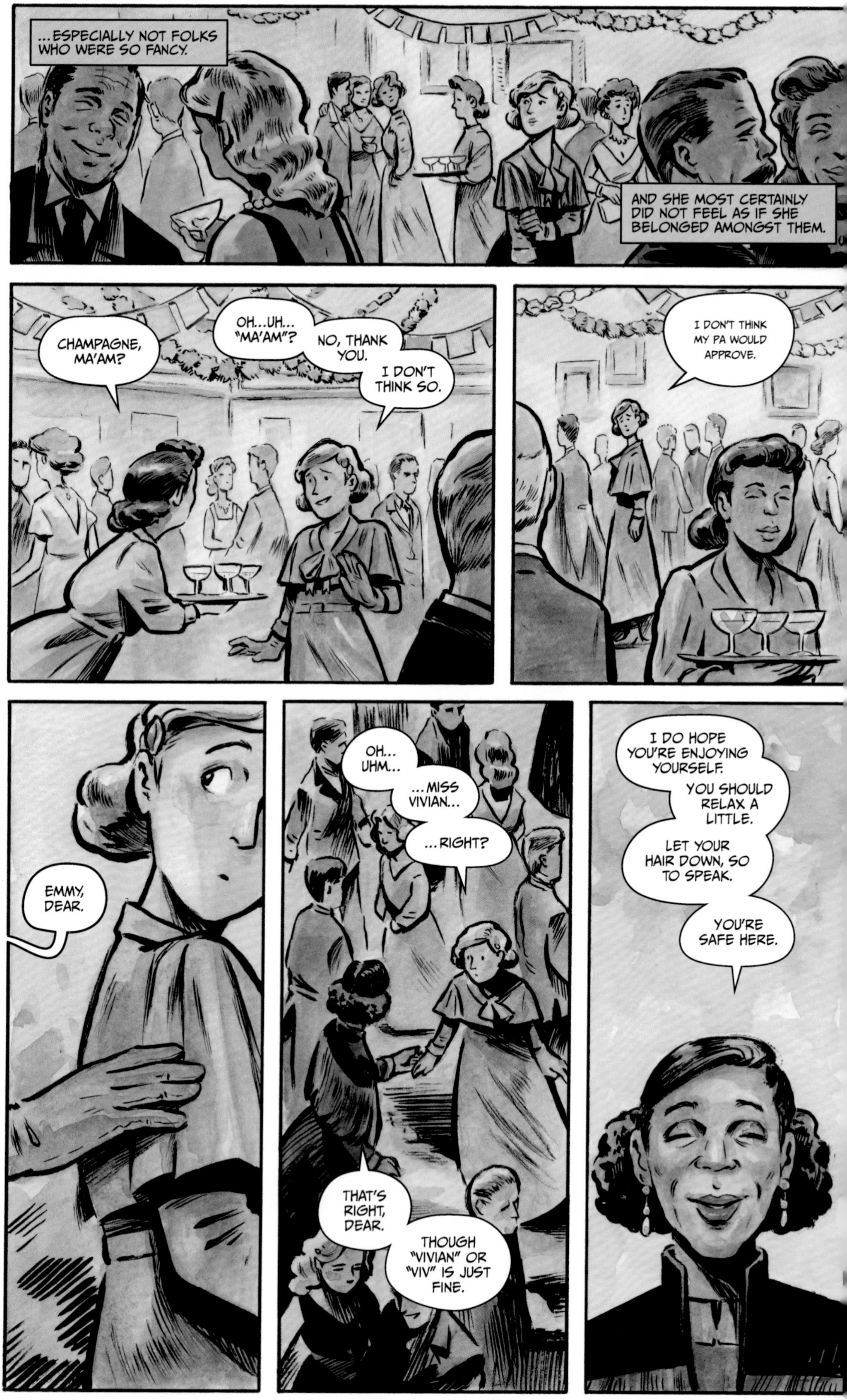
...ESPECIALLY NOT FOLKS WHO WERE SO FANCY.
AND SHE MOST CERTAINLY DID NOT FEEL AS IF SHE BELONGED AMONGST THEM.
CHAMPAGNE, MA'AM?
OH...UH... "MA'AM"?
NO, THANK YOU.
I DON'T THINK SO.
I DON'T THINK MY PA WOULD APPROVE.
EMMY, DEAR.
OH... UHM...
...MISS VIVIAN...
...RIGHT?
THAT'S RIGHT, DEAR.
THOUGH "VIVIAN" OR "VIV" IS JUST FINE.
I DO HOPE YOU'RE ENJOYING YOURSELF.
YOU SHOULD RELAX A LITTLE.
LET YOUR HAIR DOWN, SO TO SPEAK.
YOU'RE SAFE HERE.

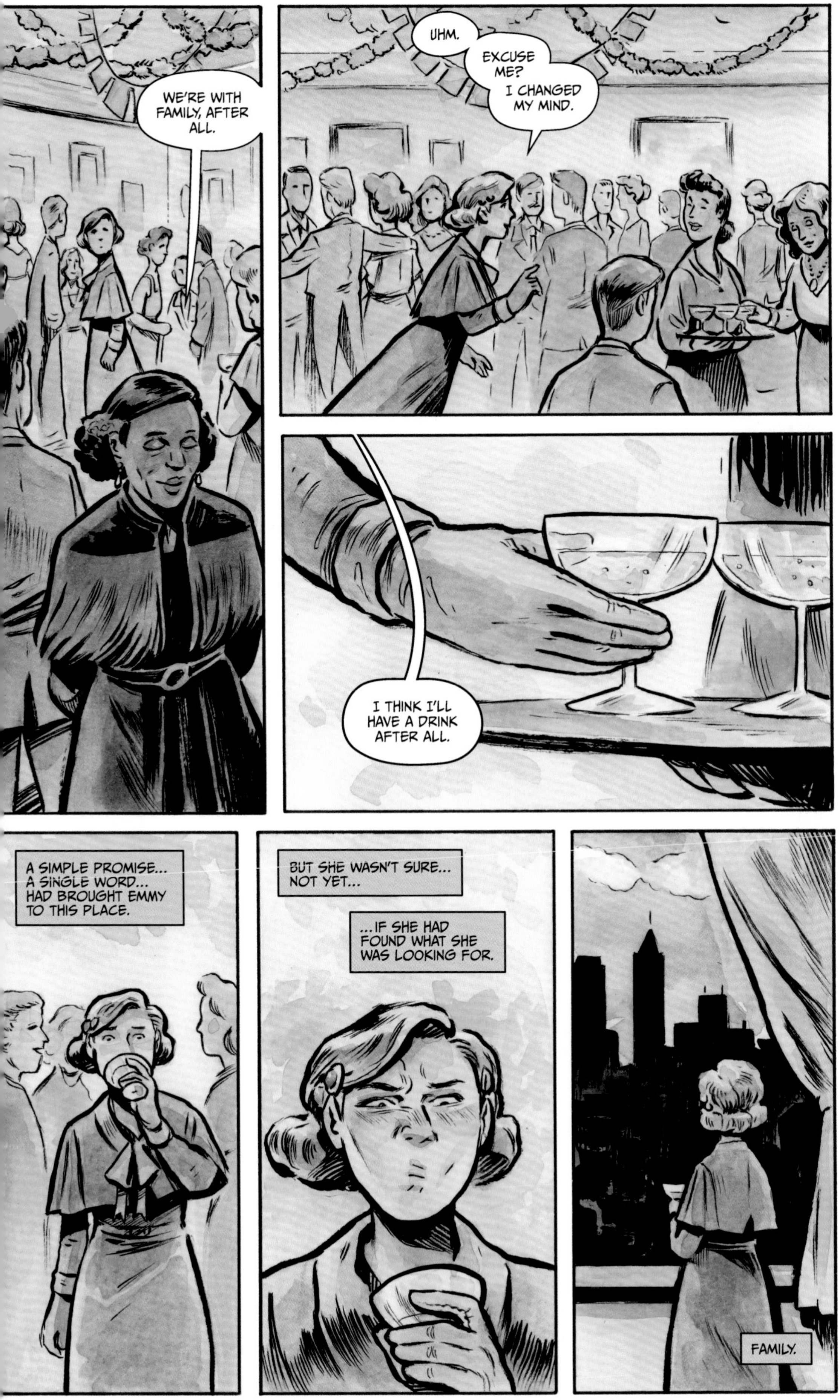
WE'RE WITH FAMILY, AFTER ALL.
UHM.
EXCUSE ME?
I CHANGED MY MIND.
I THINK I'LL HAVE A DRINK AFTER ALL.
A SIMPLE PROMISE... A SINGLE WORD... HAD BROUGHT EMMY TO THIS PLACE.
BUT SHE WASN'T SURE... NOT YET...
...IF SHE HAD FOUND WHAT SHE WAS LOOKING FOR.
FAMILY.

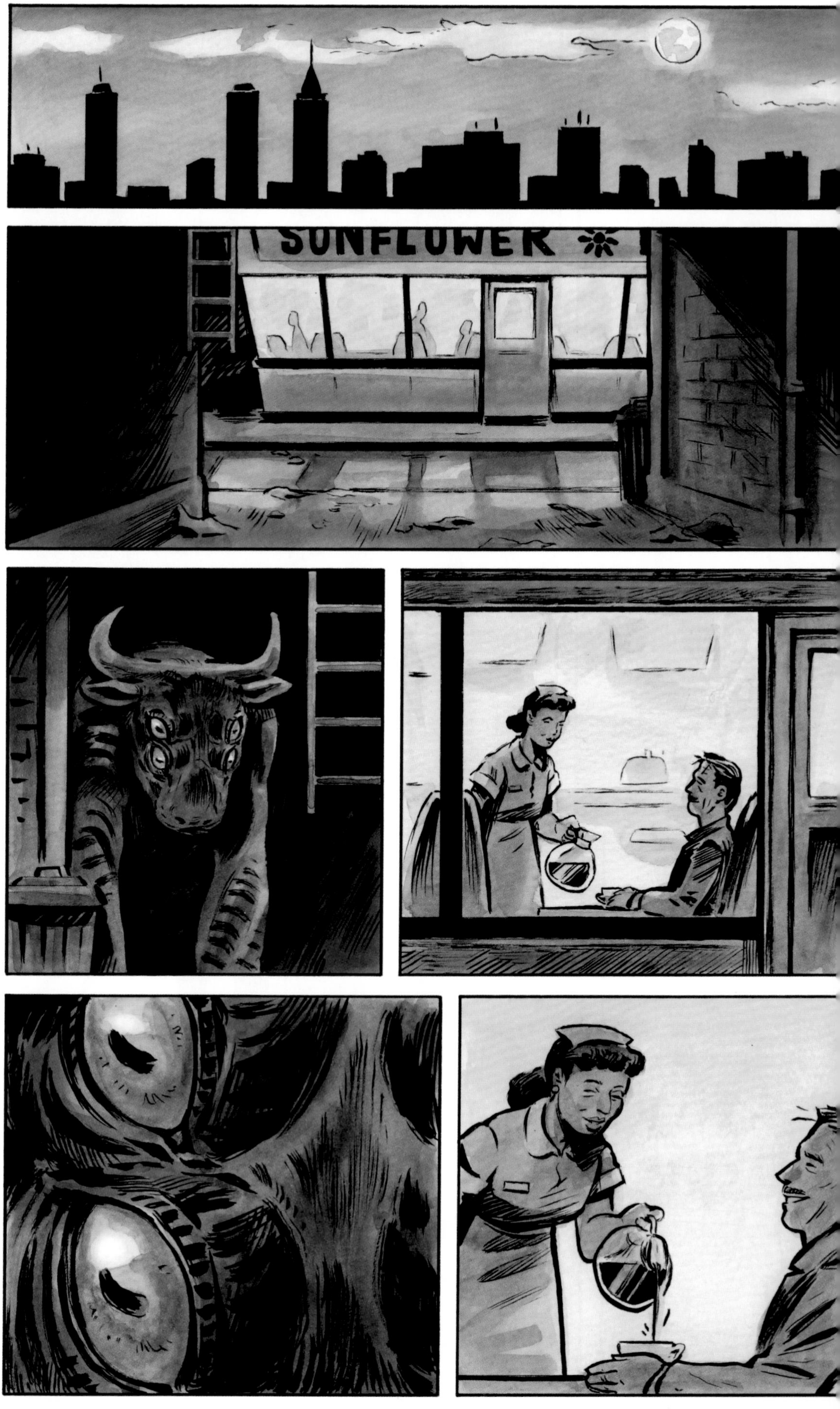
SUNFLOWER

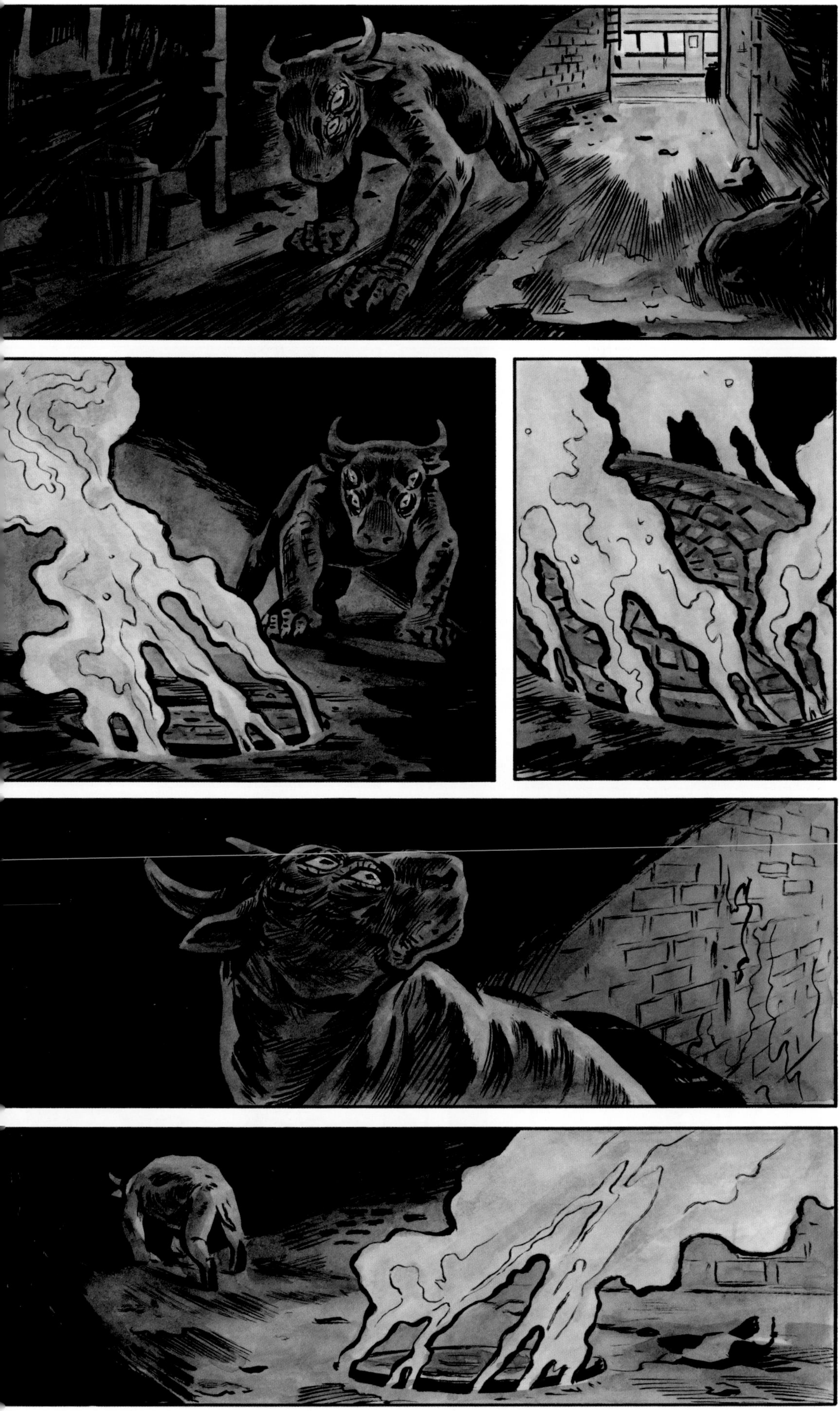

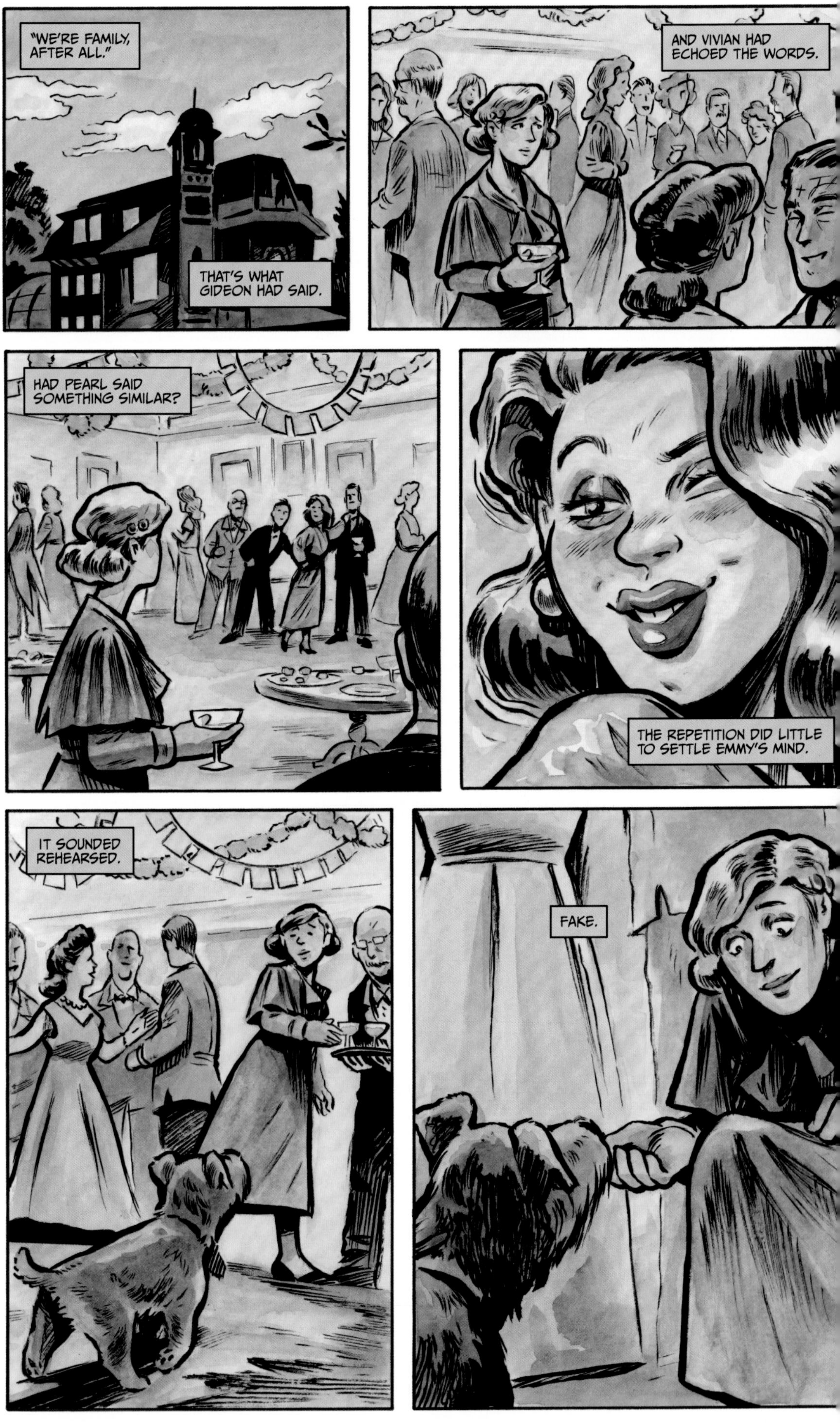
"WE'RE FAMILY, AFTER ALL."
THAT'S WHAT GIDEON HAD SAID.
AND VIVIAN HAD ECHOED THE WORDS.
HAD PEARL SAID SOMETHING SIMILAR?
THE REPETITION DID LITTLE TO SETTLE EMMY'S MIND.
IT SOUNDED REHEARSED.
FAKE.

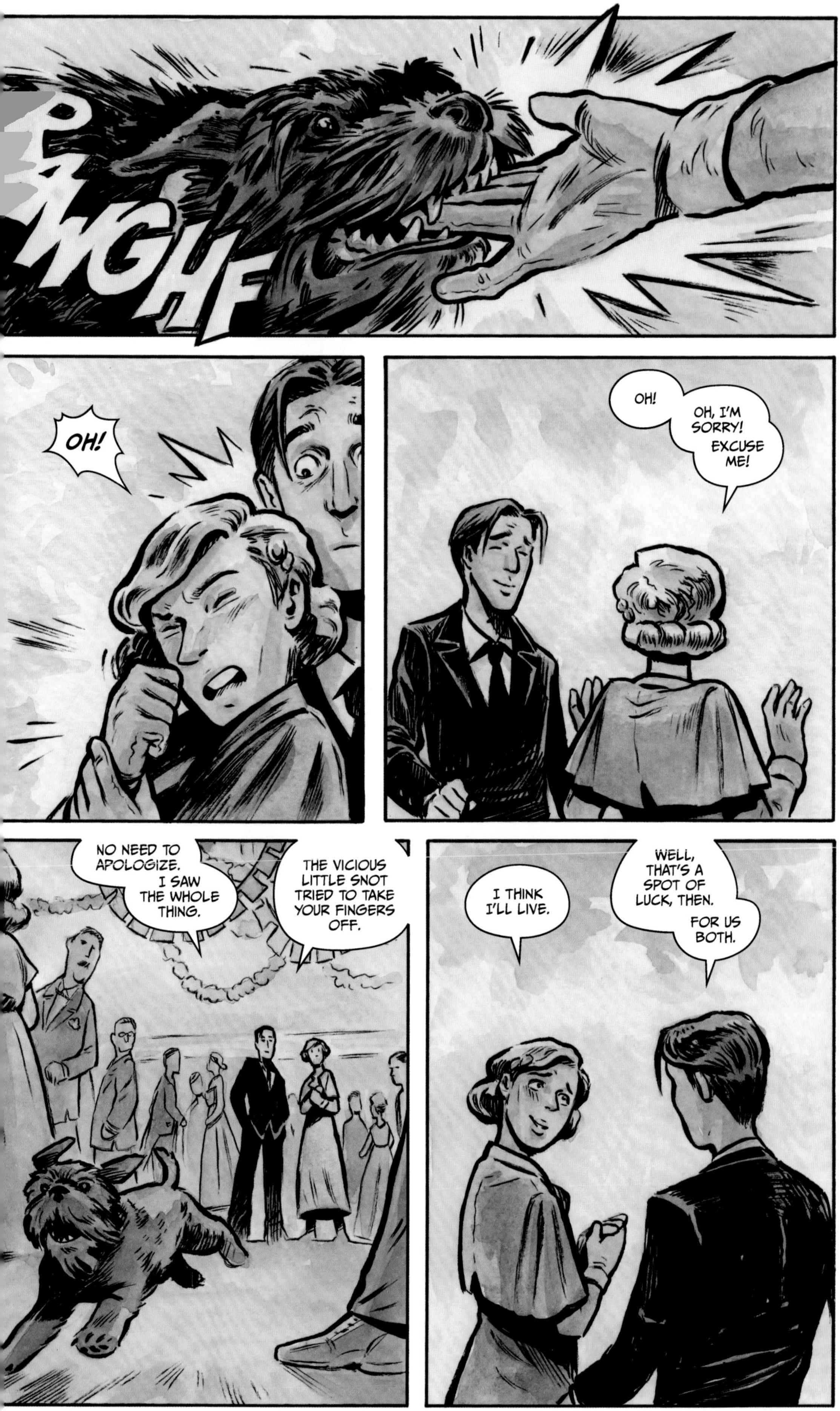
RWGHF
OH!
OH!
OH, I'M SORRY!
EXCUSE ME!
NO NEED TO APOLOGIZE.
I SAW THE WHOLE THING.
THE VICIOUS LITTLE SNOT TRIED TO TAKE YOUR FINGERS OFF.
I THINK I'LL LIVE.
WELL, THAT'S A SPOT OF LUCK, THEN.
FOR US BOTH.

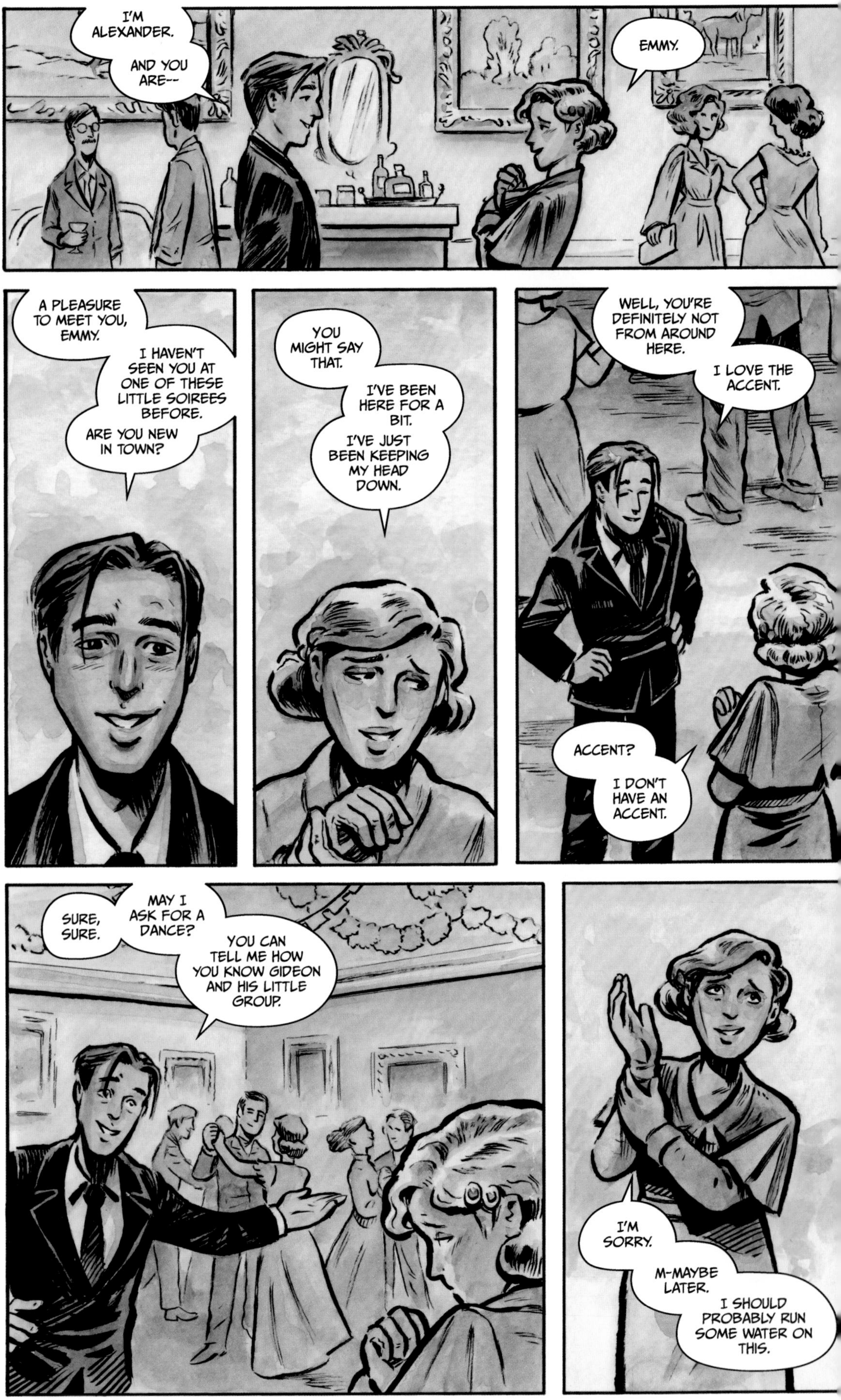
I'M ALEXANDER.
AND YOU ARE--
EMMY.
A PLEASURE TO MEET YOU, EMMY.
I HAVEN'T SEEN YOU AT ONE OF THESE LITTLE SOIREES BEFORE.
ARE YOU NEW IN TOWN?
YOU MIGHT SAY THAT.
I'VE BEEN HERE FOR A BIT.
I'VE JUST BEEN KEEPING MY HEAD DOWN.
WELL, YOU'RE DEFINITELY NOT FROM AROUND HERE.
I LOVE THE ACCENT.
ACCENT?
I DON'T HAVE AN ACCENT.
SURE, SURE.
MAY I ASK FOR A DANCE?
YOU CAN TELL ME HOW YOU KNOW GIDEON AND HIS LITTLE GROUP.
I'M SORRY.
M-MAYBE LATER.
I SHOULD PROBABLY RUN SOME WATER ON THIS.

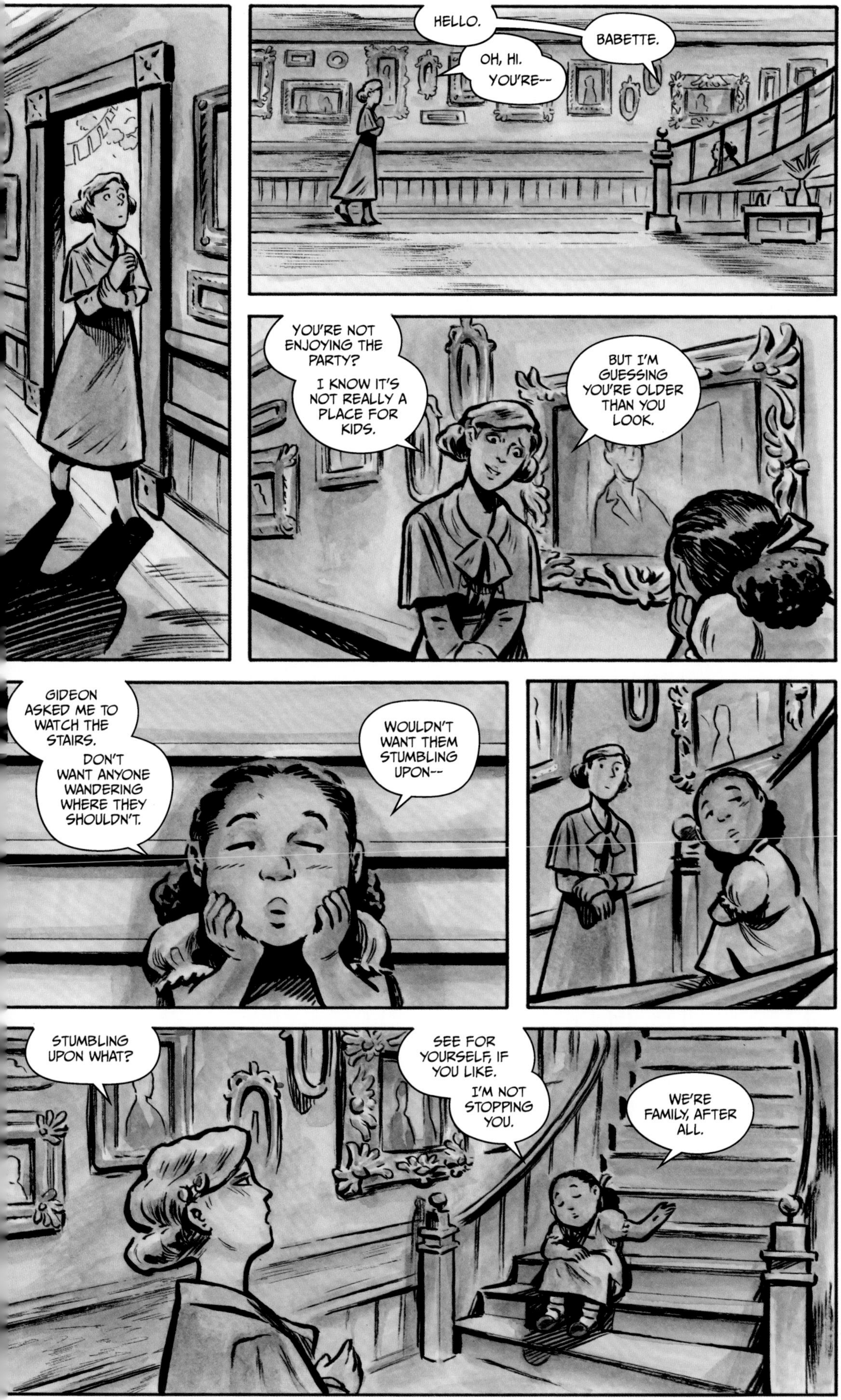
HELLO.
BABETTE.
OH, HI.
YOU'RE--
YOU'RE NOT ENJOYING THE PARTY?
I KNOW IT'S NOT REALLY A PLACE FOR KIDS.
BUT I'M GUESSING YOU'RE OLDER THAN YOU LOOK.
GIDEON ASKED ME TO WATCH THE STAIRS.
DON'T WANT ANYONE WANDERING WHERE THEY SHOULDN'T.
WOULDN'T WANT THEM STUMBLING UPON--
STUMBLING UPON WHAT?
SEE FOR YOURSELF, IF YOU LIKE.
I'M NOT STOPPING YOU.
WE'RE FAMILY, AFTER ALL.

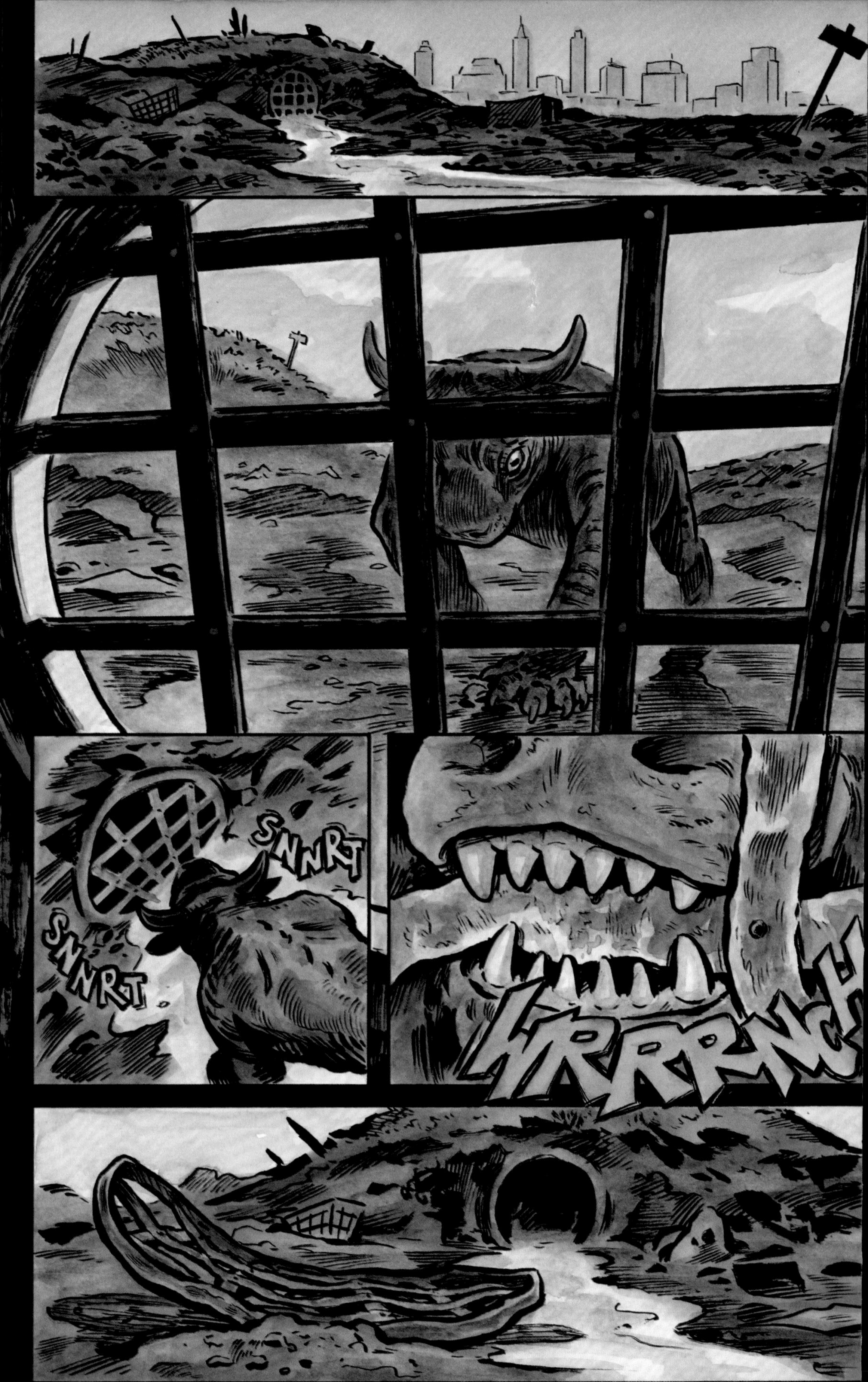
SNNRT
SNNRT
WRRNCH

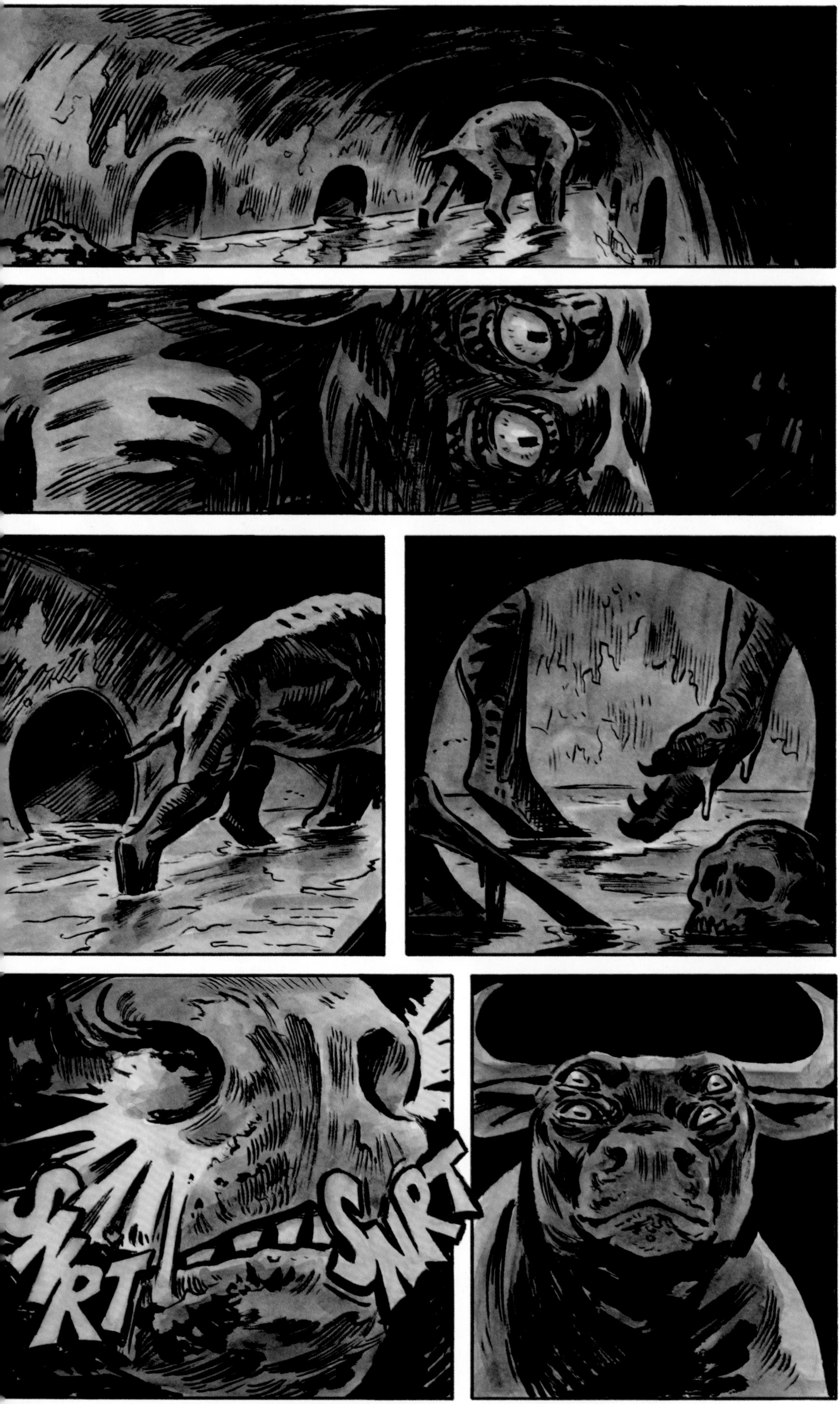
SNRT
SNRT

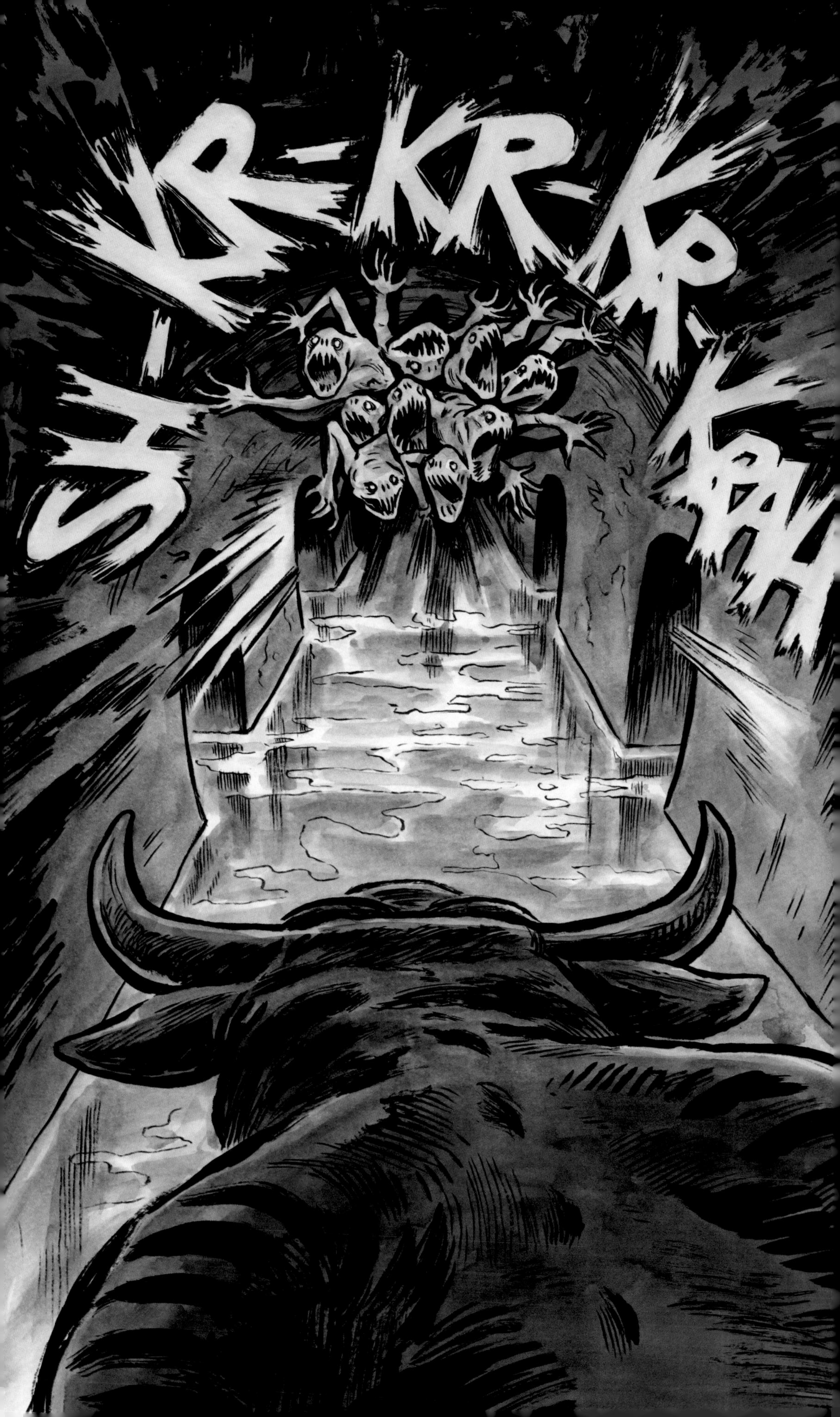
SH-KR-KR-KR-KRAH

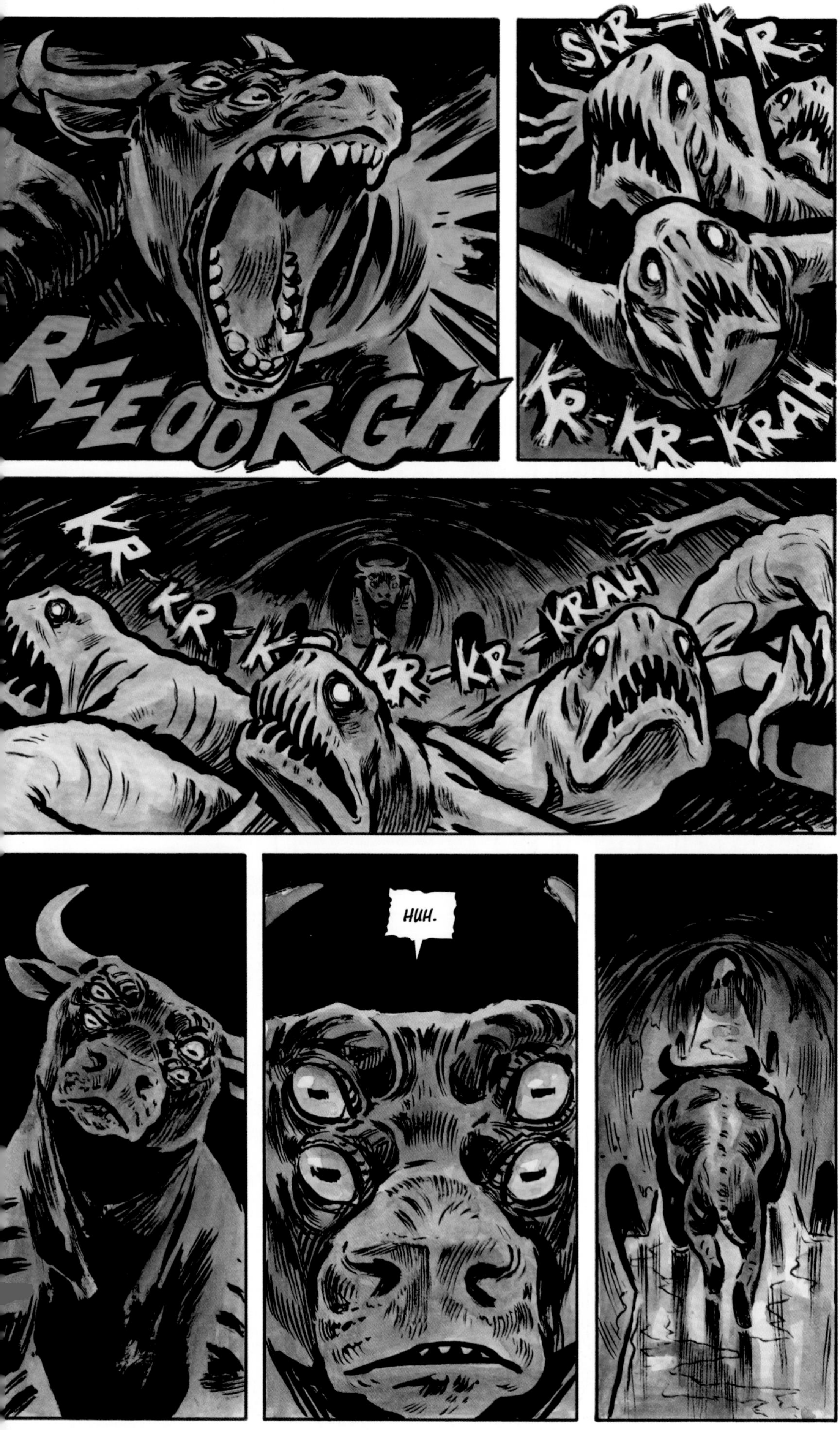
REEOORGH
SKR-KR
KR-KR-KRAH
KR-KR-K
KR-KR-KRAH
HUH.

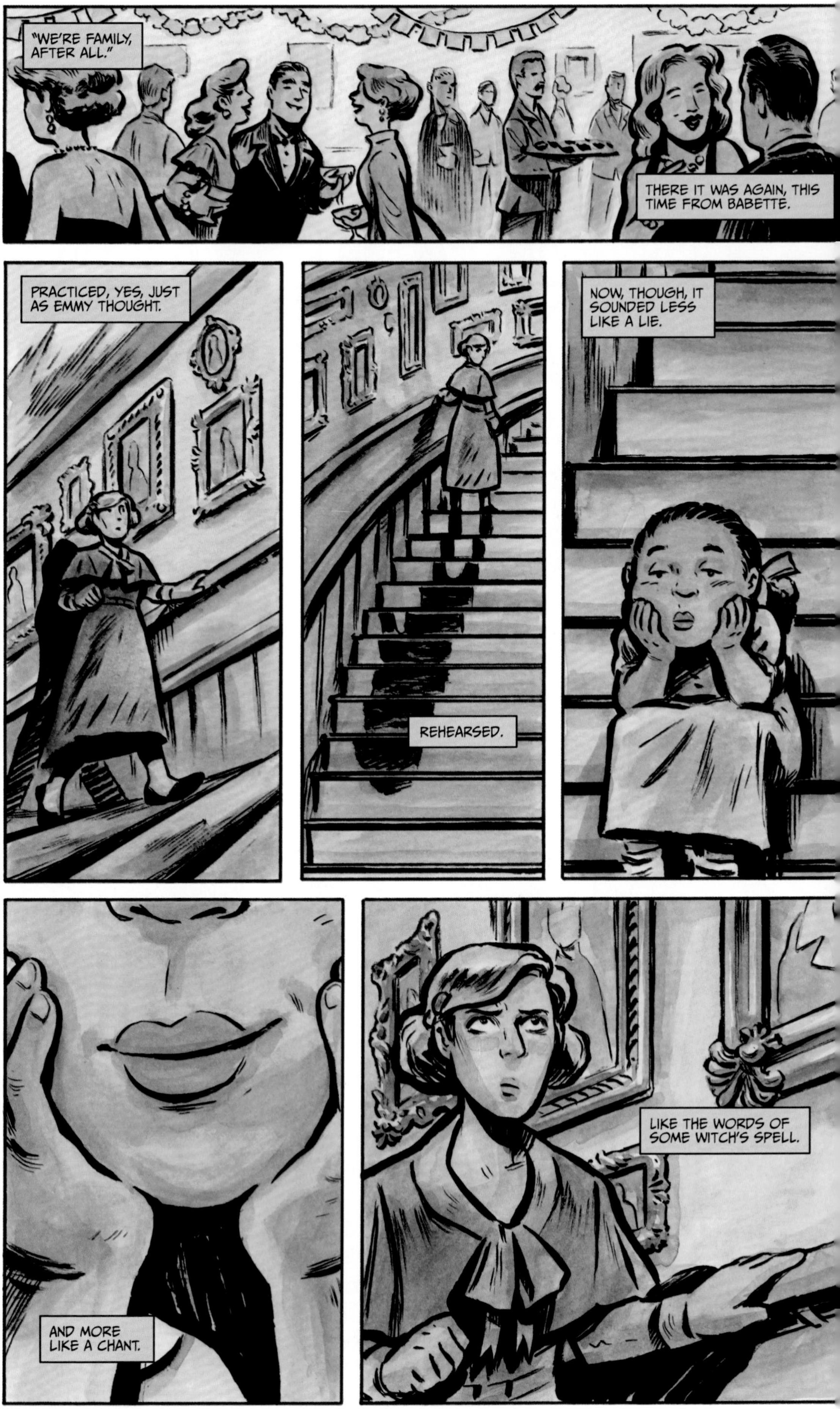
"WE'RE FAMILY, AFTER ALL."
THERE IT WAS AGAIN, THIS TIME FROM BABETTE.
PRACTICED, YES, JUST AS EMMY THOUGHT.
REHEARSED.
NOW, THOUGH, IT SOUNDED LESS LIKE A LIE.
AND MORE LIKE A CHANT.
LIKE THE WORDS OF SOME WITCH'S SPELL.

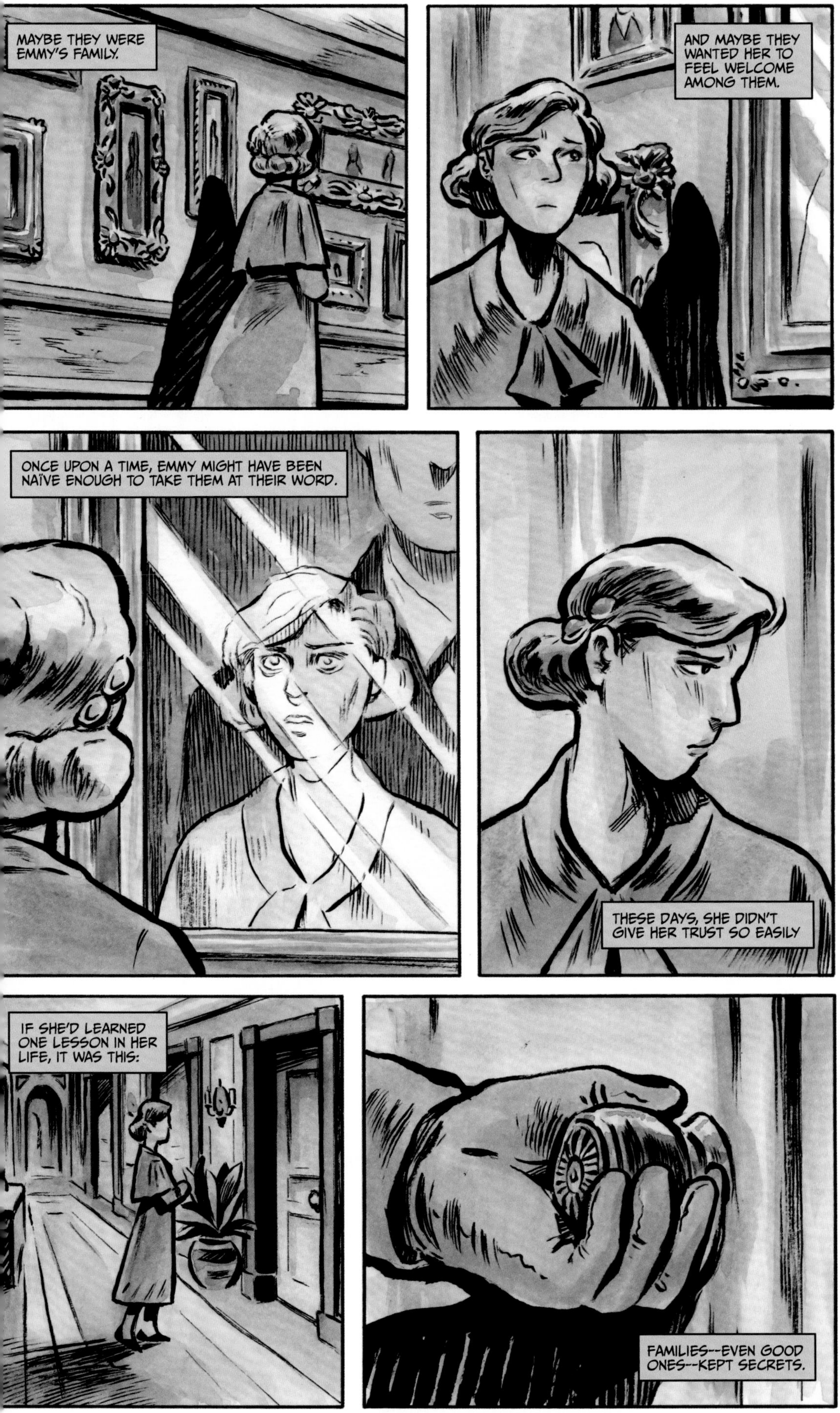
MAYBE THEY WERE EMMY'S FAMILY.
AND MAYBE THEY WANTED HER TO FEEL WELCOME AMONG THEM.
ONCE UPON A TIME, EMMY MIGHT HAVE BEEN NAÏVE ENOUGH TO TAKE THEM AT THEIR WORD.
THESE DAYS, SHE DIDN'T GIVE HER TRUST SO EASILY
IF SHE'D LEARNED ONE LESSON IN HER LIFE, IT WAS THIS:
FAMILIES--EVEN GOOD ONES--KEPT SECRETS.

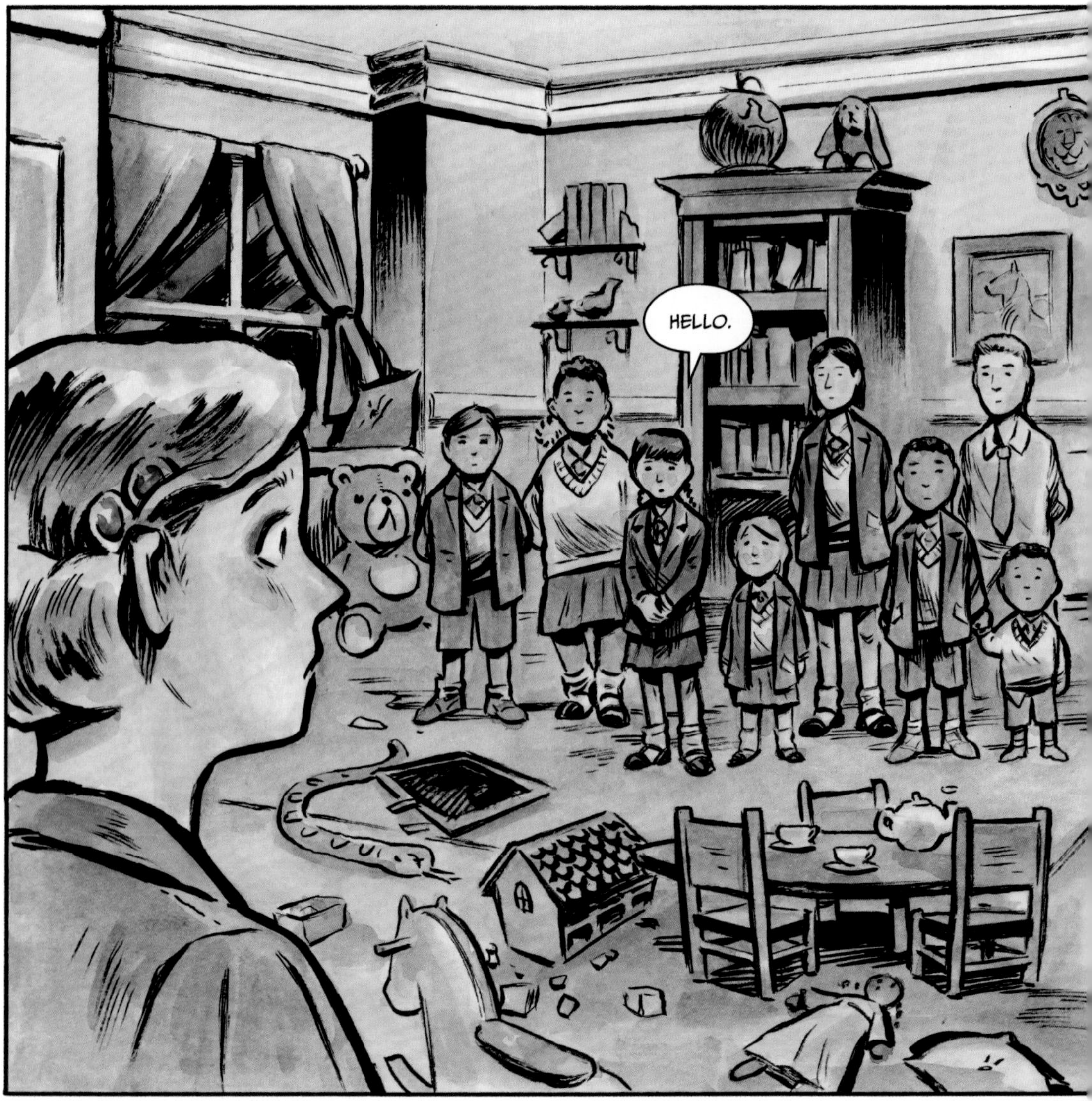
HELLO.

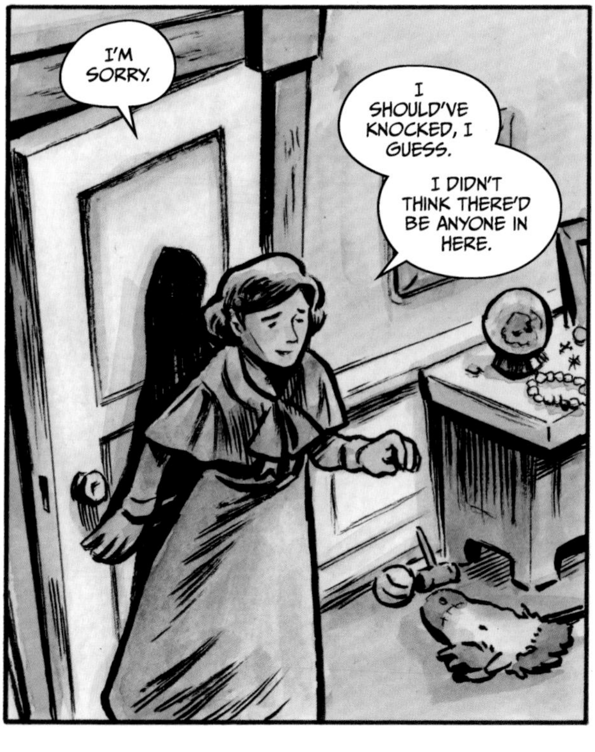
I'M SORRY.
I SHOULD'VE KNOCKED, I GUESS.
I DIDN'T THINK THERE'D BE ANYONE IN HERE.

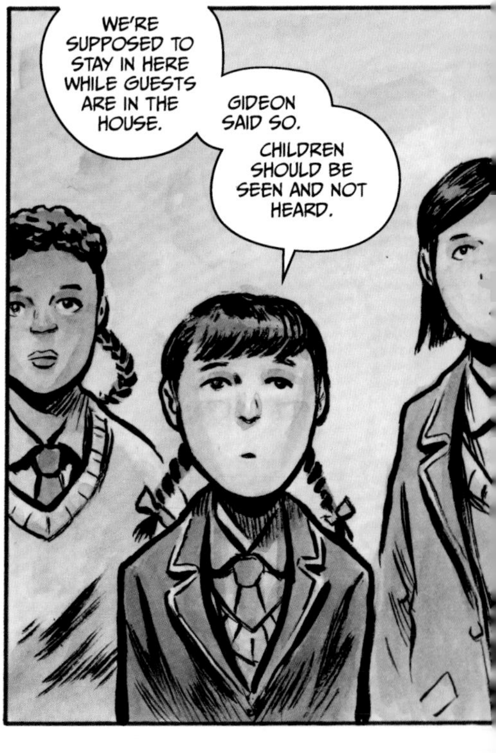
WE'RE SUPPOSED TO STAY IN HERE WHILE GUESTS ARE IN THE HOUSE.
GIDEON SAID SO.
CHILDREN SHOULD BE SEEN AND NOT HEARD.

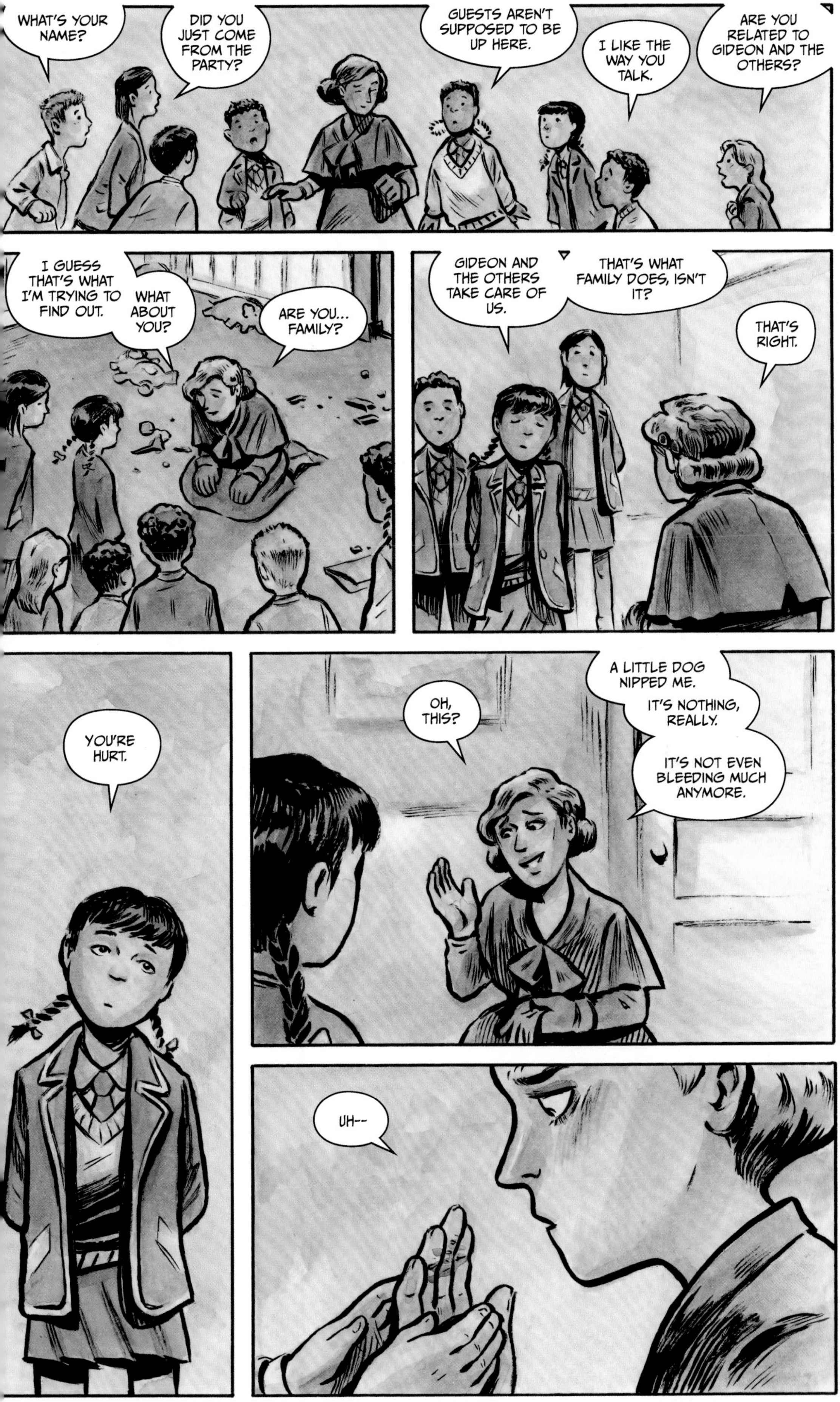
WHAT'S YOUR NAME?
DID YOU JUST COME FROM THE PARTY?
GUESTS AREN'T SUPPOSED TO BE UP HERE.
I LIKE THE WAY YOU TALK.
ARE YOU RELATED TO GIDEON AND THE OTHERS?
I GUESS THAT'S WHAT I'M TRYING TO FIND OUT.
WHAT ABOUT YOU?
ARE YOU... FAMILY?
GIDEON AND THE OTHERS TAKE CARE OF US.
THAT'S WHAT FAMILY DOES, ISN'T IT?
THAT'S RIGHT.
YOU'RE HURT.
OH, THIS?
A LITTLE DOG NIPPED ME.
IT'S NOTHING, REALLY.
IT'S NOT EVEN BLEEDING MUCH ANYMORE.
UH--

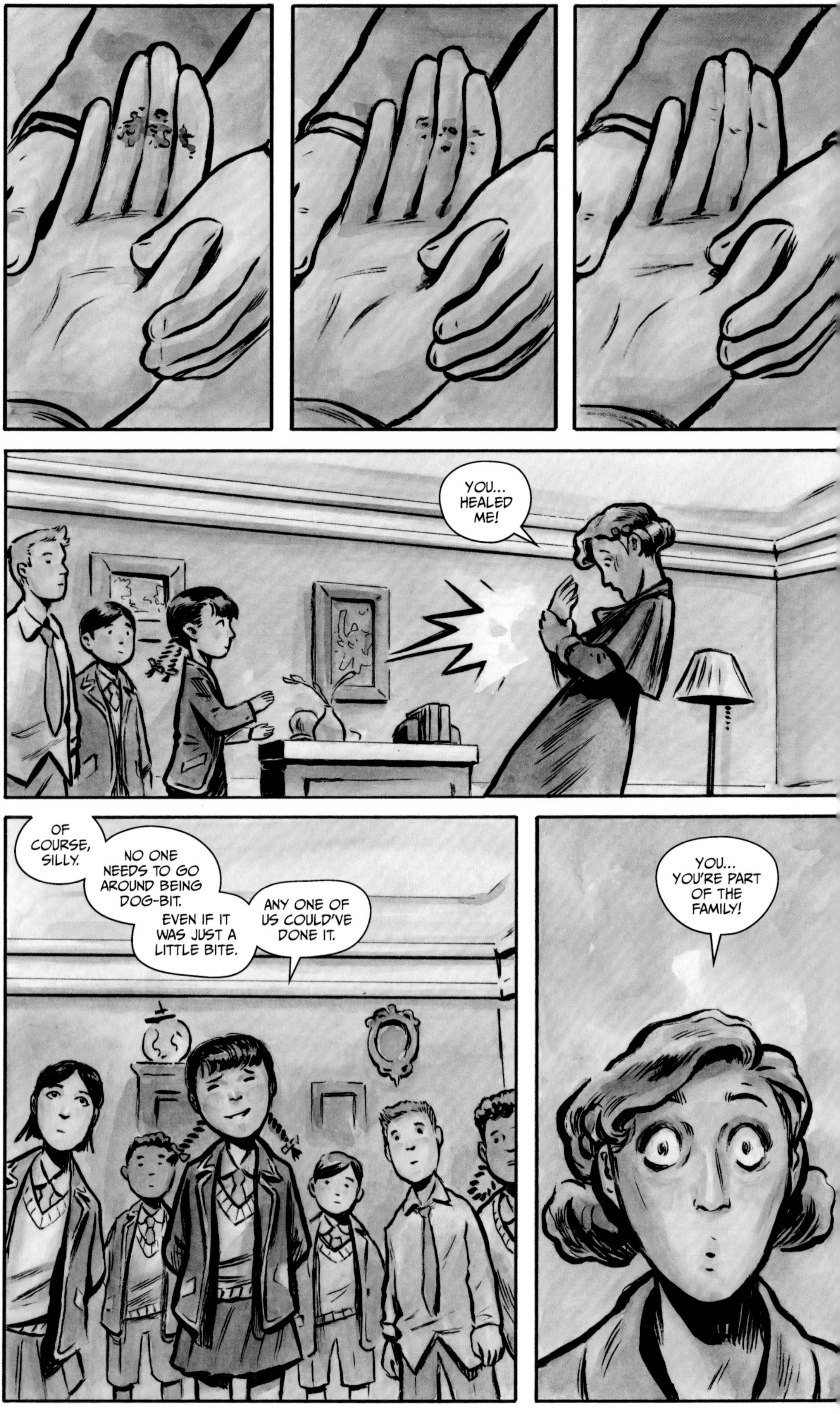
YOU... HEALED ME!
OF COURSE, SILLY.
NO ONE NEEDS TO GO AROUND BEING DOG-BIT.
EVEN IF IT WAS JUST A LITTLE BITE.
ANY ONE OF US COULD'VE DONE IT.
YOU... YOU'RE PART OF THE FAMILY!

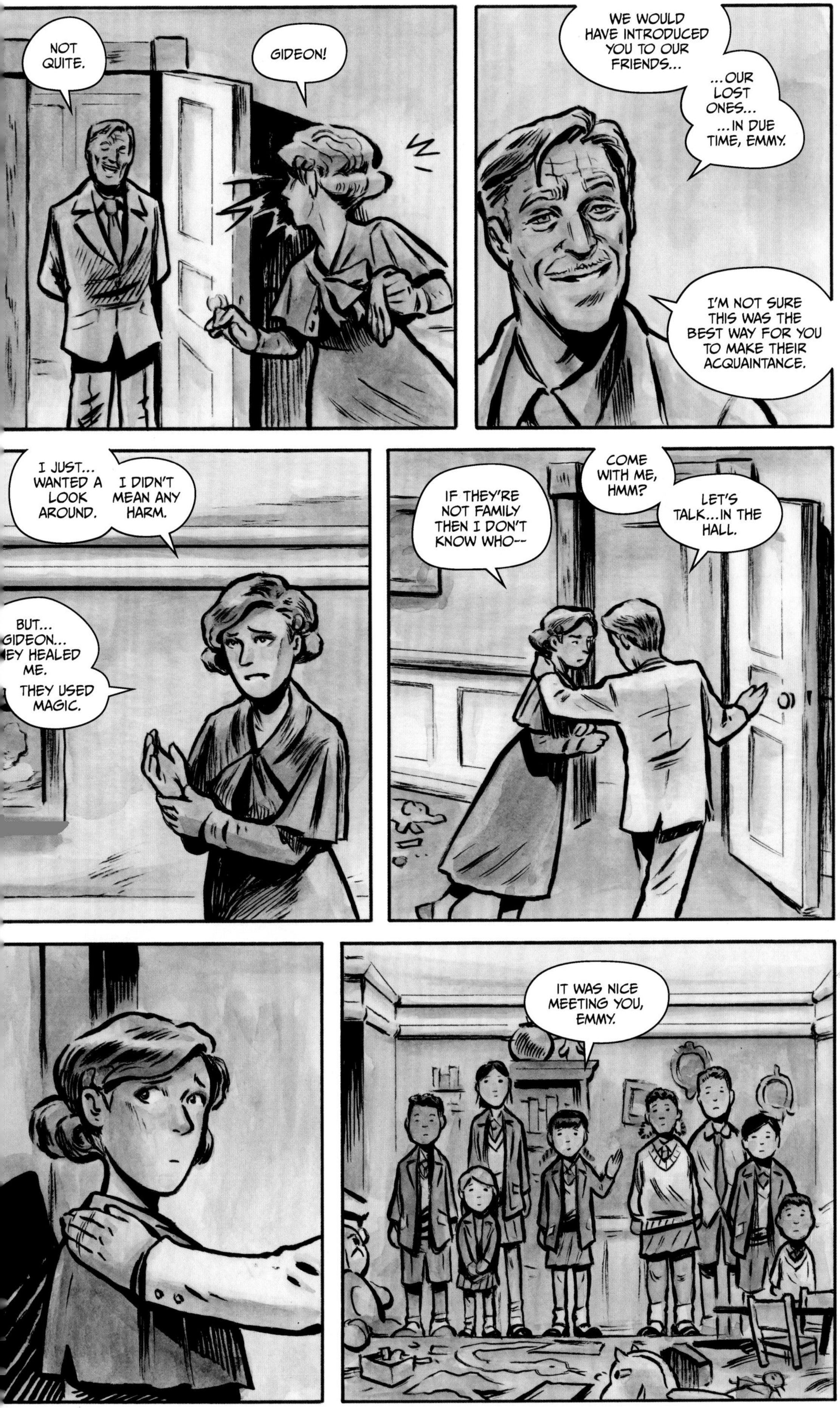
NOT QUITE.
GIDEON!
WE WOULD HAVE INTRODUCED YOU TO OUR FRIENDS...
...OUR LOST ONES...
...IN DUE TIME, EMMY.
I'M NOT SURE THIS WAS THE BEST WAY FOR YOU TO MAKE THEIR ACQUAINTANCE.
I JUST... WANTED A LOOK AROUND.
I DIDN'T MEAN ANY HARM.
BUT... GIDEON... EY HEALED ME.
THEY USED MAGIC.
IF THEY'RE NOT FAMILY THEN I DON'T KNOW WHO--
COME WITH ME, HMM?
LET'S TALK...IN THE HALL.
IT WAS NICE MEETING YOU, EMMY.

WHO ARE THEY?

THERE ARE SO MANY OF THEM.

AND THEY CAN USE MAGIC.

WHERE DID THEY COME FROM?

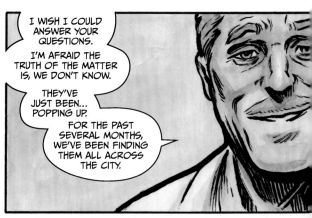

I WISH I COULD ANSWER YOUR QUESTIONS.

I'M AFRAID THE TRUTH OF THE MATTER IS, WE DON'T KNOW.

THEY'VE JUST BEEN... POPPING UP.

FOR THE PAST SEVERAL MONTHS, WE'VE BEEN FINDING THEM ALL ACROSS THE CITY.

LIKE YOU FOUND ME.

NOT QUITE, NOT QUITE.

WE KNOW WHO YOU ARE, EMMY.

WE KNOW WHERE YOU CAME FROM.

BUT THESE CHILDREN ARE... A MYSTERY.

BUT, EMMY, I NEED YOU TO LISTEN TO ME.

WE'VE TAKEN THE LOST ONES UNDER OUR ROOF.

SO THAT WE MIGHT UNDERSTAND THEM.

SO WE MIGHT TEACH THEM.

BUT YOU SHOULD BE CAREFUL AROUND THEM.

YOU SHOULDN'T VISIT THEM WHILE YOU'RE ALONE.

THEY MAY LOOK HARMLESS BUT BELIEVE ME...

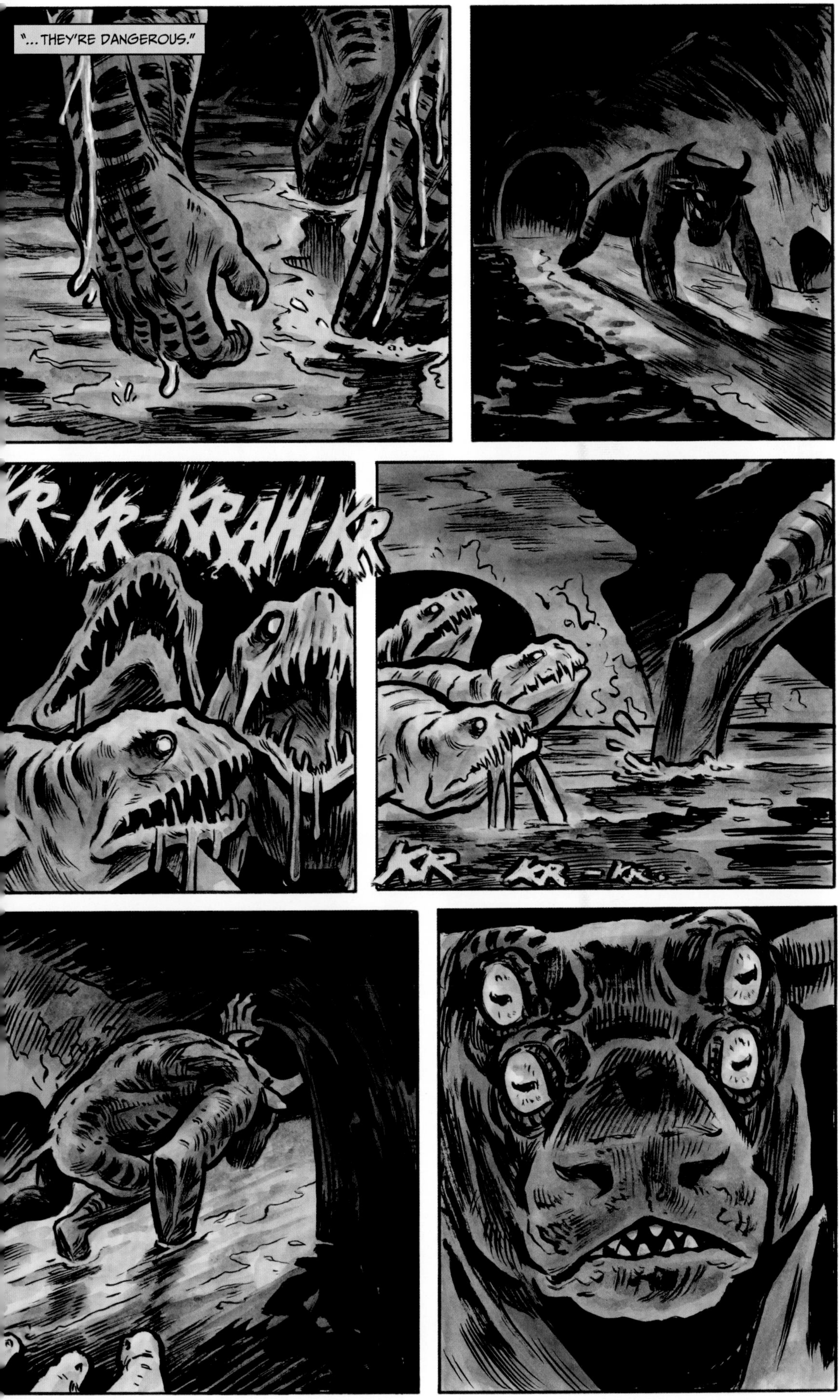
"... THEY'RE DANGEROUS."
KR-KR-KRAH-KR
KR KR-KR

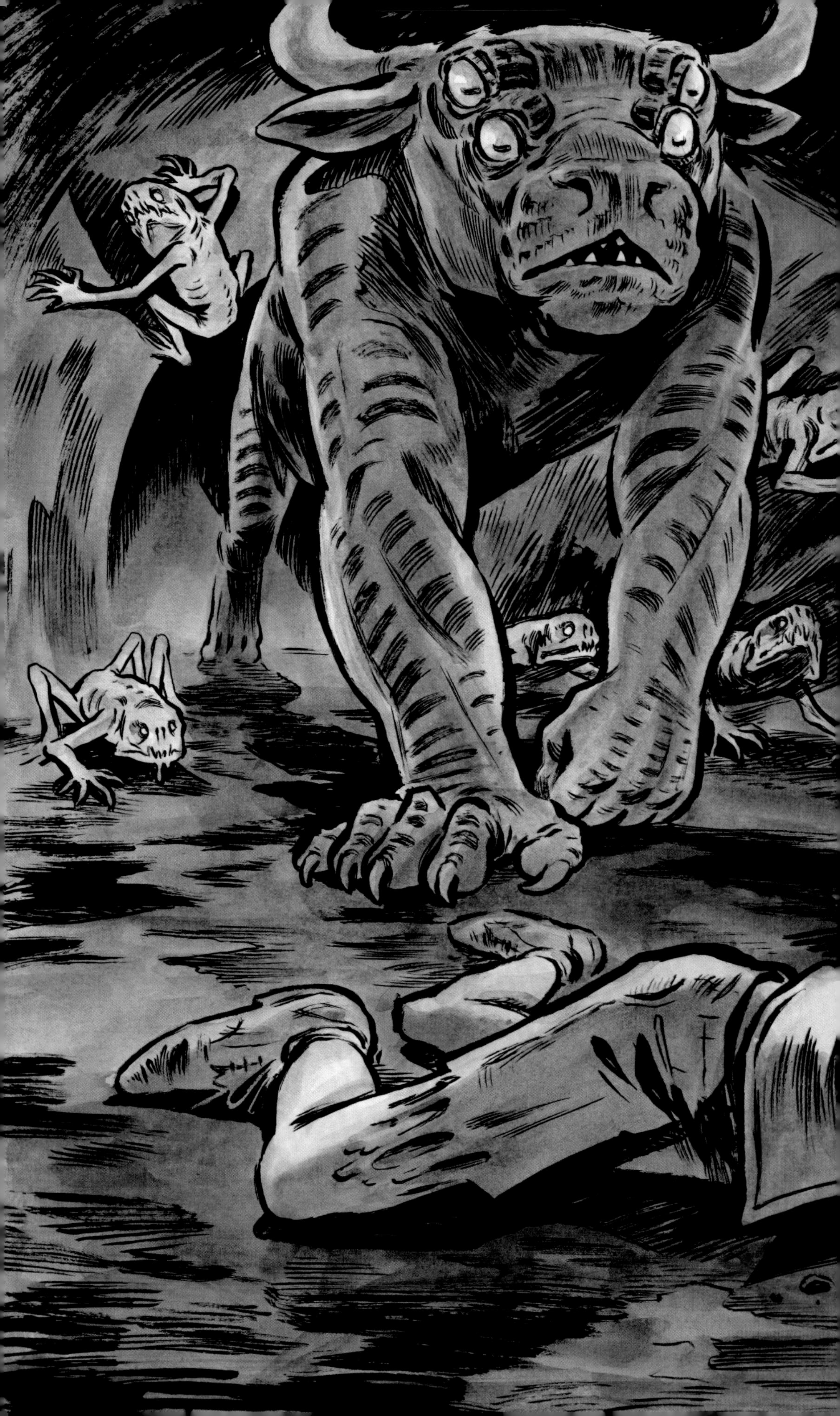

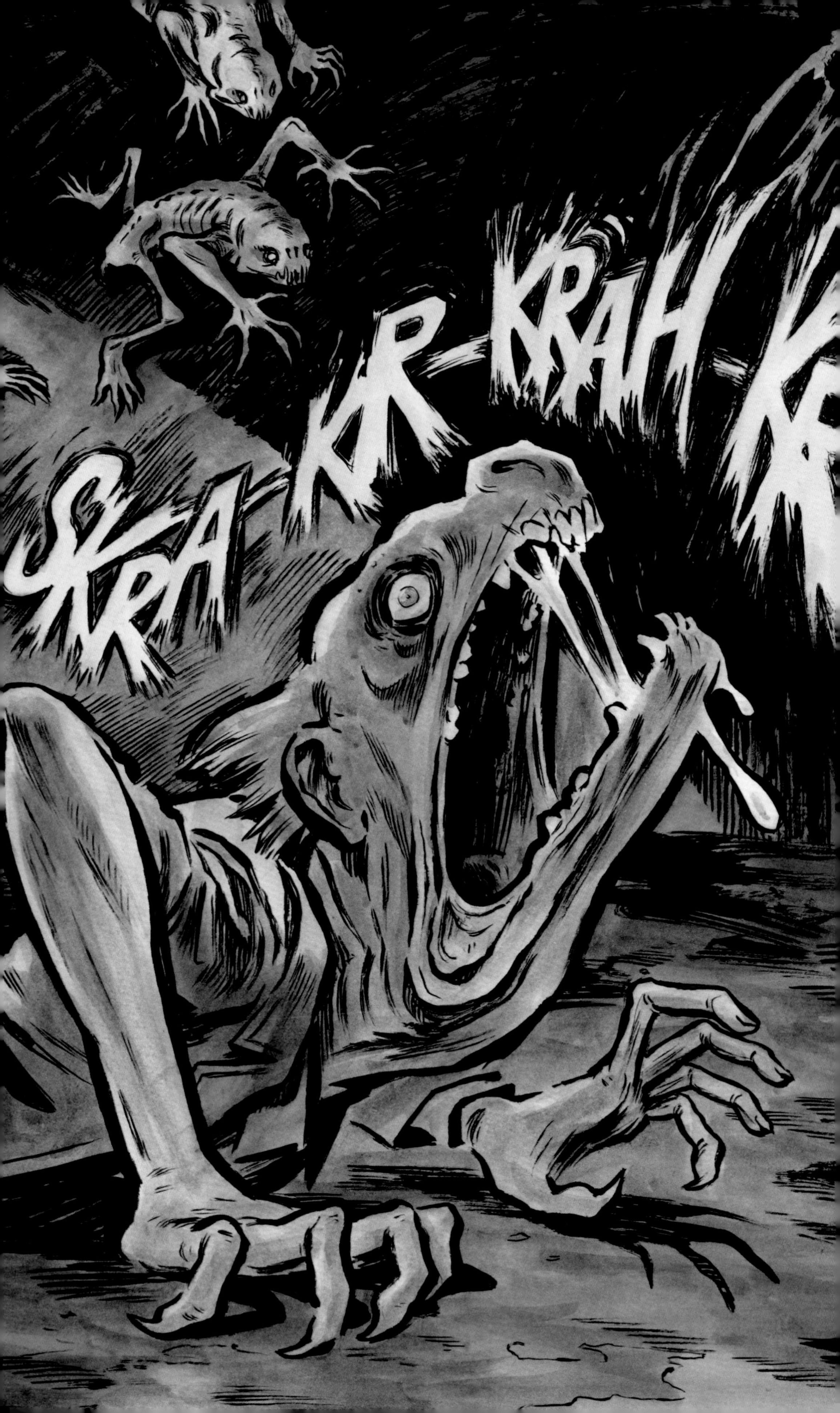
SKRA-KR-KRAH-KR

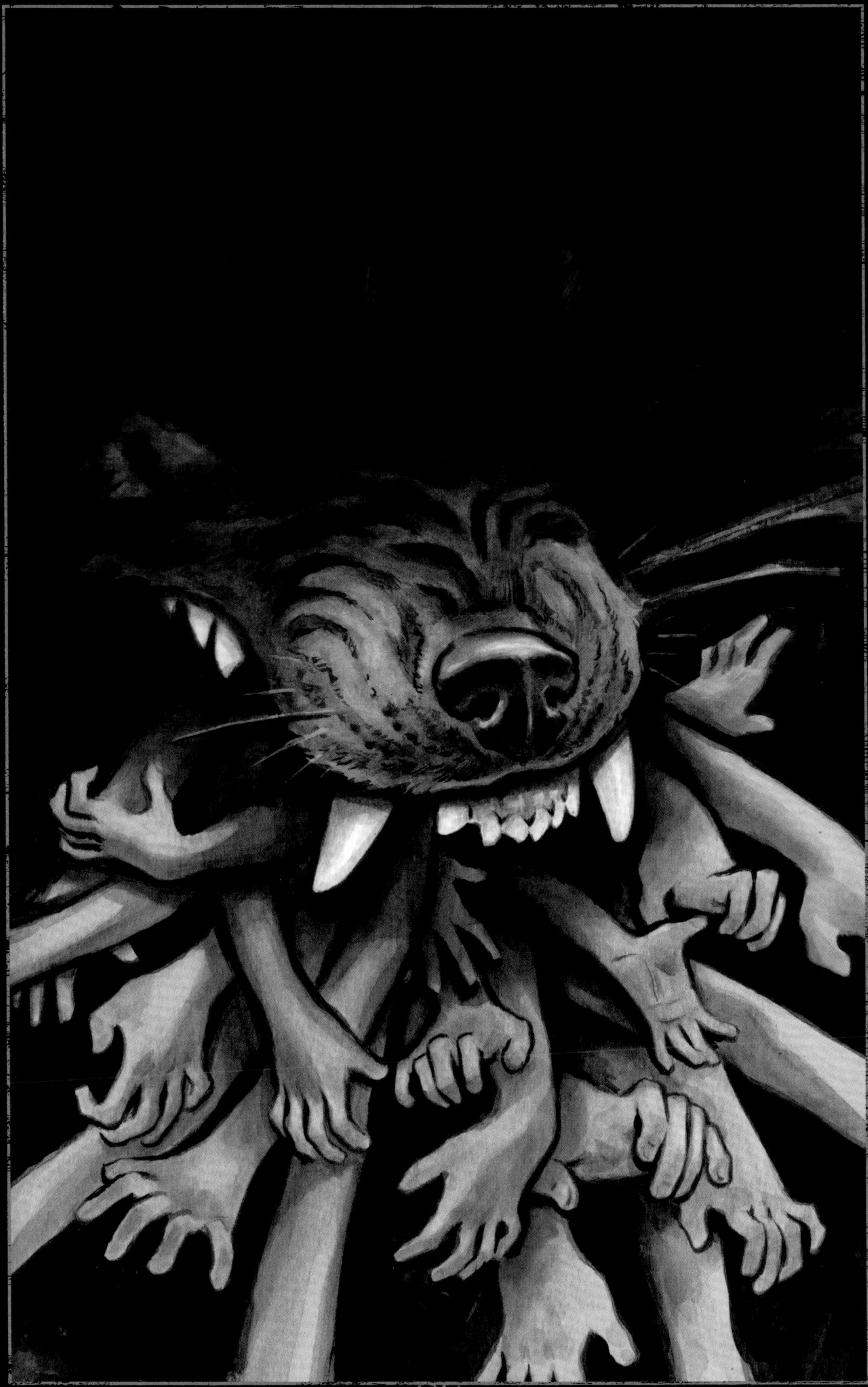

THREE

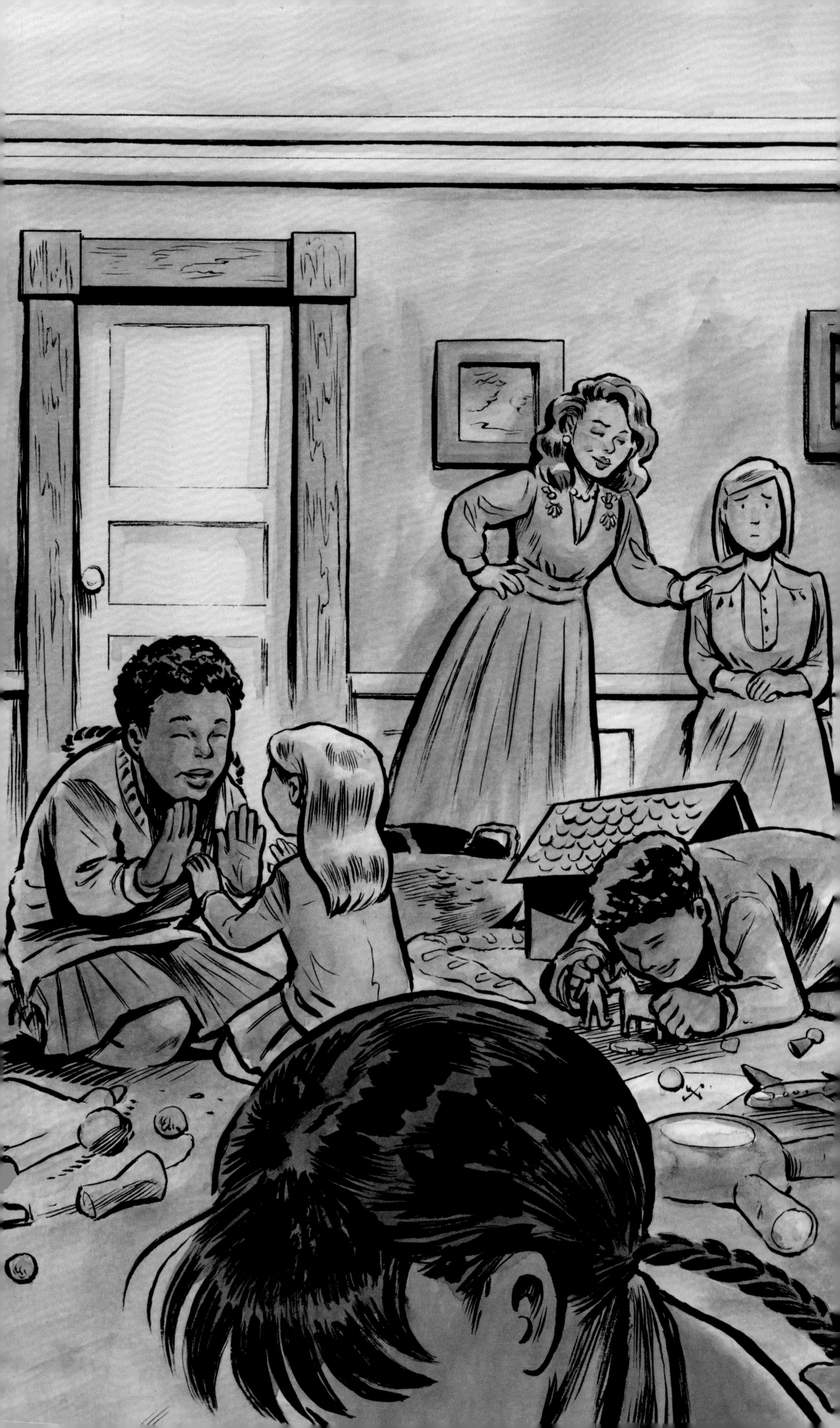

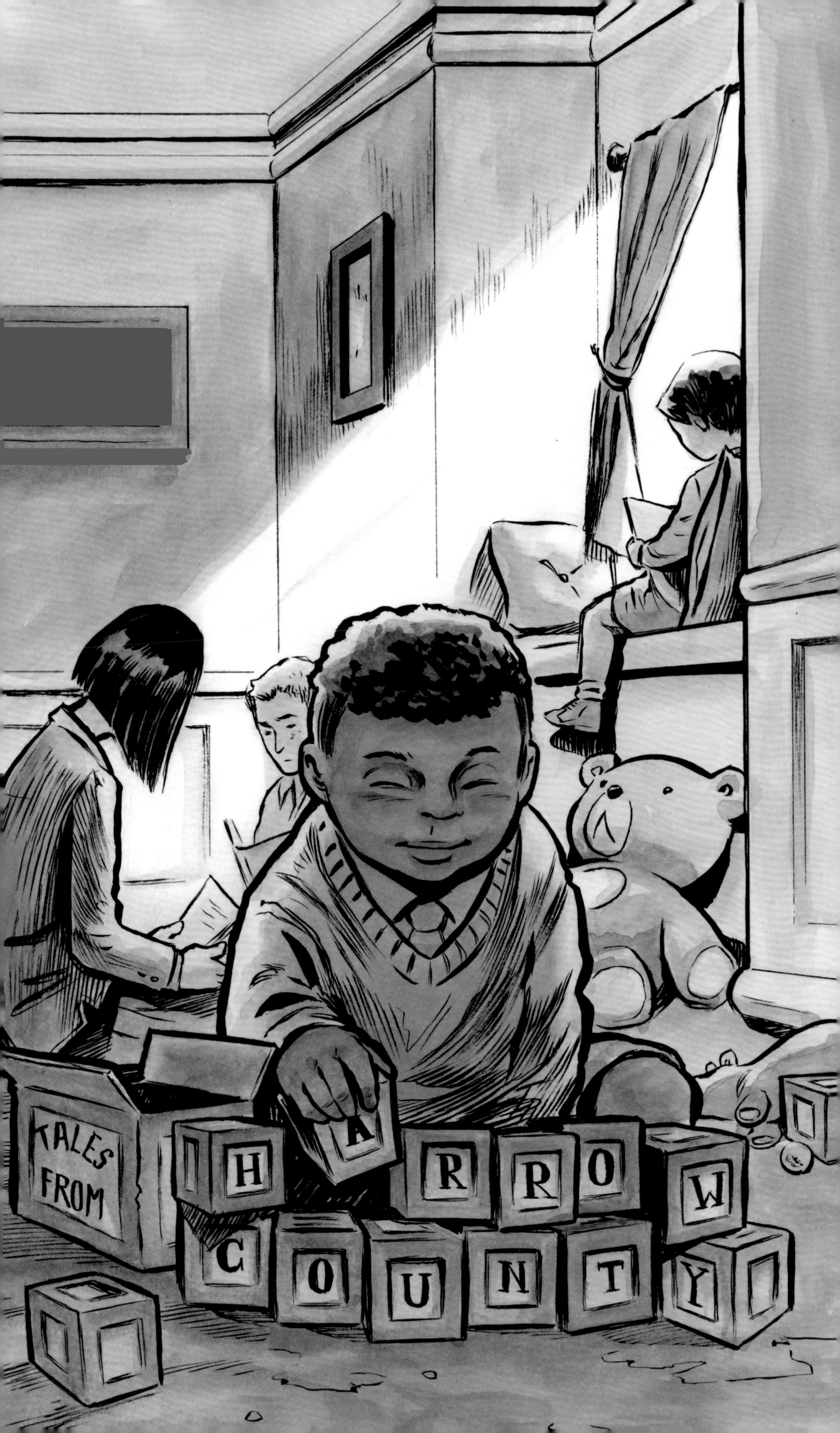
TALES FROM
HARROW
COUNTY

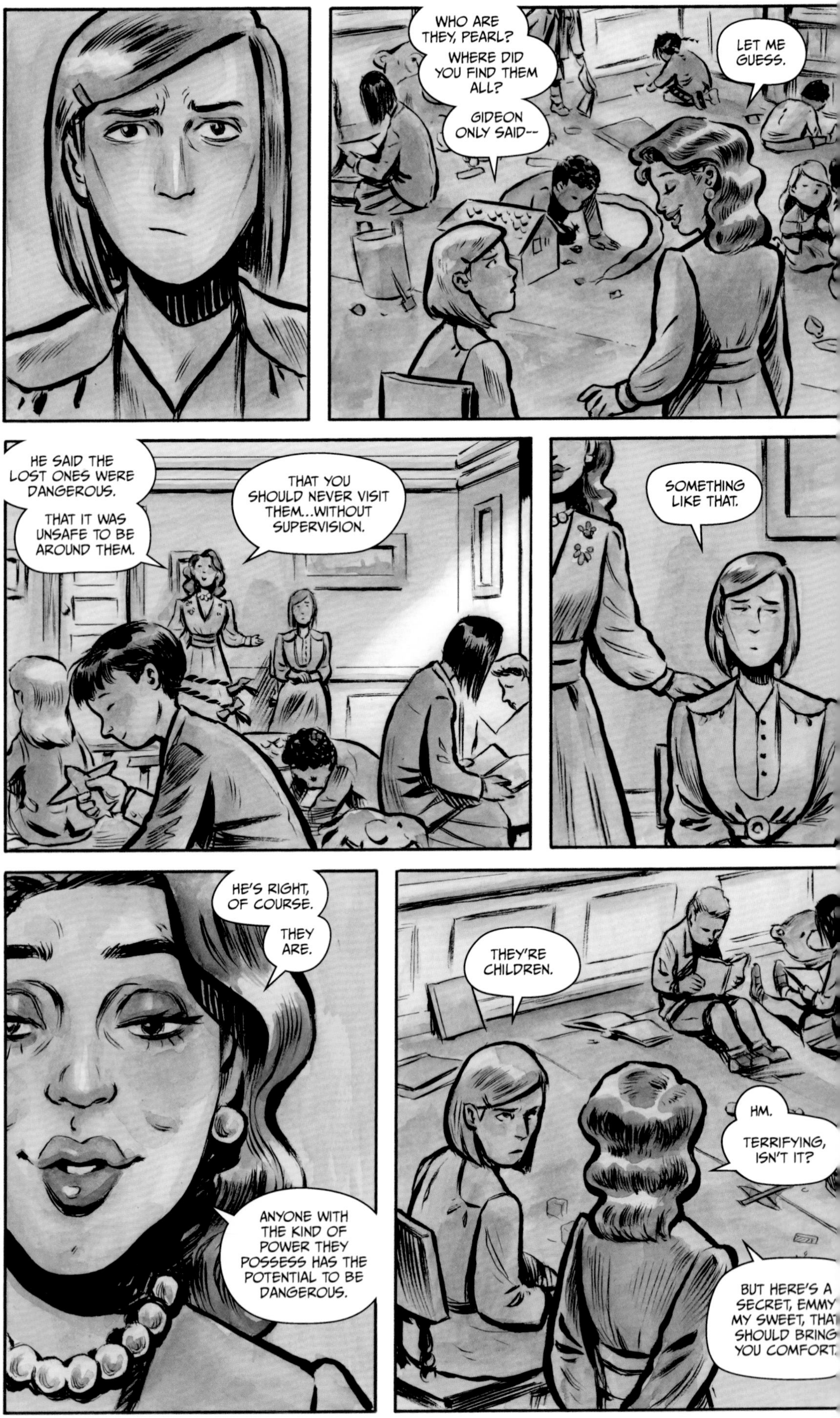
WHO ARE THEY, PEARL?
WHERE DID YOU FIND THEM ALL?
GIDEON ONLY SAID--
LET ME GUESS.
HE SAID THE LOST ONES WERE DANGEROUS.
THAT IT WAS UNSAFE TO BE AROUND THEM.
THAT YOU SHOULD NEVER VISIT THEM...WITHOUT SUPERVISION.
SOMETHING LIKE THAT.
HE'S RIGHT, OF COURSE.
THEY ARE.
ANYONE WITH THE KIND OF POWER THEY POSSESS HAS THE POTENTIAL TO BE DANGEROUS.
THEY'RE CHILDREN.
HM.
TERRIFYING, ISN'T IT?
BUT HERE'S A SECRET, EMMY MY SWEET, THAT SHOULD BRING YOU COMFORT.

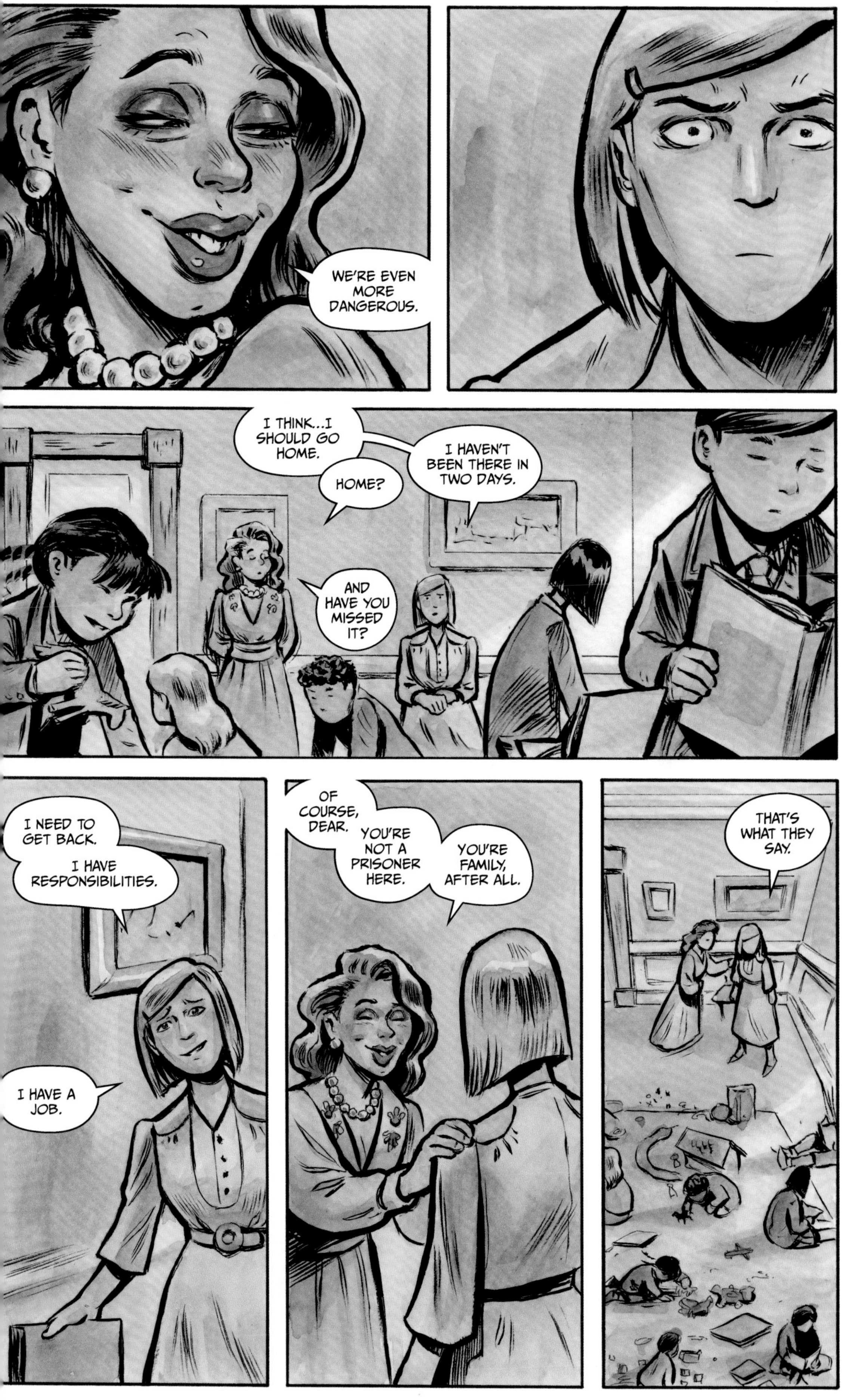
WE'RE EVEN MORE DANGEROUS.
I THINK...I SHOULD GO HOME.
HOME?
I HAVEN'T BEEN THERE IN TWO DAYS.
AND HAVE YOU MISSED IT?
I NEED TO GET BACK.
I HAVE RESPONSIBILITIES.
I HAVE A JOB.
OF COURSE, DEAR.
YOU'RE NOT A PRISONER HERE.
YOU'RE FAMILY, AFTER ALL.
THAT'S WHAT THEY SAY.

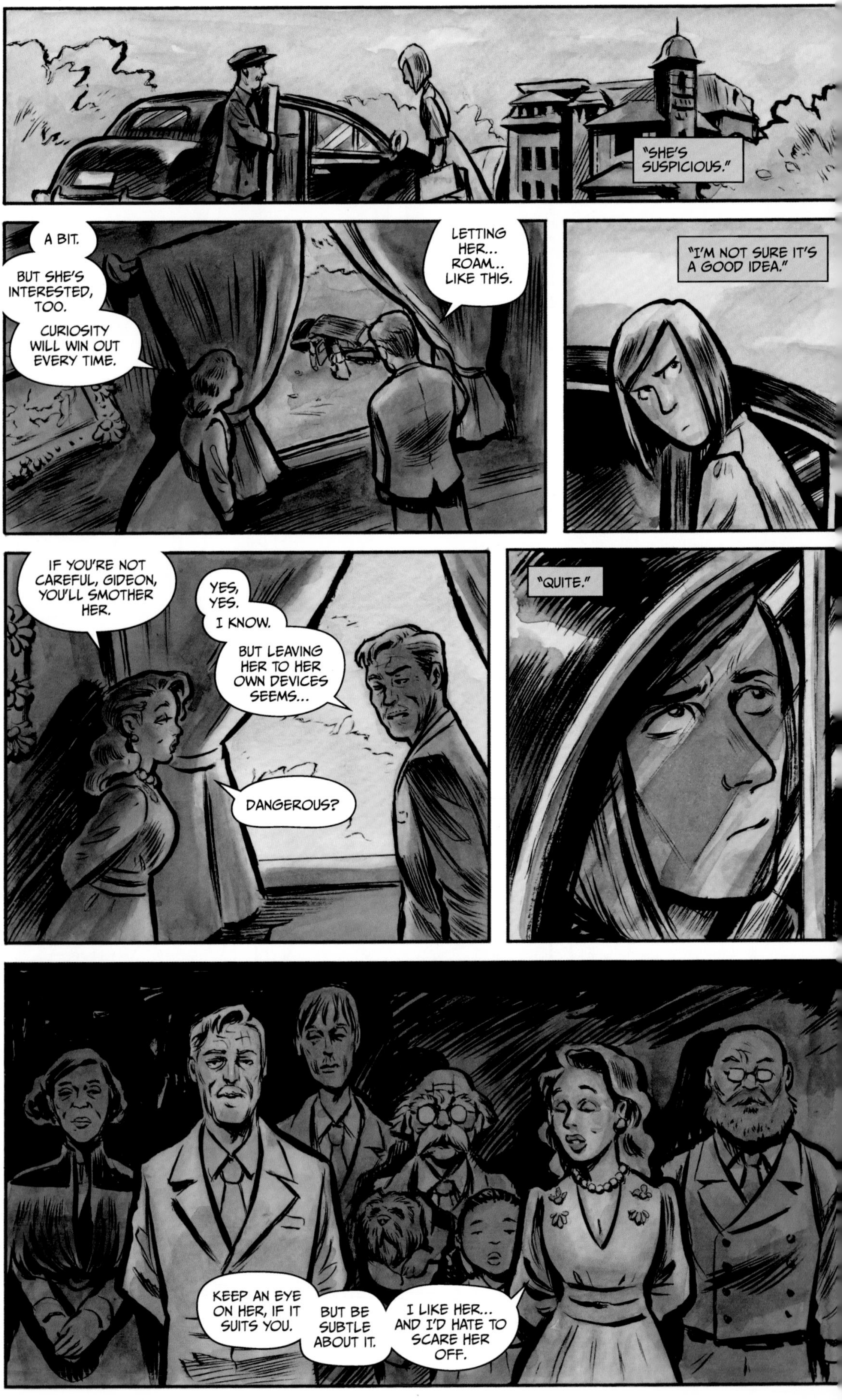
"SHE'S SUSPICIOUS."
A BIT.
BUT SHE'S INTERESTED, TOO.
CURIOSITY WILL WIN OUT EVERY TIME.
LETTING HER... ROAM.. LIKE THIS.
"I'M NOT SURE IT'S A GOOD IDEA."
IF YOU'RE NOT CAREFUL, GIDEON, YOU'LL SMOTHER HER.
YES, YES.
I KNOW.
BUT LEAVING HER TO HER OWN DEVICES SEEMS...
DANGEROUS?
"QUITE."
KEEP AN EYE ON HER, IF IT SUITS YOU.
BUT BE SUBTLE ABOUT IT.
I LIKE HER... AND I'D HATE TO SCARE HER OFF.

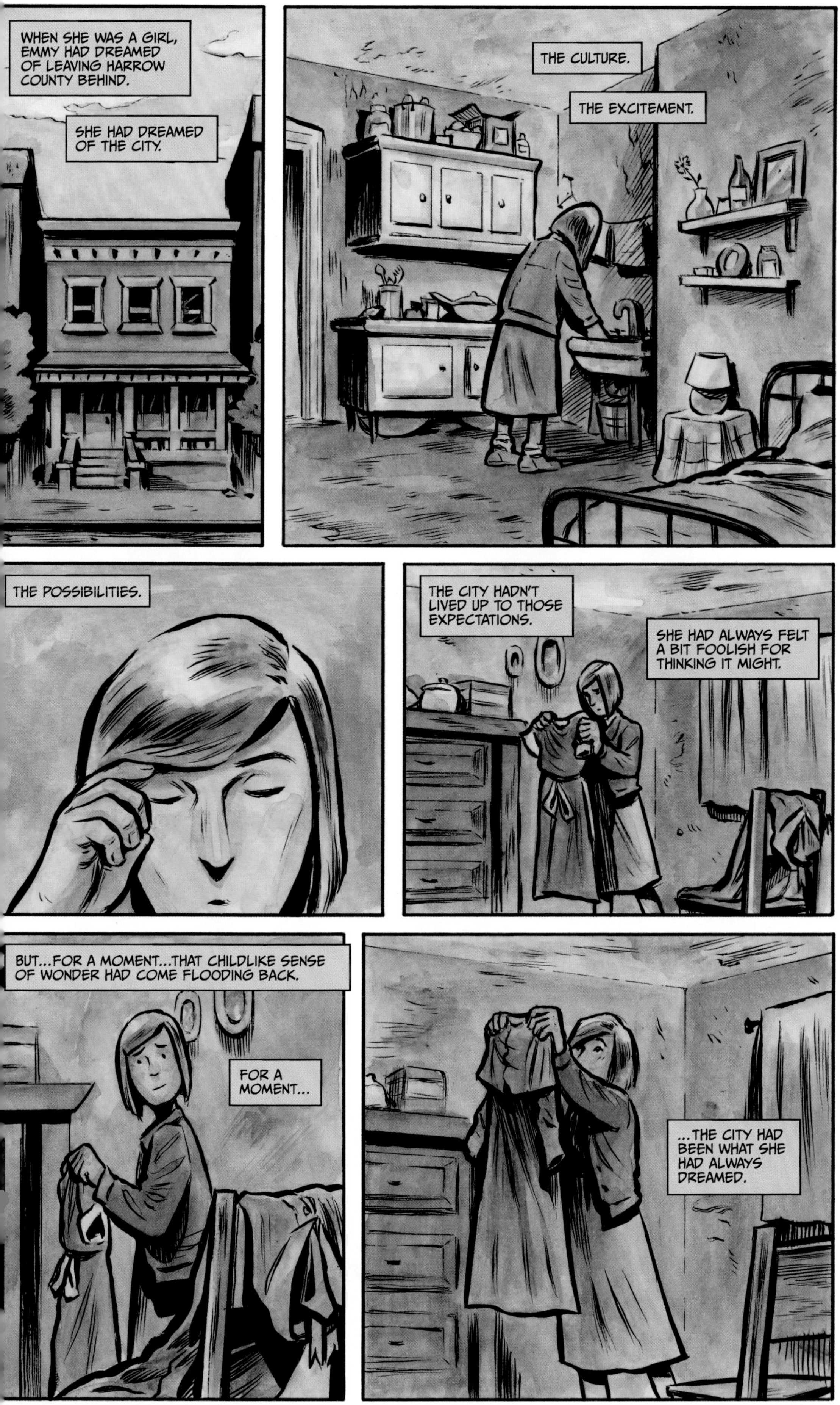
WHEN SHE WAS A GIRL, EMMY HAD DREAMED OF LEAVING HARROW COUNTY BEHIND.
SHE HAD DREAMED OF THE CITY.
THE CULTURE.
THE EXCITEMENT.
THE POSSIBILITIES.
THE CITY HADN'T LIVED UP TO THOSE EXPECTATIONS.
SHE HAD ALWAYS FELT A BIT FOOLISH FOR THINKING IT MIGHT.
BUT...FOR A MOMENT...THAT CHILDLIKE SENSE OF WONDER HAD COME FLOODING BACK.
FOR A MOMENT...
...THE CITY HAD BEEN WHAT SHE HAD ALWAYS DREAMED.

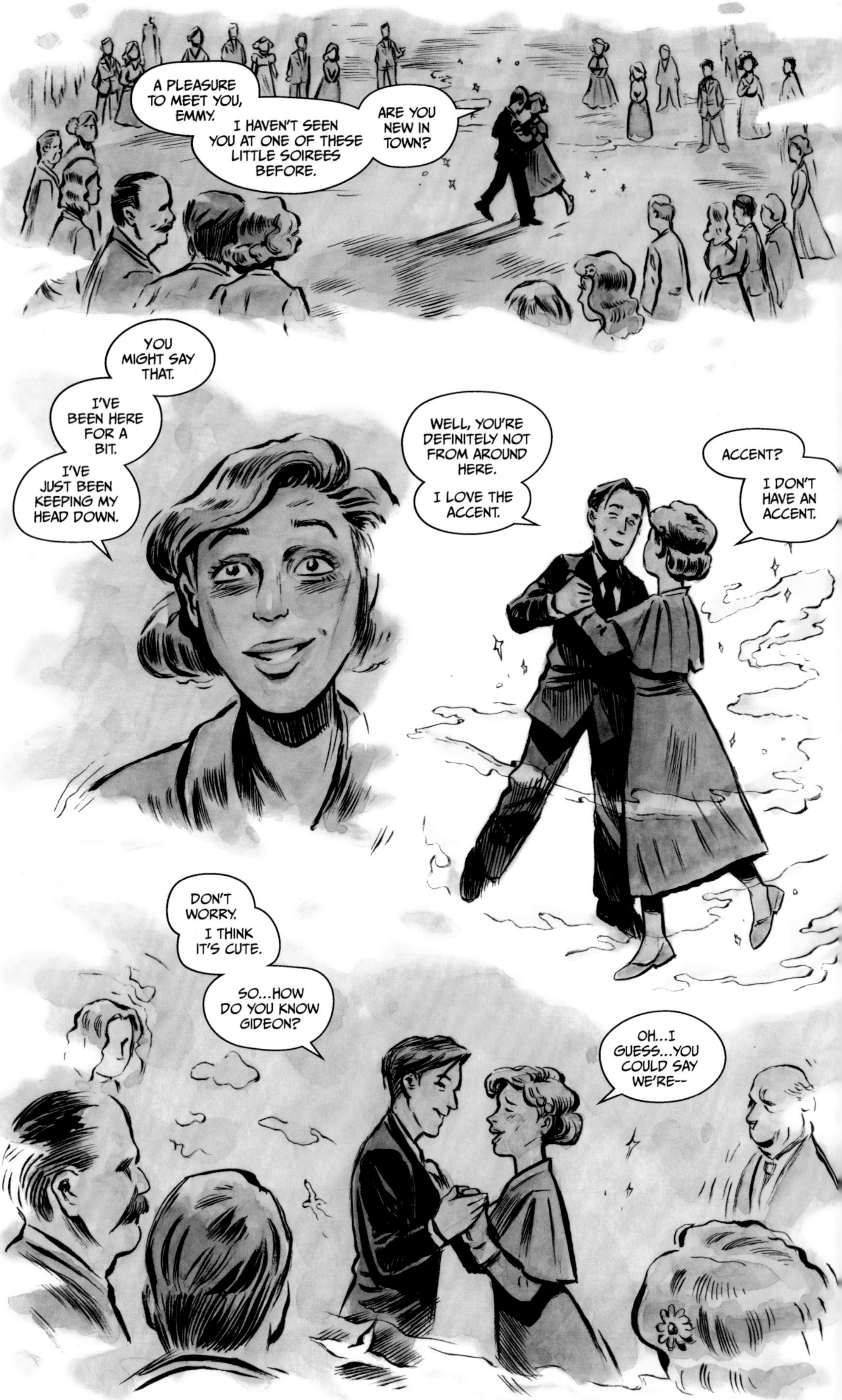

A PLEASURE TO MEET YOU, EMMY.
I HAVEN'T SEEN YOU AT ONE OF THESE LITTLE SOIREES BEFORE.
ARE YOU NEW IN TOWN?
YOU MIGHT SAY THAT.
I'VE BEEN HERE FOR A BIT.
I'VE JUST BEEN KEEPING MY HEAD DOWN.
WELL, YOU'RE DEFINITELY NOT FROM AROUND HERE.
I LOVE THE ACCENT.
ACCENT?
I DON'T HAVE AN ACCENT.
DON'T WORRY.
I THINK IT'S CUTE.
SO...HOW DO YOU KNOW GIDEON?
OH...I GUESS...YOU COULD SAY WE'RE--

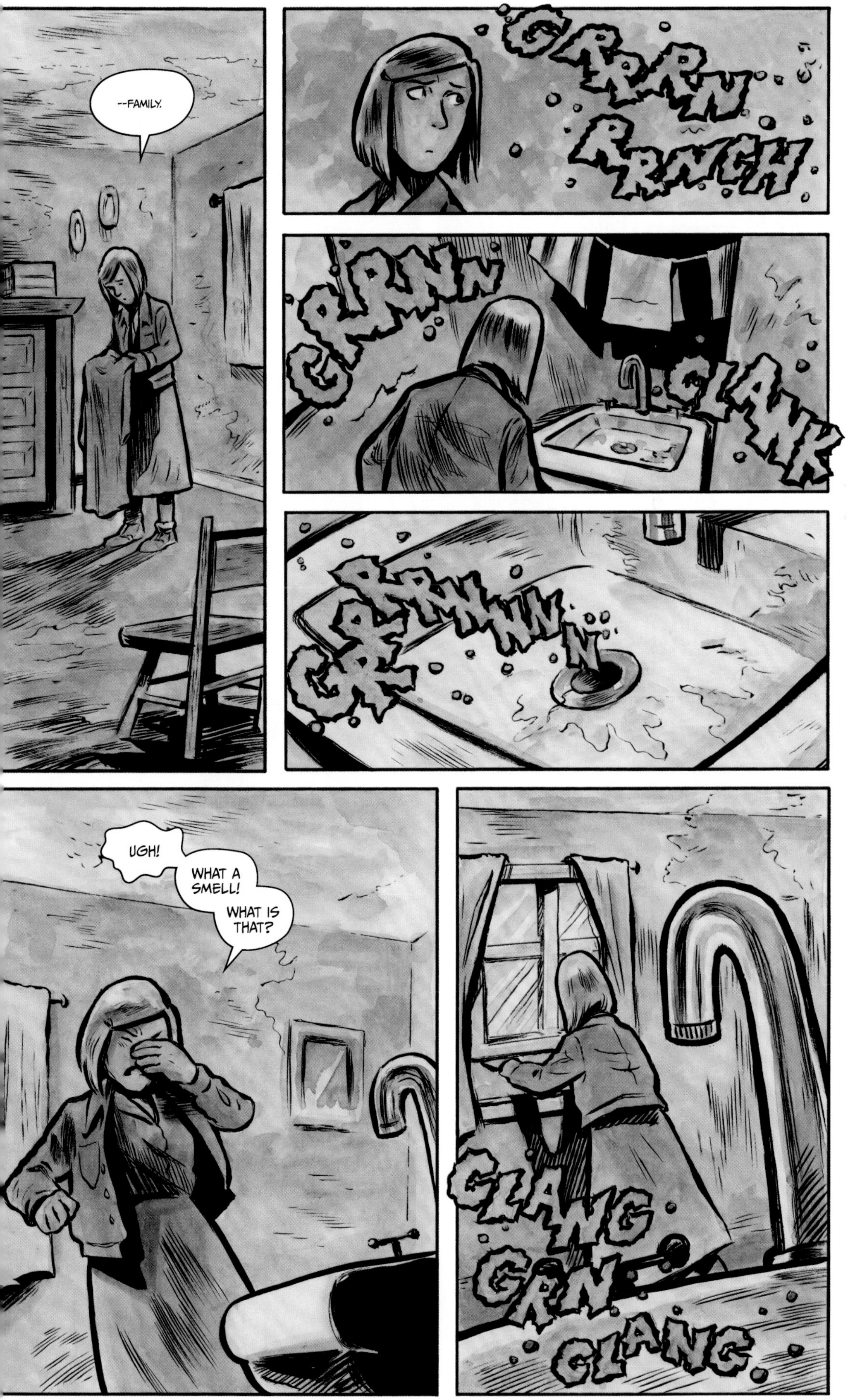
--FAMILY.
GRRRN
RRNCH
GRRNN
CLANK
GRRNNNN
UGH!
WHAT A SMELL!
WHAT IS THAT?
CLANG
GRN
CLANG

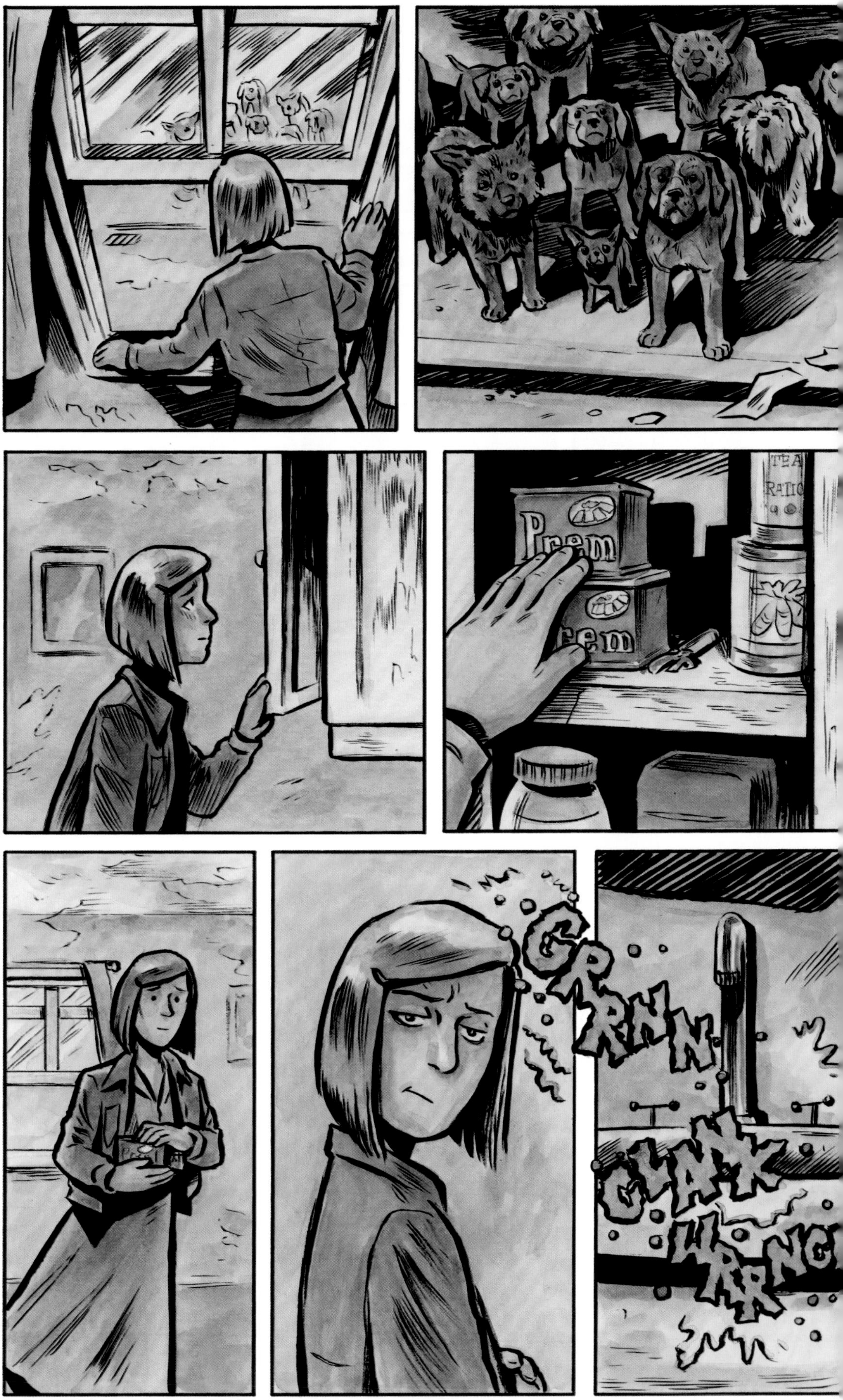
Prem
Prem
TEA RATIO
GRRHN
CLANK
WARRNG

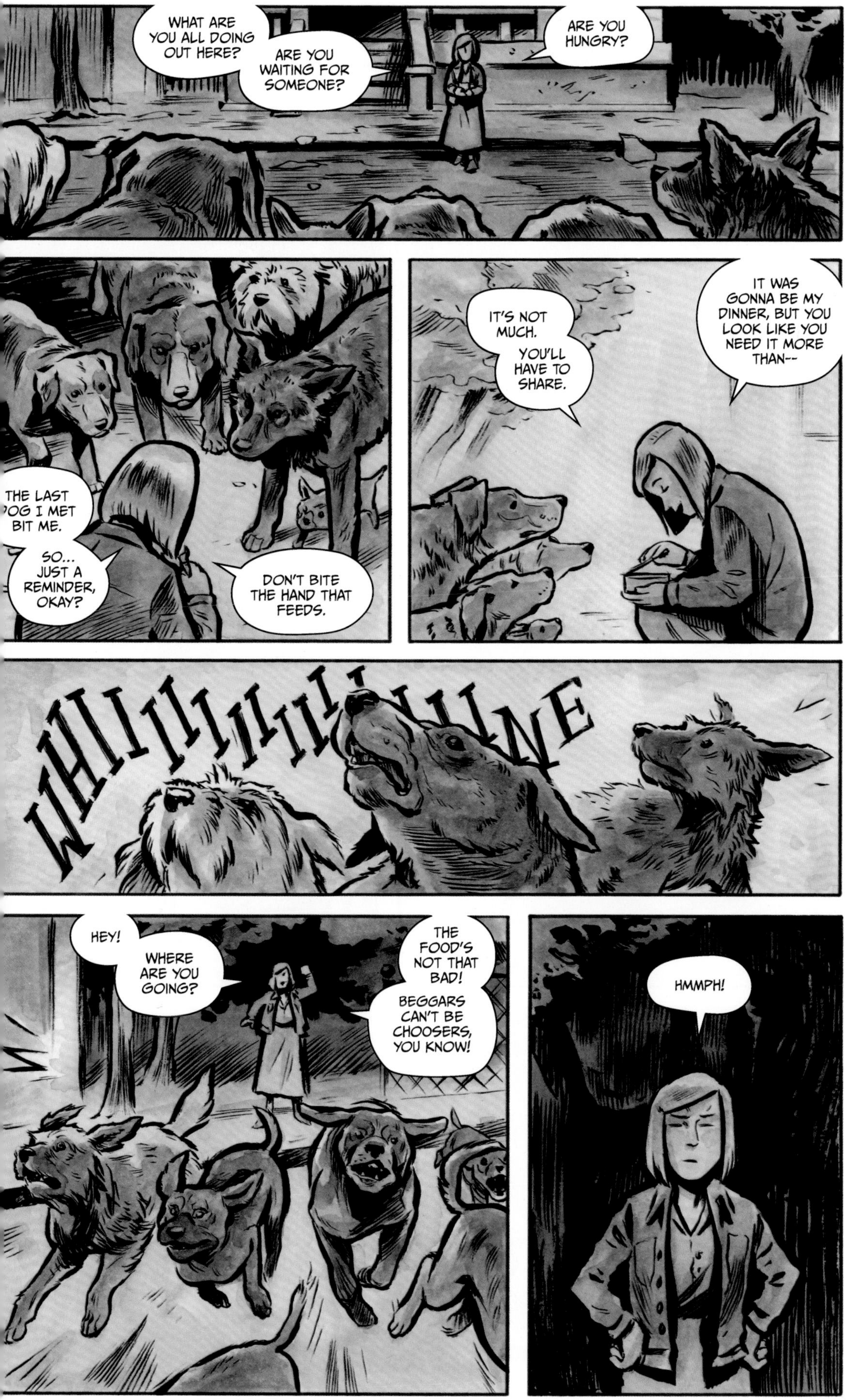
WHAT ARE YOU ALL DOING OUT HERE?
ARE YOU WAITING FOR SOMEONE?
ARE YOU HUNGRY?
THE LAST DOG I MET BIT ME.
SO... JUST A REMINDER, OKAY?
DON'T BITE THE HAND THAT FEEDS.
IT'S NOT MUCH.
YOU'LL HAVE TO SHARE.
IT WAS GONNA BE MY DINNER, BUT YOU LOOK LIKE YOU NEED IT MORE THAN--
WHIIIIIIIIIINE
HEY!
WHERE ARE YOU GOING?
THE FOOD'S NOT THAT BAD!
BEGGARS CAN'T BE CHOOSERS, YOU KNOW!
HMMPH!

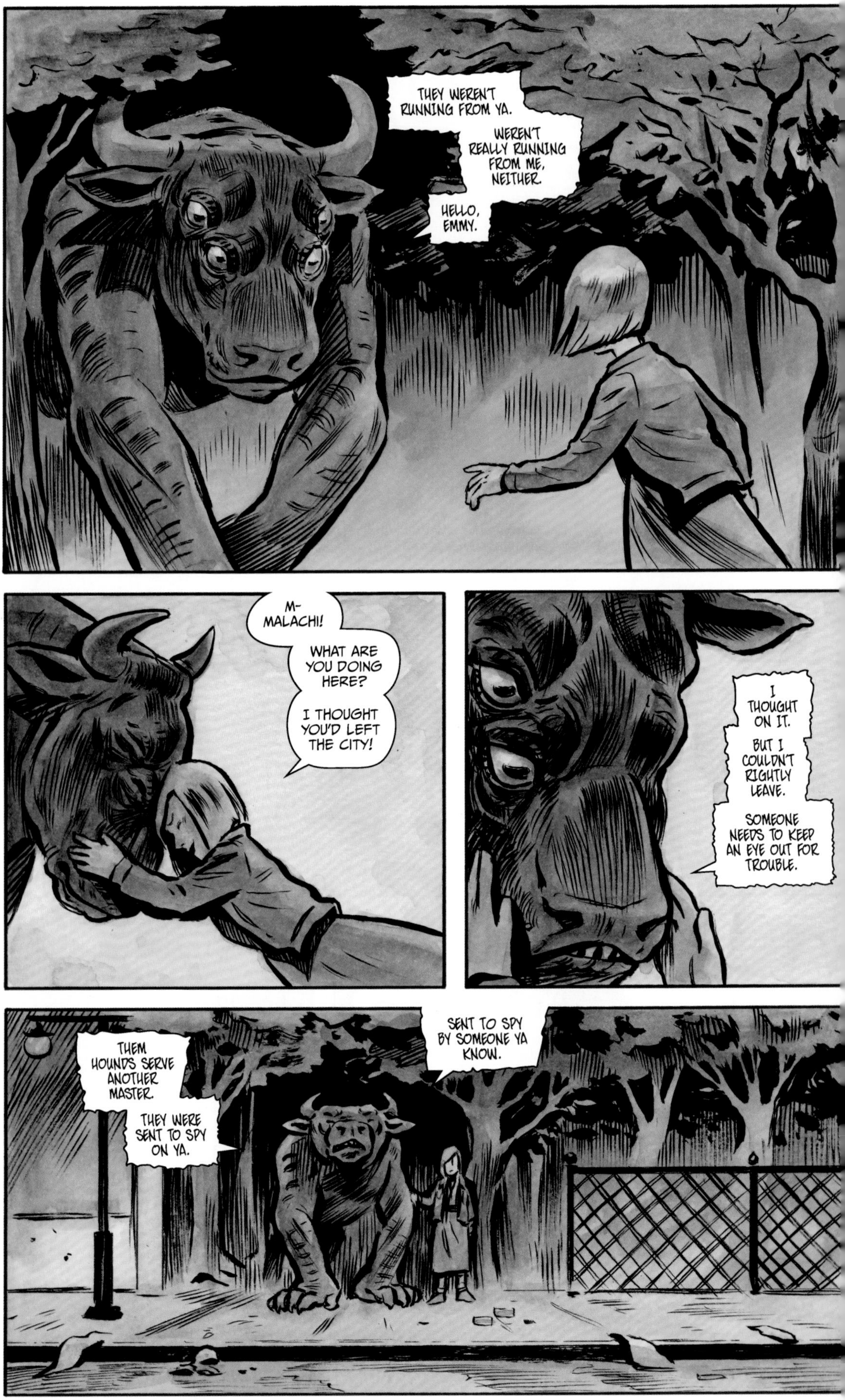
THEY WEREN'T RUNNING FROM YA.
WEREN'T REALLY RUNNING FROM ME, NEITHER.
HELLO, EMMY.
M-MALACHI!
WHAT ARE YOU DOING HERE?
I THOUGHT YOU'D LEFT THE CITY!
I THOUGHT ON IT.
BUT I COULDN'T RIGHTLY LEAVE.
SOMEONE NEEDS TO KEEP AN EYE OUT FOR TROUBLE.
THEM HOUNDS SERVE ANOTHER MASTER.
THEY WERE SENT TO SPY ON YA.
SENT TO SPY BY SOMEONE YA KNOW.

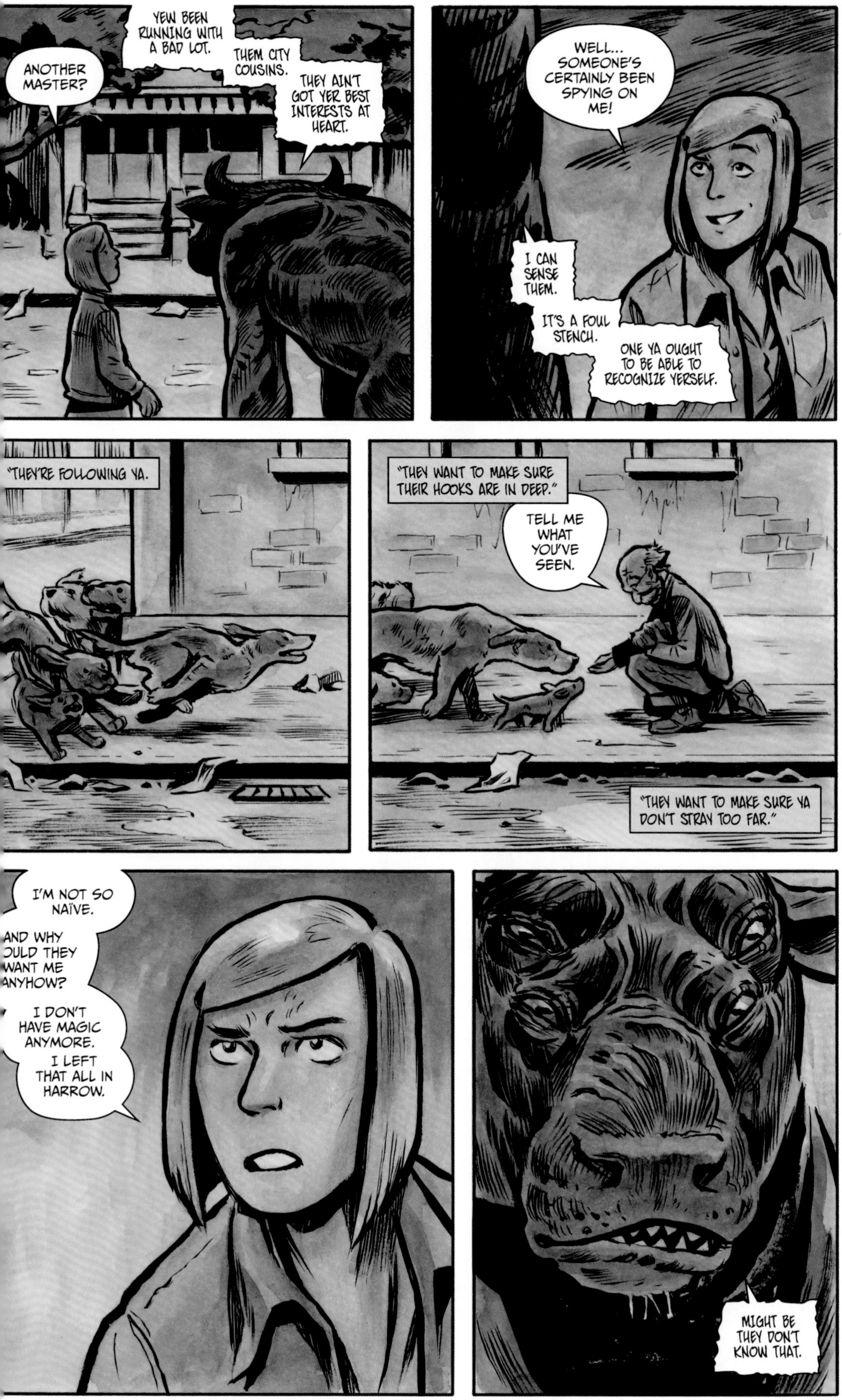
ANOTHER MASTER?
YEW BEEN RUNNING WITH A BAD LOT.
THEM CITY COUSINS.
THEY AIN'T GOT YER BEST INTERESTS AT HEART.
WELL... SOMEONE'S CERTAINLY BEEN SPYING ON ME!
I CAN SENSE THEM.
IT'S A FOUL STENCH.
ONE YA OUGHT TO BE ABLE TO RECOGNIZE YERSELF.
"THEY'RE FOLLOWING YA.
"THEY WANT TO MAKE SURE THEIR HOOKS ARE IN DEEP."
TELL ME WHAT YOU'VE SEEN.
"THEY WANT TO MAKE SURE YA DON'T STRAY TOO FAR."
I'M NOT SO NAÏVE.
AND WHY OULD THEY WANT ME ANYHOW?
I DON'T HAVE MAGIC ANYMORE.
I LEFT THAT ALL IN HARROW.
MIGHT BE THEY DON'T KNOW THAT.

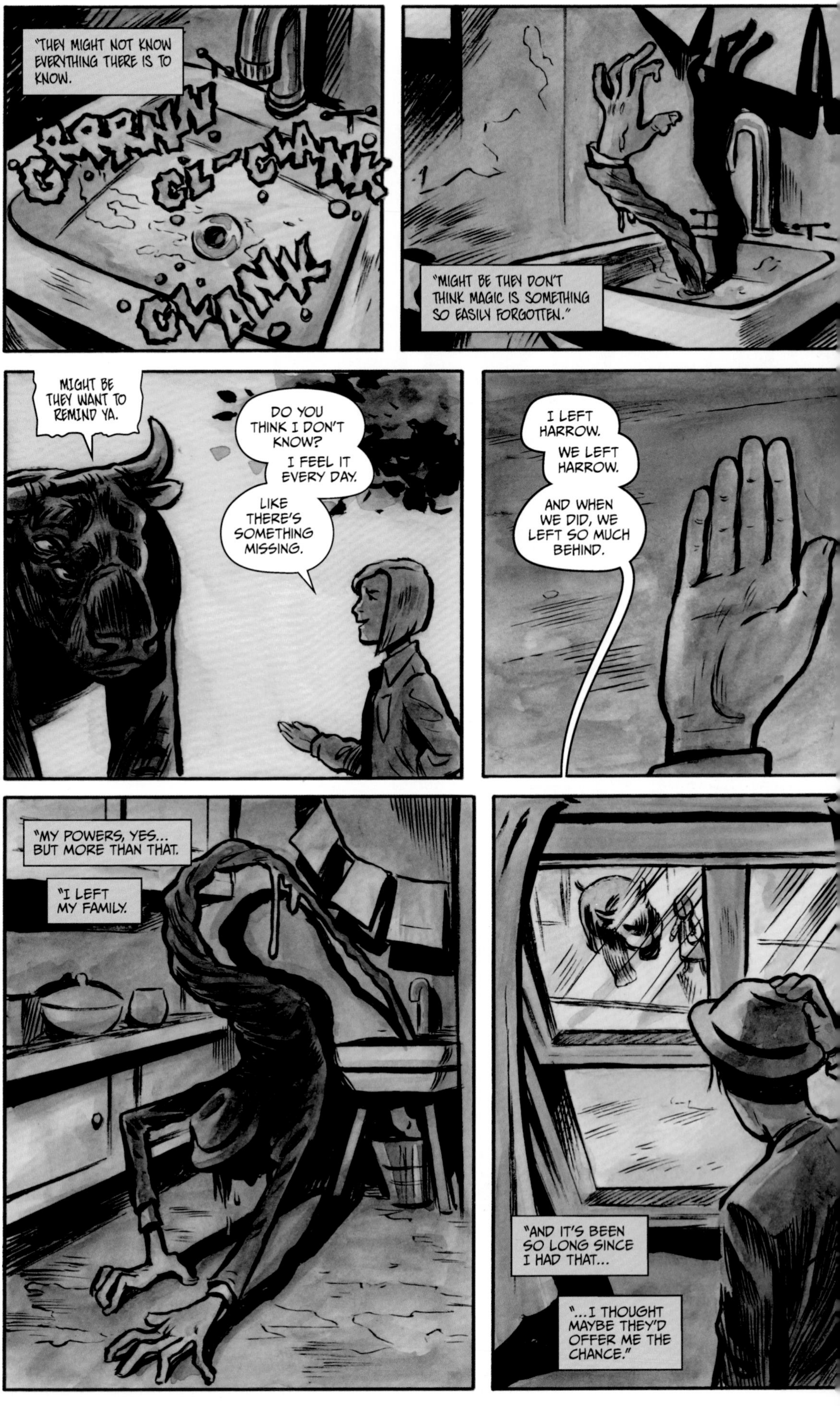
"THEY MIGHT NOT KNOW EVERYTHING THERE IS TO KNOW.
GRRRNN
CL-CLANK
CLANK
"MIGHT BE THEY DON'T THINK MAGIC IS SOMETHING SO EASILY FORGOTTEN."
MIGHT BE THEY WANT TO REMIND YA.
DO YOU THINK I DON'T KNOW?
I FEEL IT EVERY DAY.
LIKE THERE'S SOMETHING MISSING.
I LEFT HARROW.
WE LEFT HARROW.
AND WHEN WE DID, WE LEFT SO MUCH BEHIND.
"MY POWERS, YES... BUT MORE THAN THAT.
"I LEFT MY FAMILY.
"AND IT'S BEEN SO LONG SINCE I HAD THAT...
"...I THOUGHT MAYBE THEY'D OFFER ME THE CHANCE."

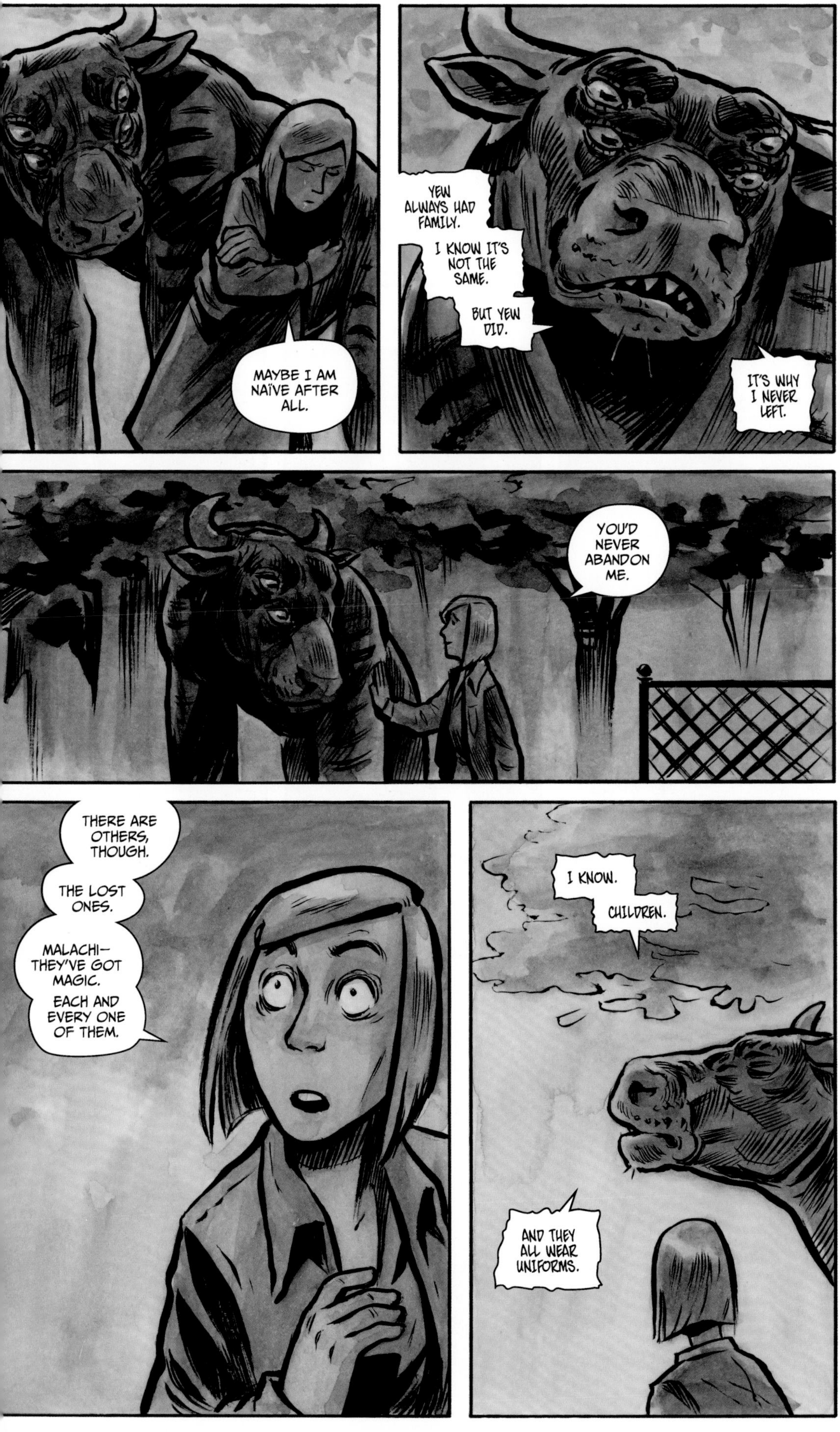
MAYBE I AM NAÏVE AFTER ALL.
YEW ALWAYS HAD FAMILY.
I KNOW IT'S NOT THE SAME.
BUT YEW DID.
IT'S WHY I NEVER LEFT.
YOU'D NEVER ABANDON ME.
THERE ARE OTHERS, THOUGH.
THE LOST ONES.
MALACHI— THEY'VE GOT MAGIC.
EACH AND EVERY ONE OF THEM.
I KNOW.
CHILDREN.
AND THEY ALL WEAR UNIFORMS.

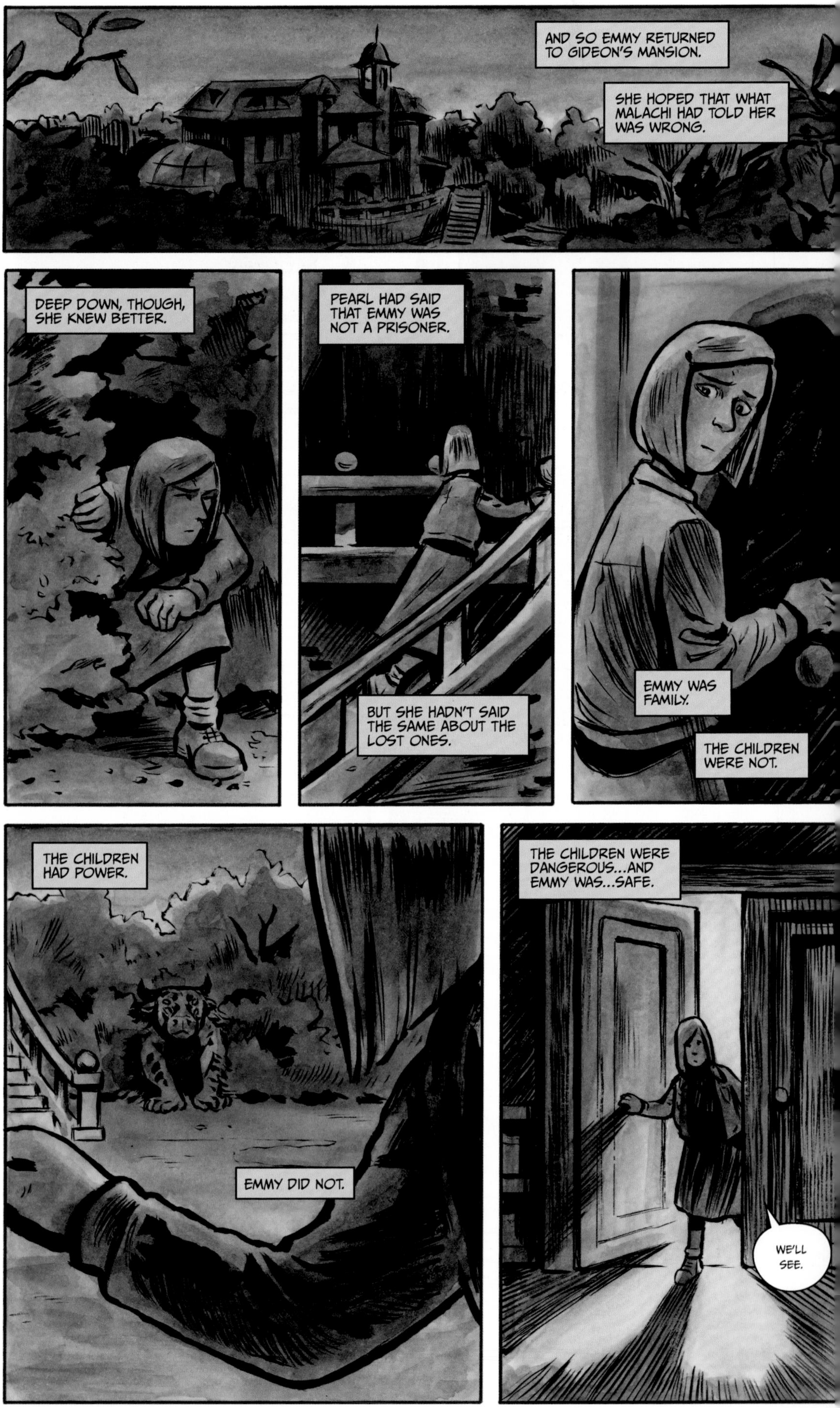
AND SO EMMY RETURNED TO GIDEON'S MANSION.
SHE HOPED THAT WHAT MALACHI HAD TOLD HER WAS WRONG.
DEEP DOWN, THOUGH, SHE KNEW BETTER.
PEARL HAD SAID THAT EMMY WAS NOT A PRISONER.
BUT SHE HADN'T SAID THE SAME ABOUT THE LOST ONES.
EMMY WAS FAMILY.
THE CHILDREN WERE NOT.
THE CHILDREN HAD POWER.
EMMY DID NOT.
THE CHILDREN WERE DANGEROUS...AND EMMY WAS...SAFE.
WE'LL SEE.

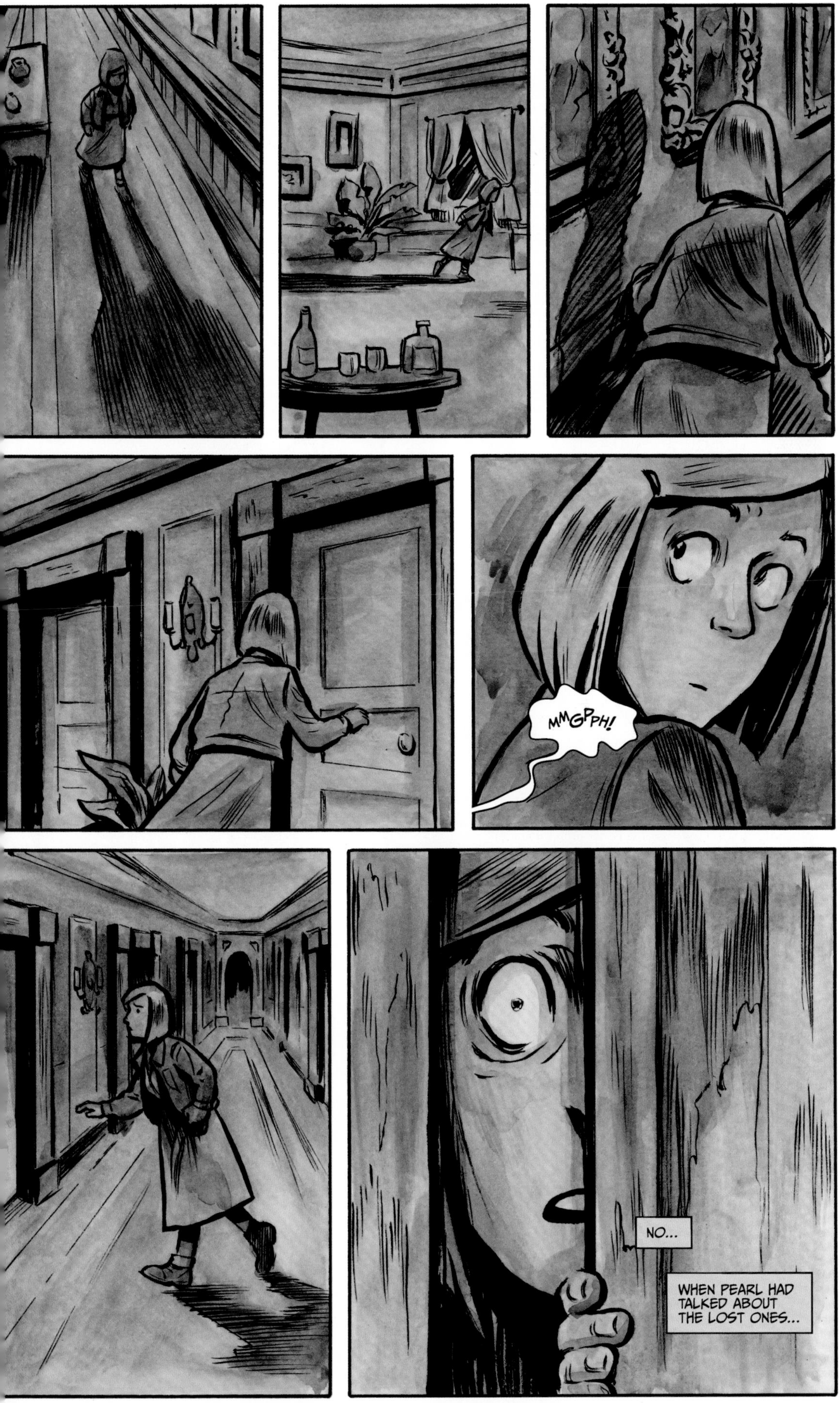
MMGPPH!
NO...
WHEN PEARL HAD TALKED ABOUT THE LOST ONES...

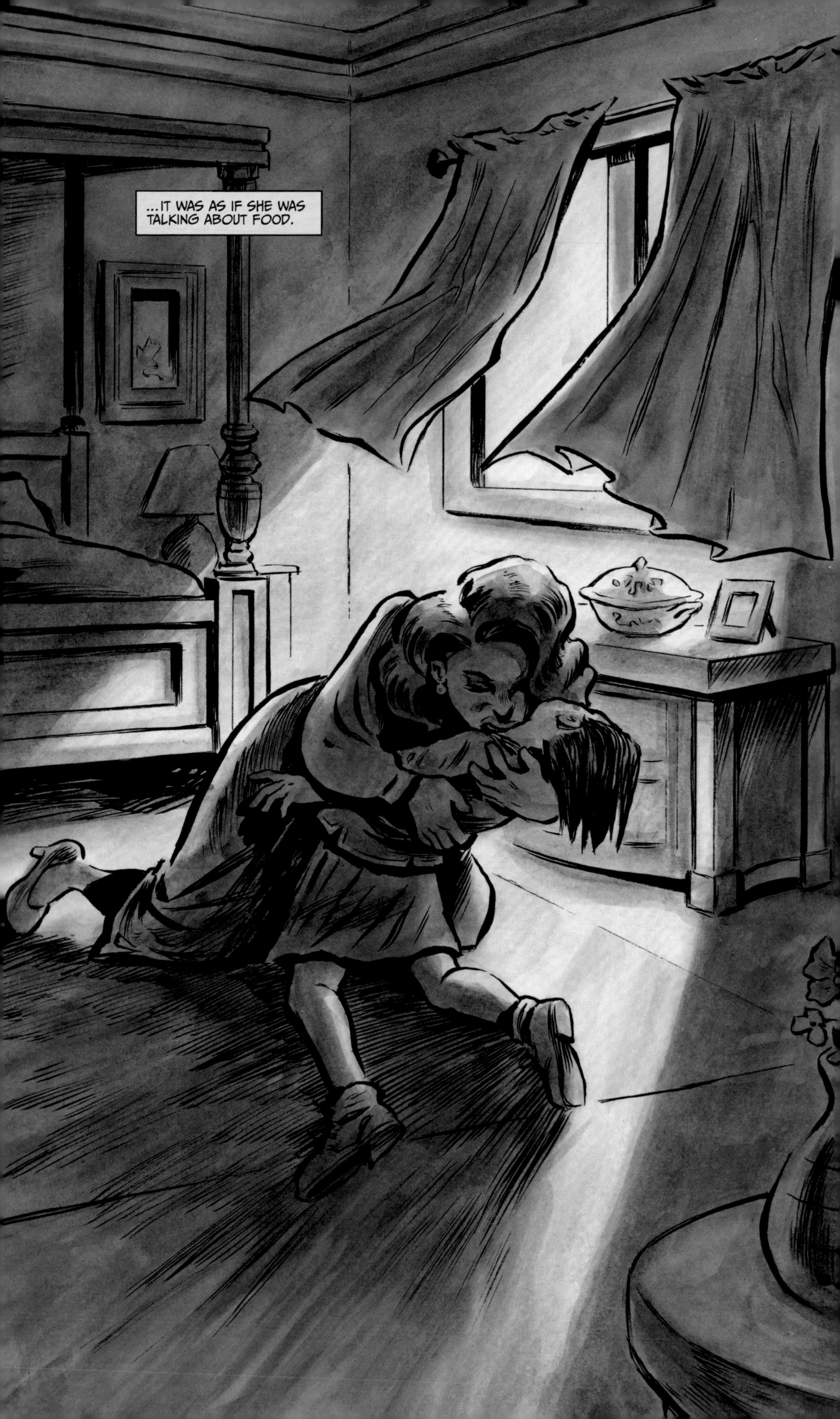
...IT WAS AS IF SHE WAS TALKING ABOUT FOOD.

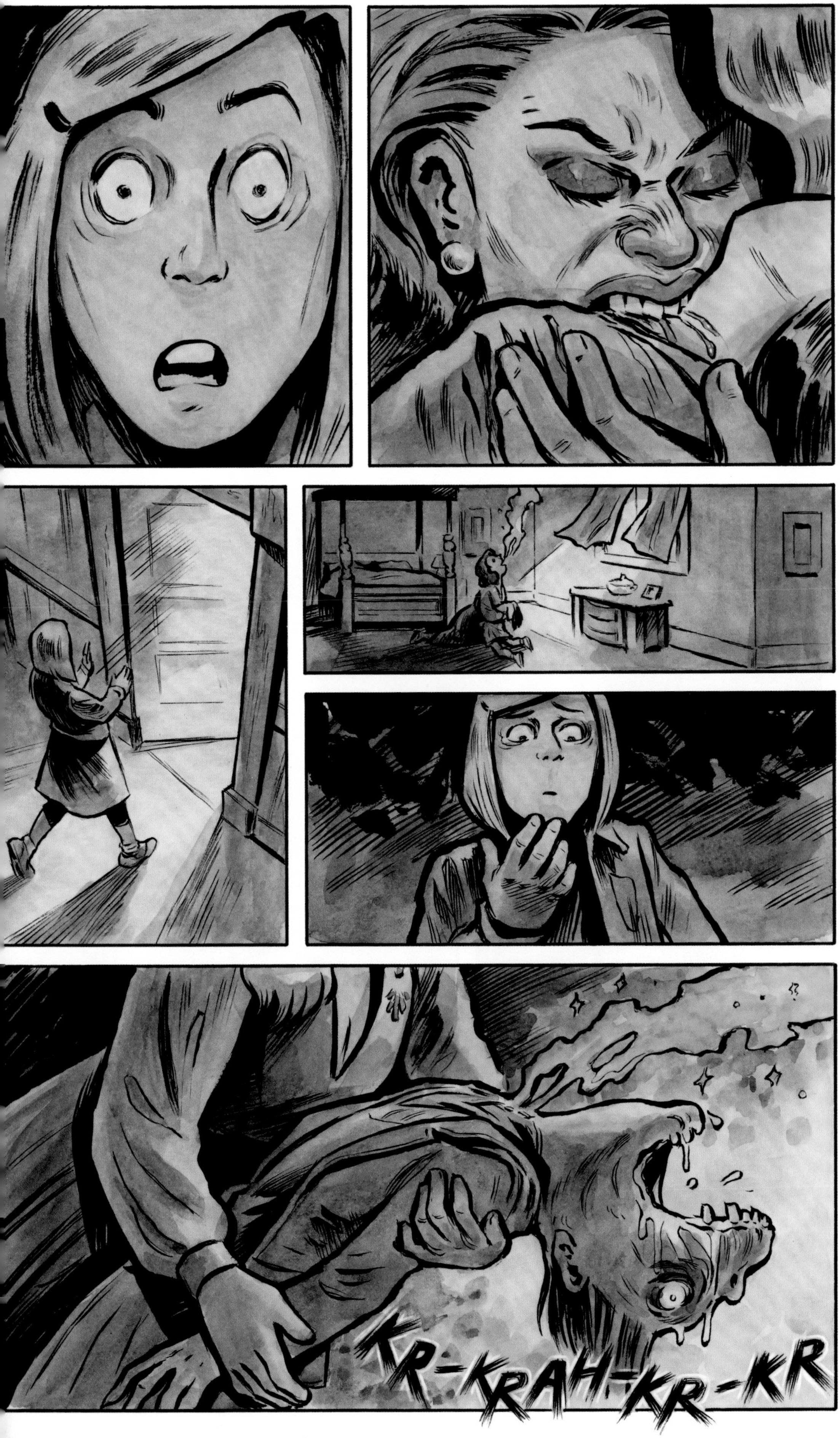
KR-KRAH-KR-KR

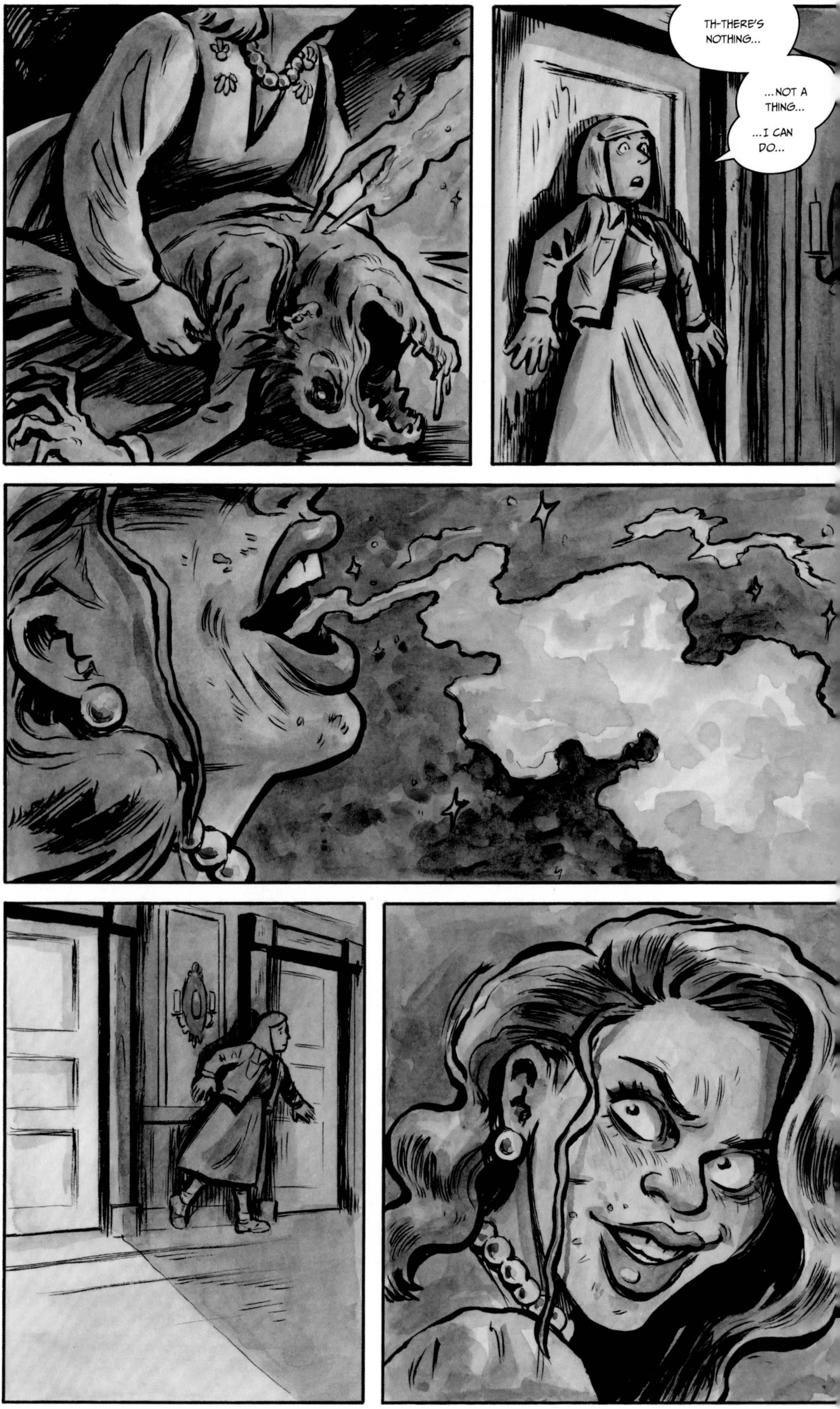
TH-THERE'S NOTHING...
...NOT A THING...
...I CAN DO...

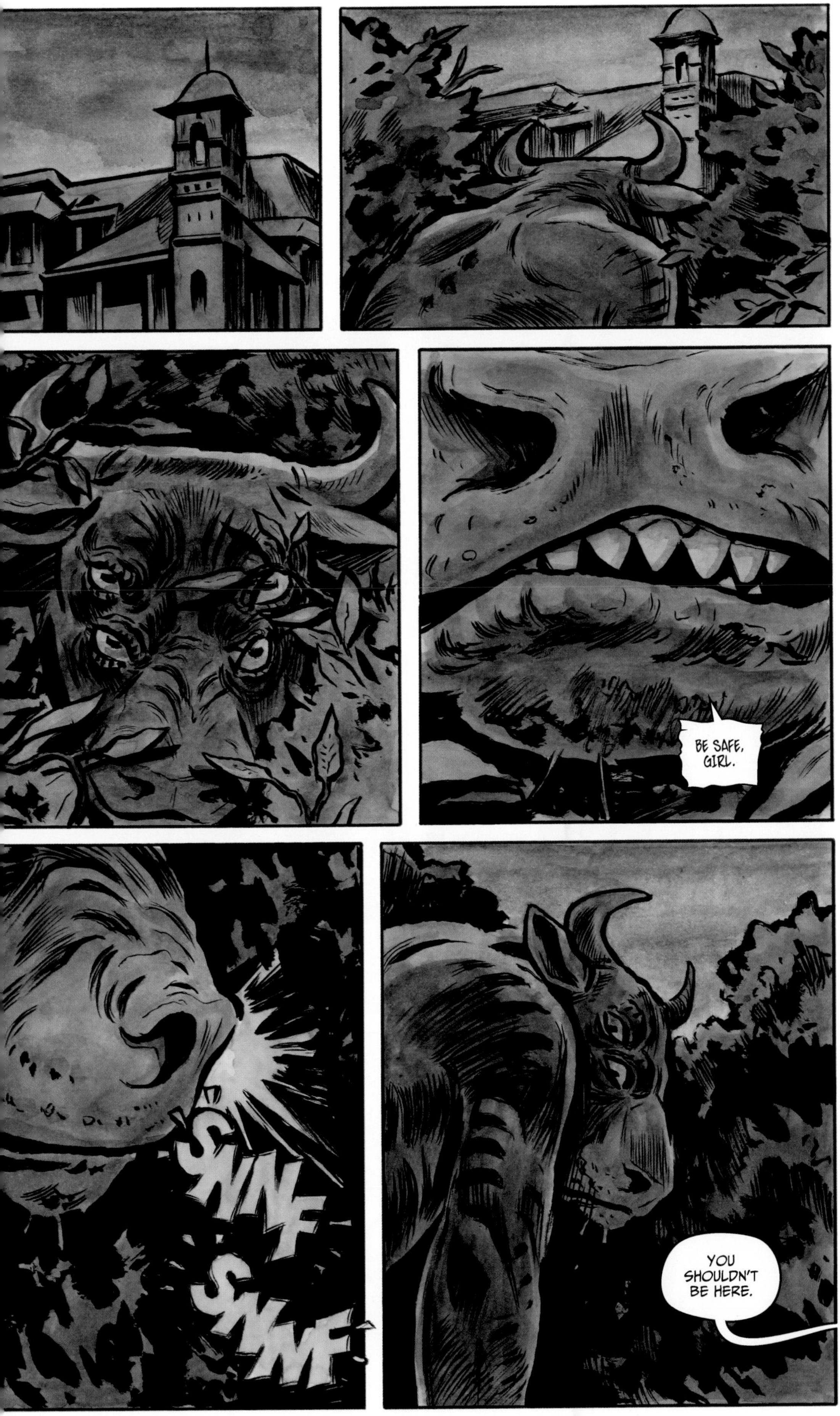
BE SAFE, GIRL.
SNNF SNNF
YOU SHOULDN'T BE HERE.

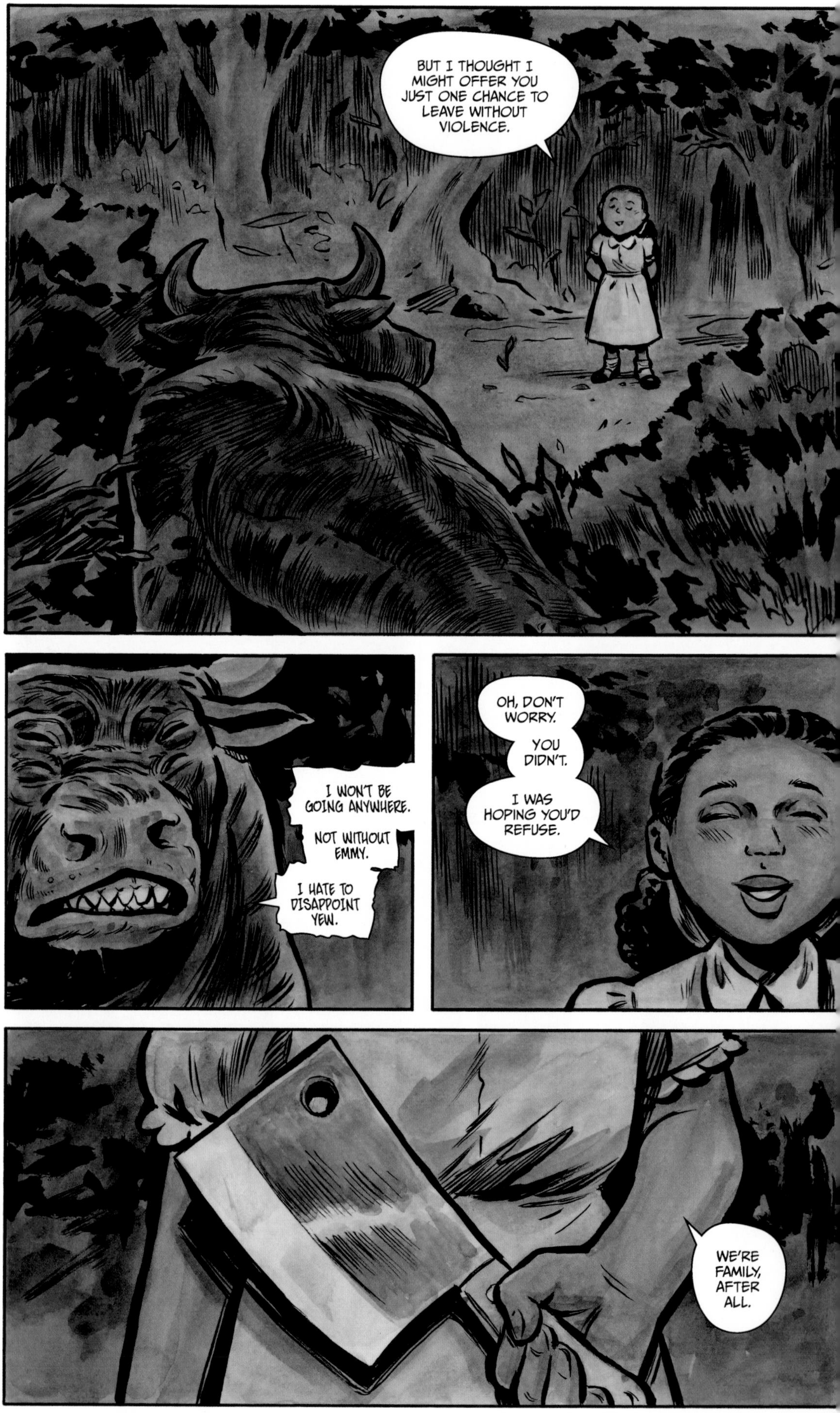
BUT I THOUGHT I MIGHT OFFER YOU JUST ONE CHANCE TO LEAVE WITHOUT VIOLENCE.
I WON'T BE GOING ANYWHERE.
NOT WITHOUT EMMY.
I HATE TO DISAPPOINT YEW.
OH, DON'T WORRY.
YOU DIDN'T.
I WAS HOPING YOU'D REFUSE.
WE'RE FAMILY, AFTER ALL.

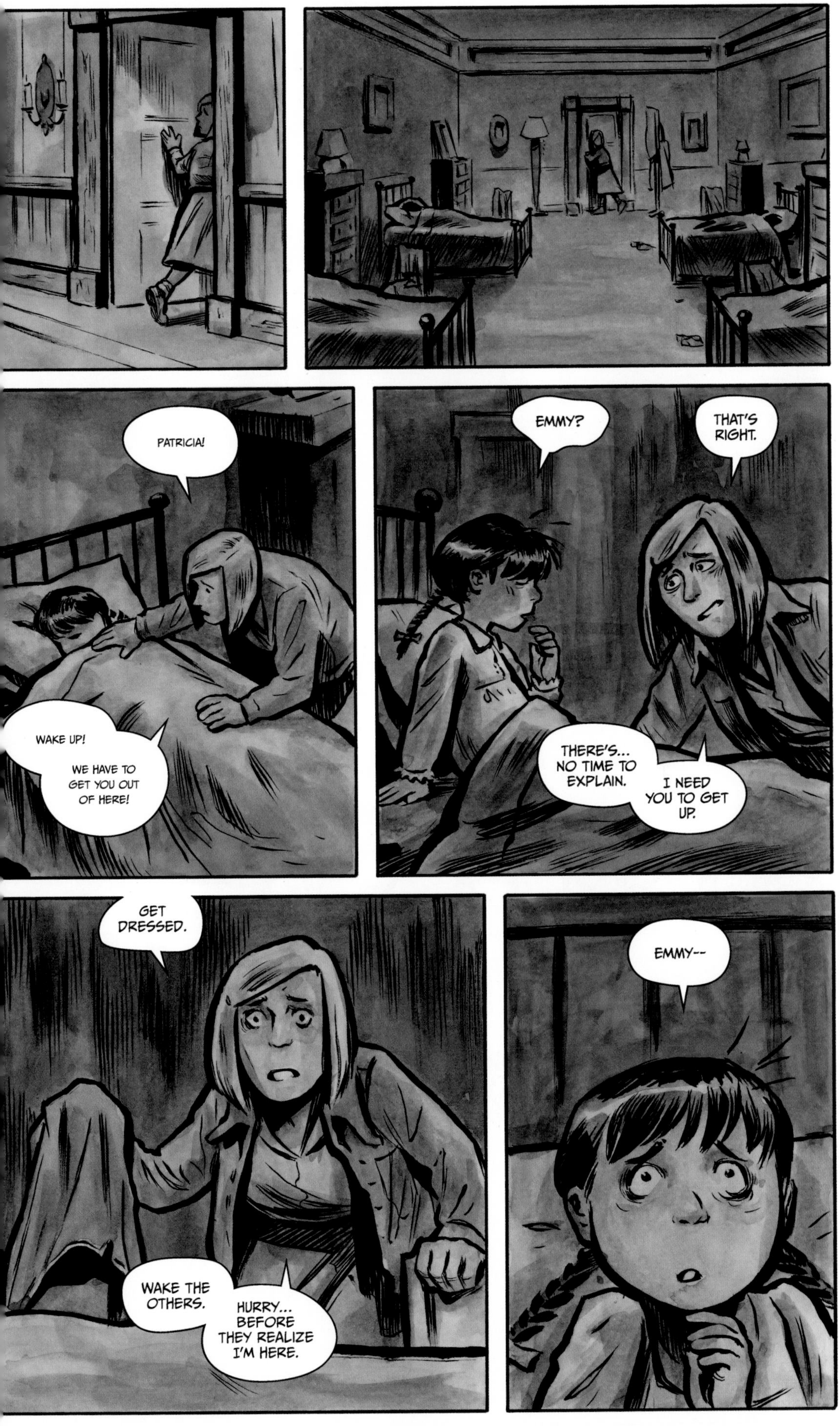
PATRICIA!
WAKE UP!
WE HAVE TO GET YOU OUT OF HERE!
EMMY?
THAT'S RIGHT.
THERE'S... NO TIME TO EXPLAIN.
I NEED YOU TO GET UP.
GET DRESSED.
WAKE THE OTHERS.
HURRY... BEFORE THEY REALIZE I'M HERE.
EMMY--

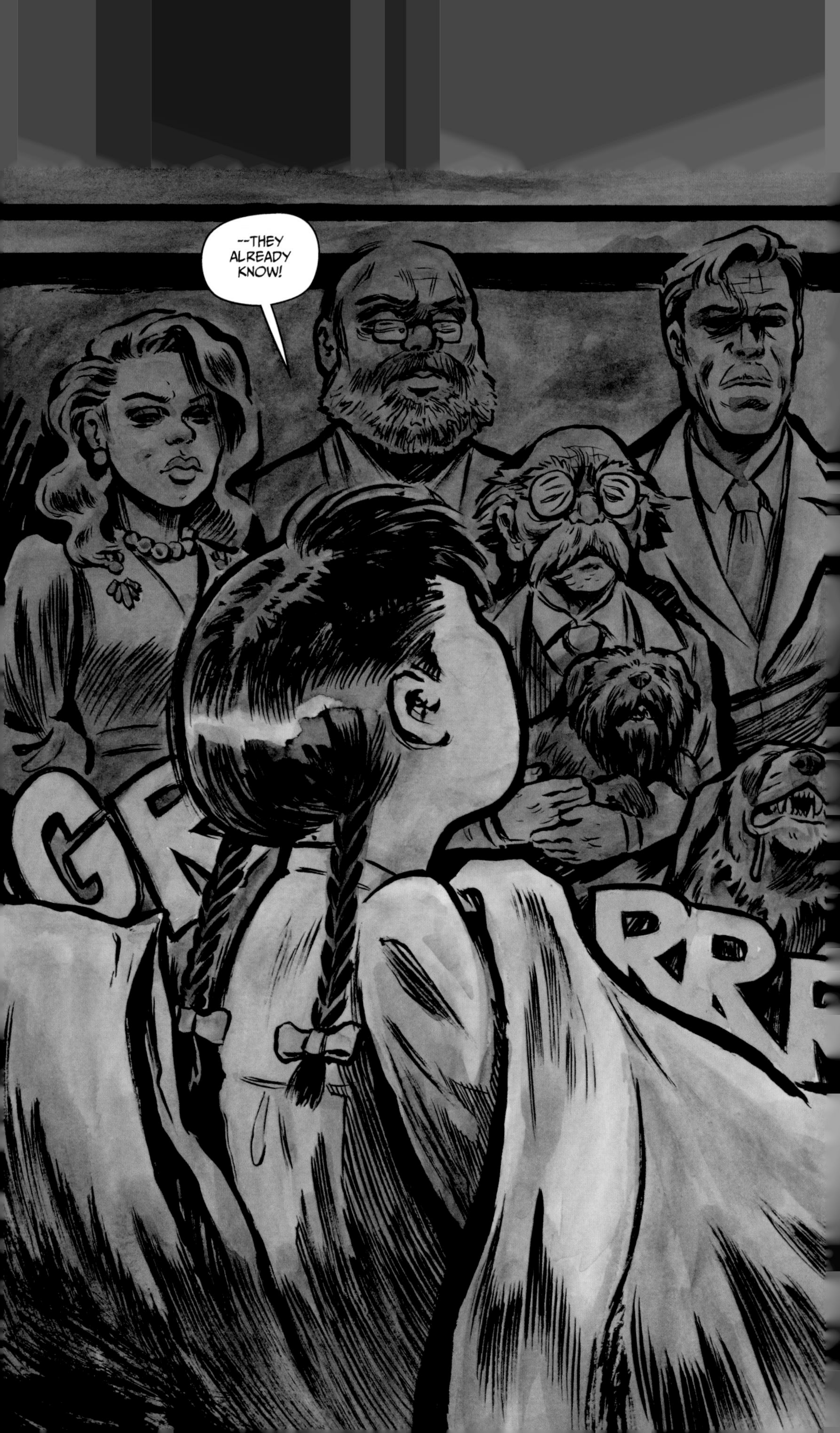
--THEY ALREADY KNOW!
GR
RRR

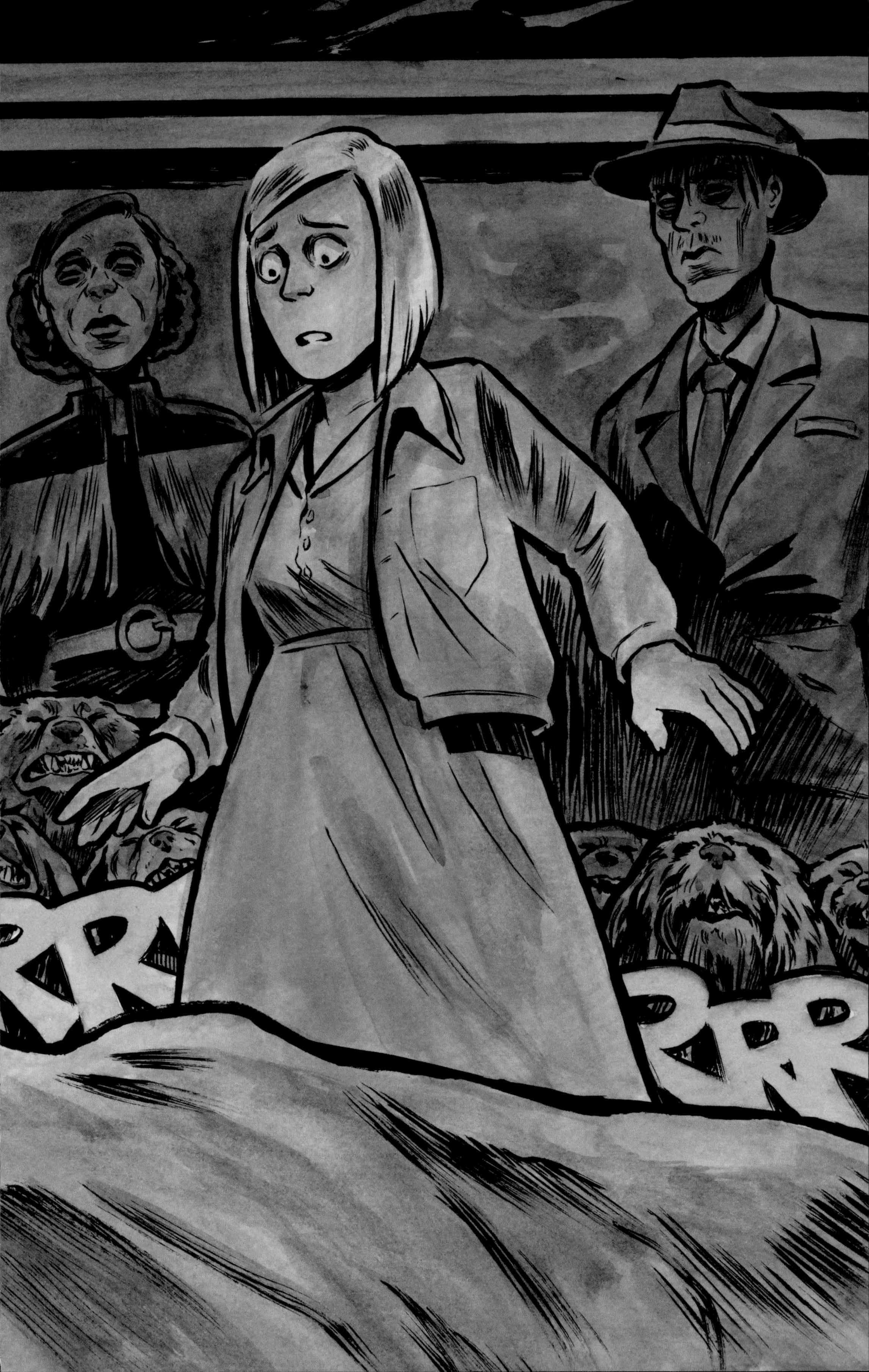
RR
RRR

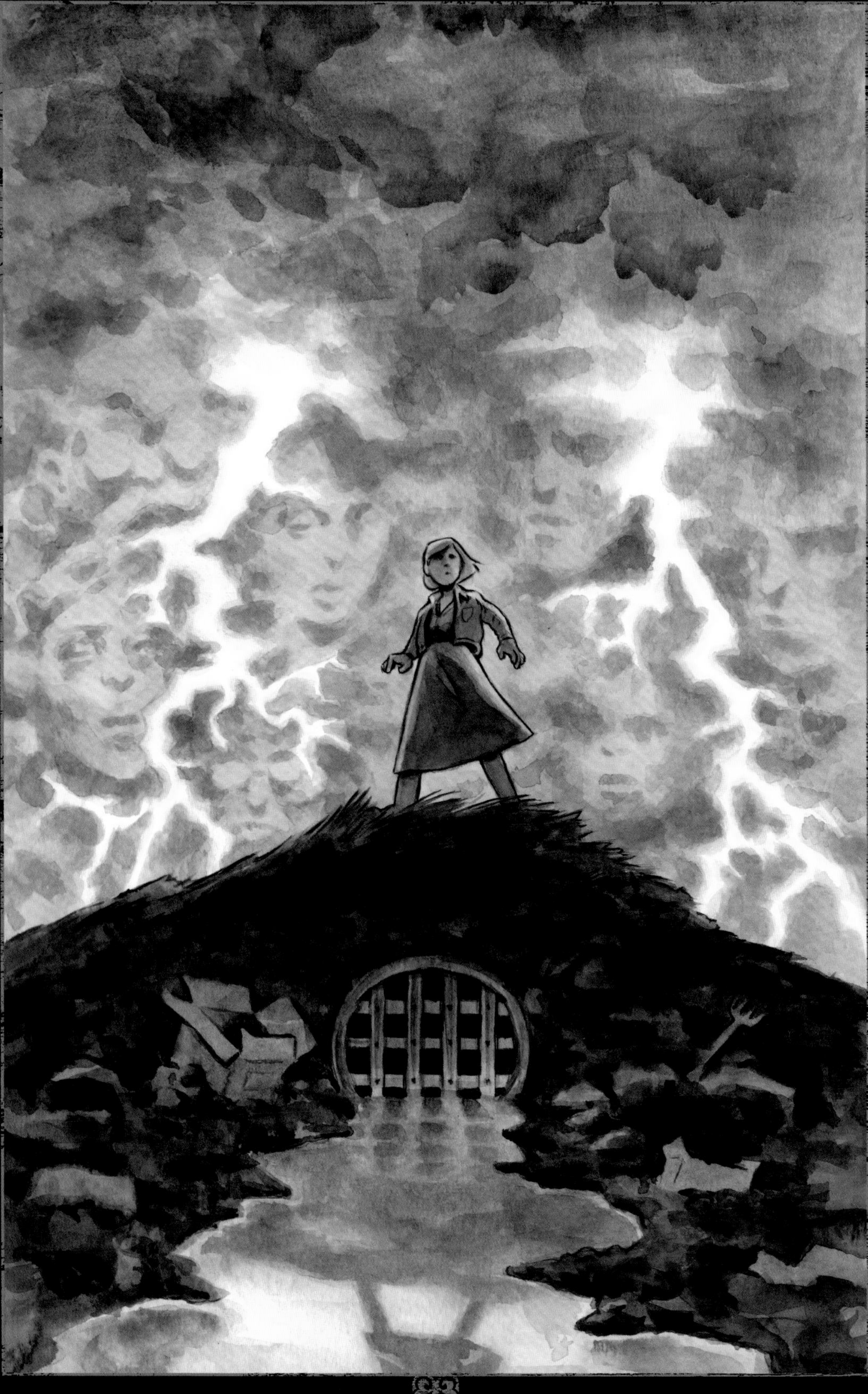

FOUR

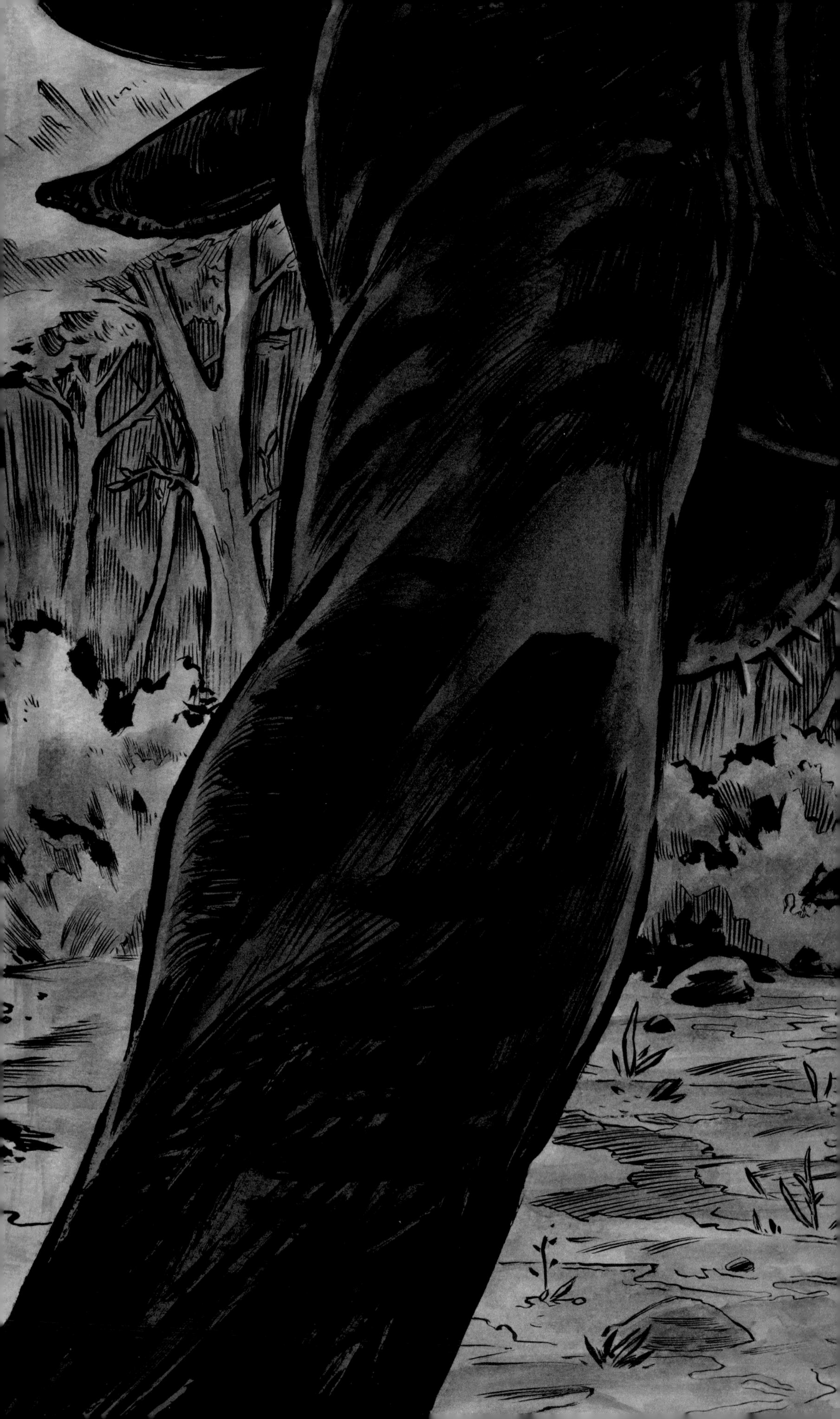

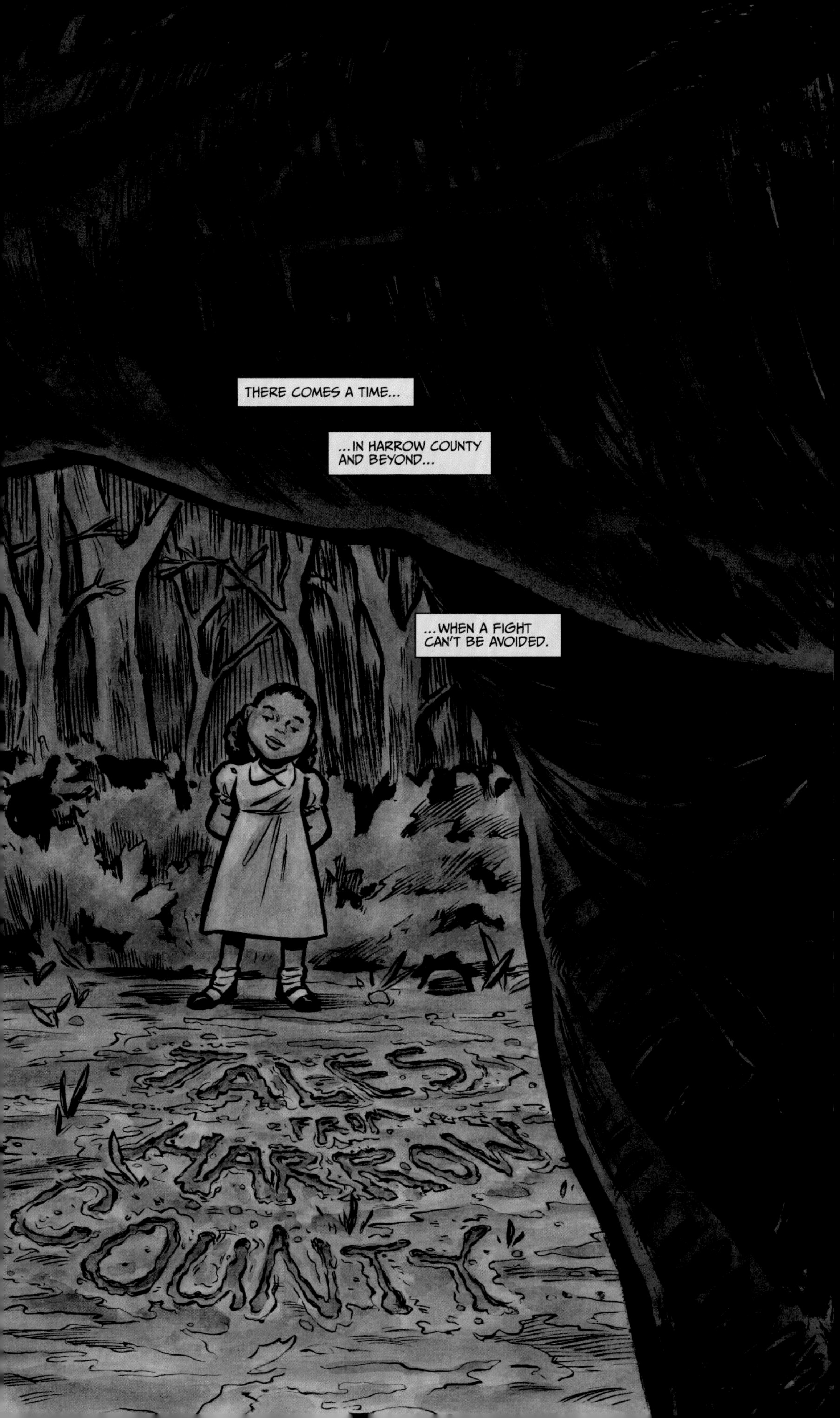
THERE COMES A TIME...
...IN HARROW COUNTY AND BEYOND...
...WHEN A FIGHT CAN'T BE AVOIDED.
TALES FROM HARROW COUNTY

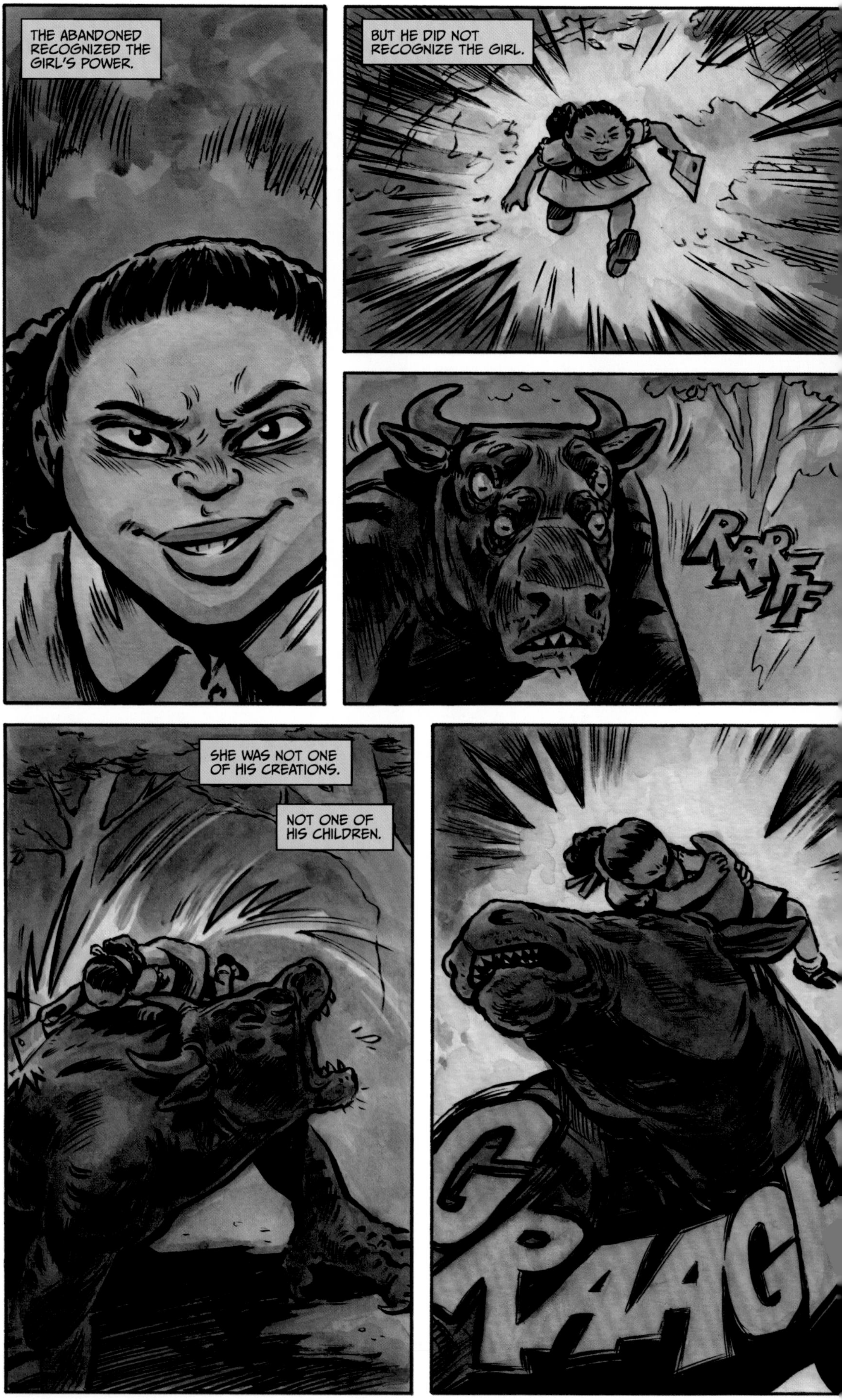
THE ABANDONED RECOGNIZED THE GIRL'S POWER.
BUT HE DID NOT RECOGNIZE THE GIRL.
RARFF
SHE WAS NOT ONE OF HIS CREATIONS.
NOT ONE OF HIS CHILDREN.
CRAAGH

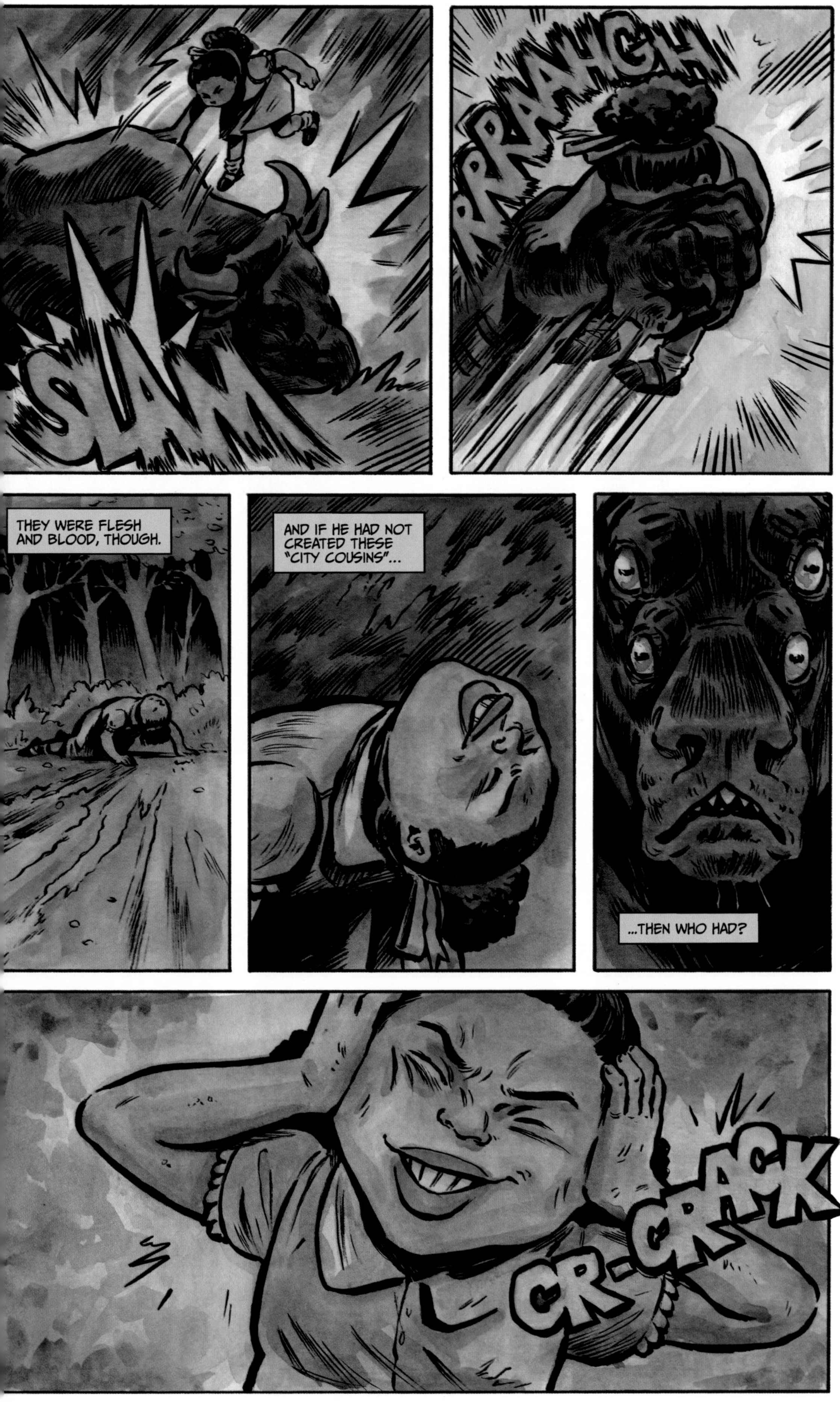
SLAM
KRRRAHGH
THEY WERE FLESH AND BLOOD, THOUGH.
AND IF HE HAD NOT CREATED THESE "CITY COUSINS"...
...THEN WHO HAD?
CR-CRACK

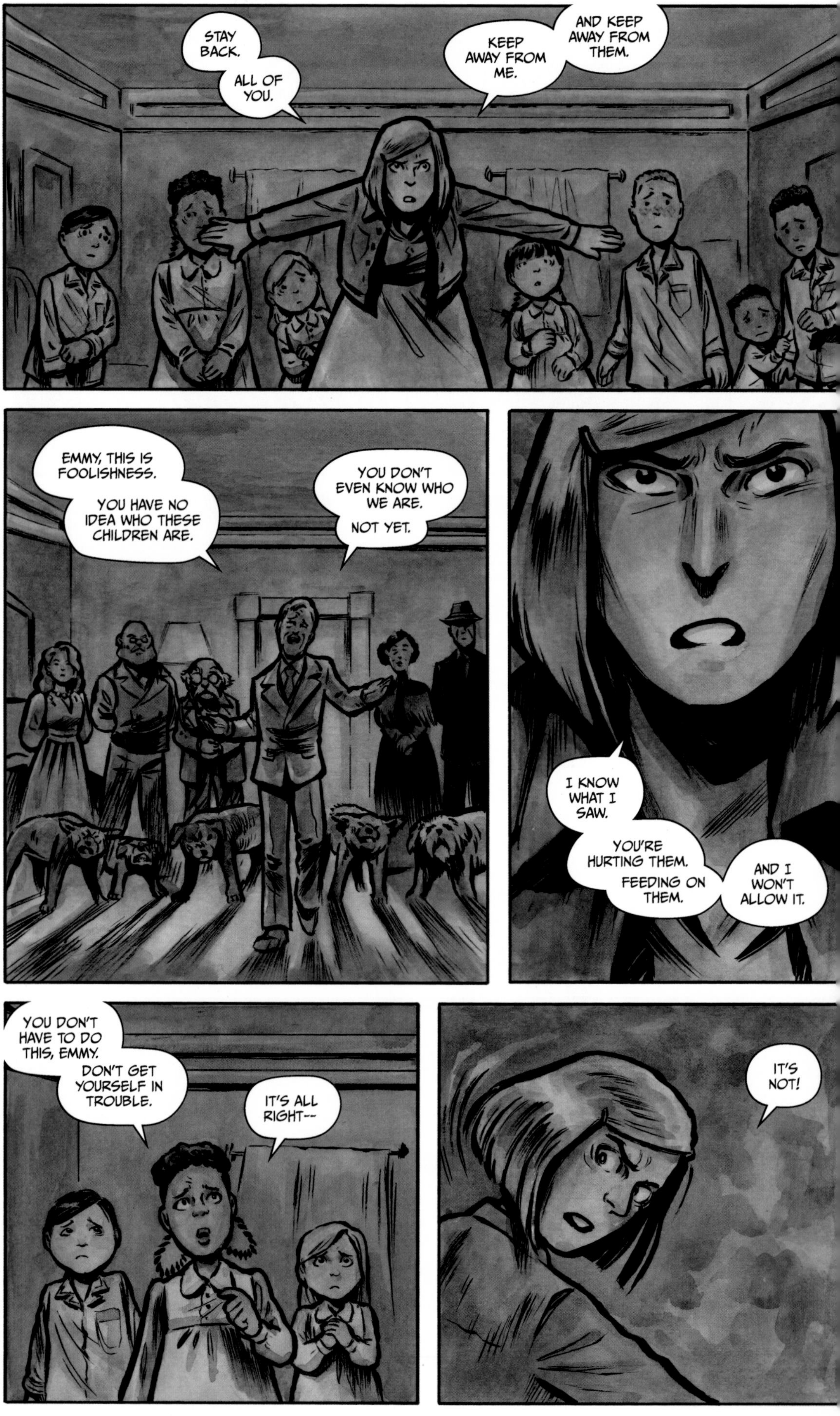
STAY BACK.
ALL OF YOU.
KEEP AWAY FROM ME.
AND KEEP AWAY FROM THEM.
EMMY, THIS IS FOOLISHNESS.
YOU HAVE NO IDEA WHO THESE CHILDREN ARE.
YOU DON'T EVEN KNOW WHO WE ARE.
NOT YET.
I KNOW WHAT I SAW.
YOU'RE HURTING THEM.
FEEDING ON THEM.
AND I WON'T ALLOW IT.
YOU DON'T HAVE TO DO THIS, EMMY.
DON'T GET YOURSELF IN TROUBLE.
IT'S ALL RIGHT--
IT'S NOT!

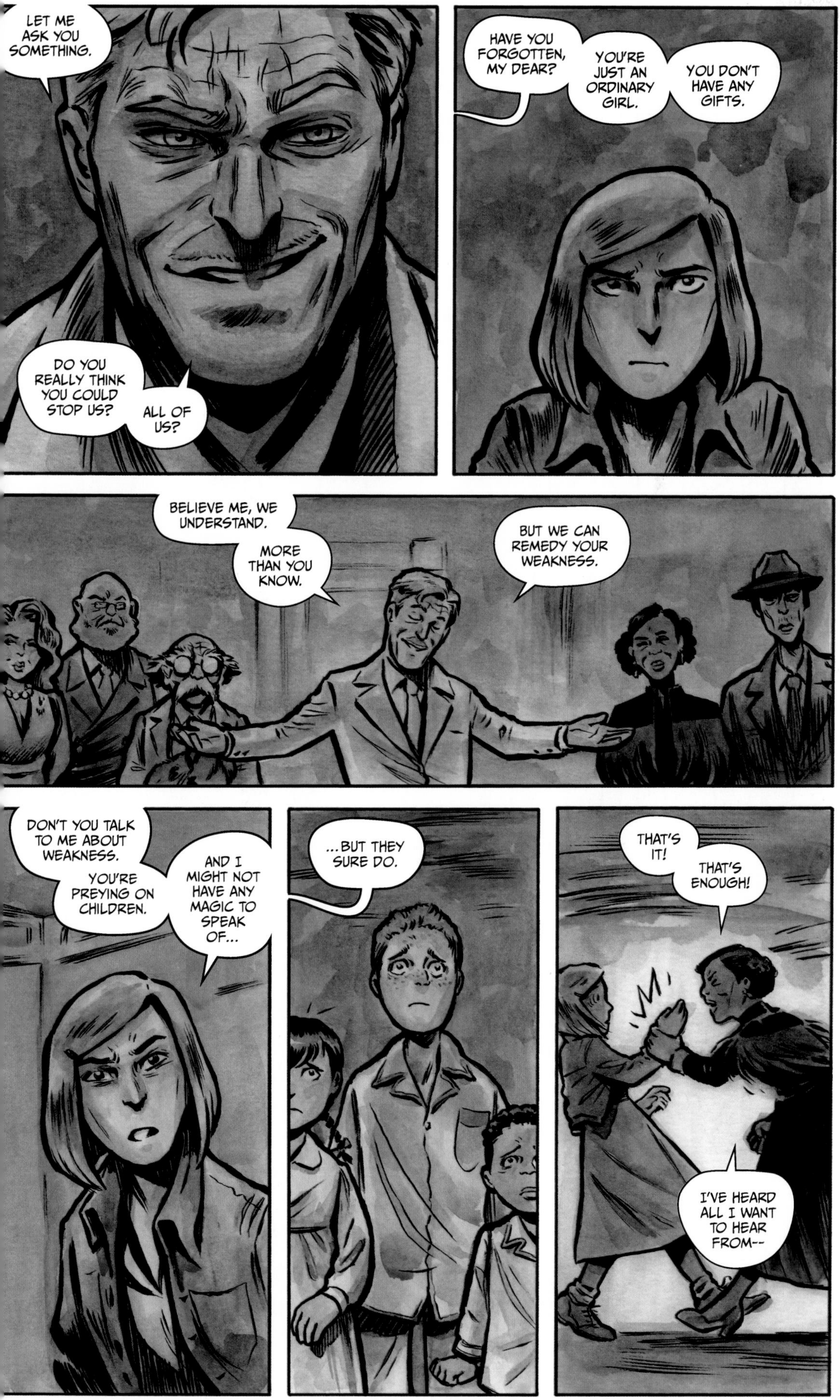
LET ME ASK YOU SOMETHING.
DO YOU REALLY THINK YOU COULD STOP US?
ALL OF US?
HAVE YOU FORGOTTEN, MY DEAR?
YOU'RE JUST AN ORDINARY GIRL.
YOU DON'T HAVE ANY GIFTS.
BELIEVE ME, WE UNDERSTAND.
MORE THAN YOU KNOW.
BUT WE CAN REMEDY YOUR WEAKNESS.
DON'T YOU TALK TO ME ABOUT WEAKNESS.
YOU'RE PREYING ON CHILDREN.
AND I MIGHT NOT HAVE ANY MAGIC TO SPEAK OF...
...BUT THEY SURE DO.
THAT'S IT!
THAT'S ENOUGH!
I'VE HEARD ALL I WANT TO HEAR FROM--

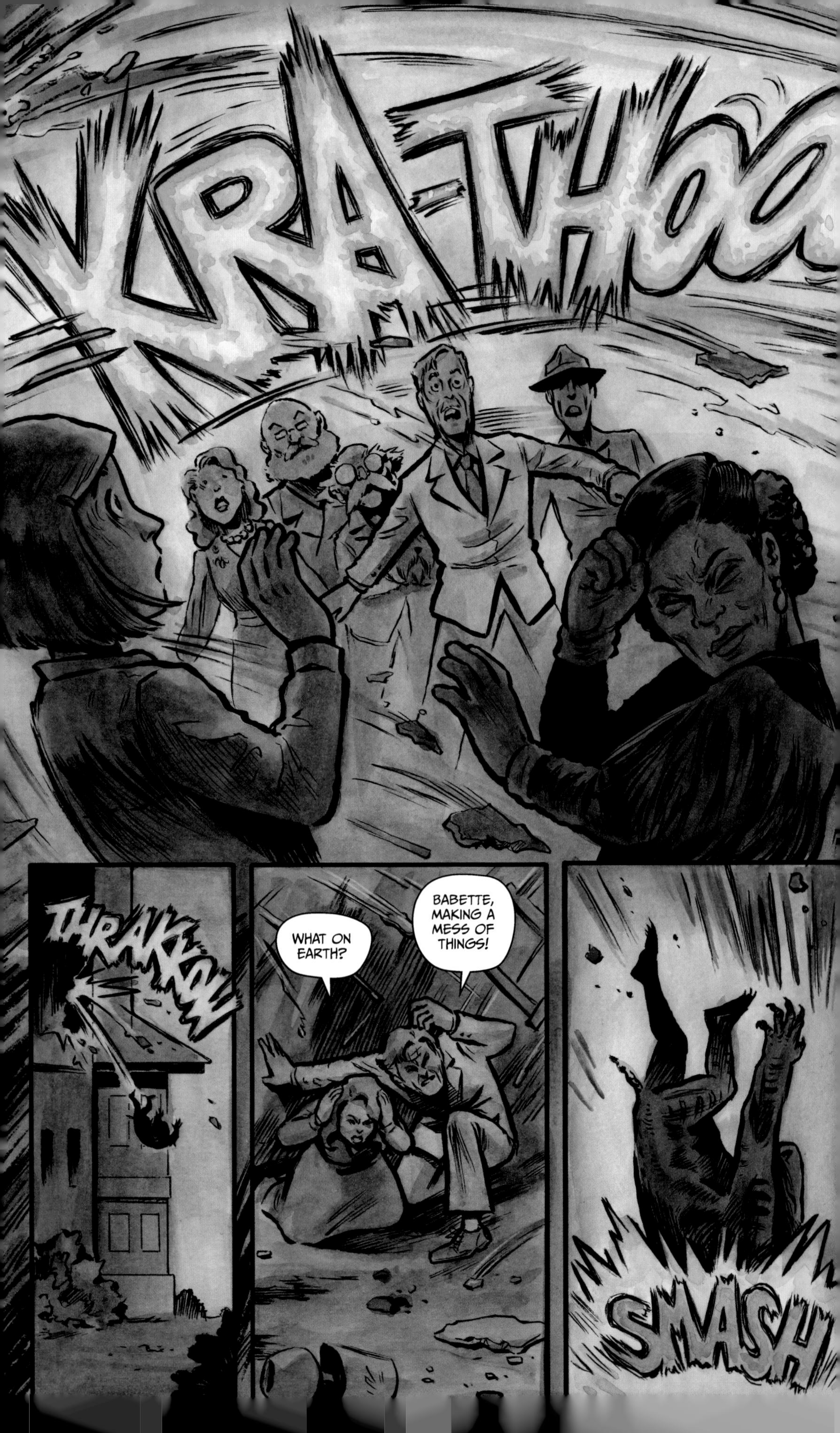
KRA-THOOM
THRAKKOW
WHAT ON EARTH?
BABETTE, MAKING A MESS OF THINGS!
SMASH

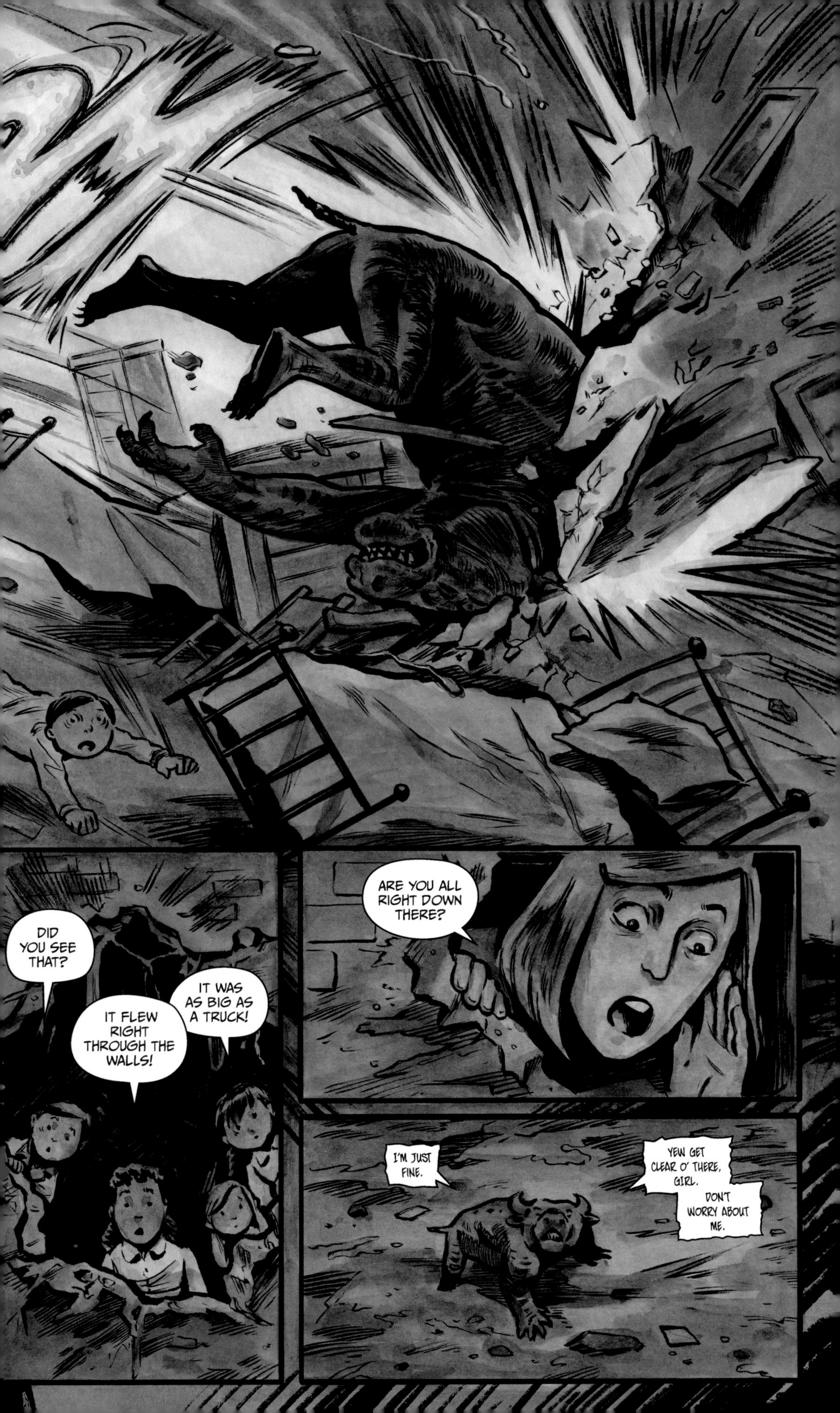
DID YOU SEE THAT?
IT FLEW RIGHT THROUGH THE WALLS!
IT WAS AS BIG AS A TRUCK!
ARE YOU ALL RIGHT DOWN THERE?
I'M JUST FINE.
YEW GET CLEAR O' THERE, GIRL.
DON'T WORRY ABOUT ME.

PATRICIA!

HELP ME GET THEM OUT OF HERE!

WE'RE LEAVING!

I'LL B[DAMNE[

GRRRRRRRRRRRRRRRR

DON'T HARM THE CHILDREN. JUST KEEP THEM AT BAY.

EMMY, THOUGH... EMMY.

TEAR HER APART.

BARK

YAP

GRAAF

BAR[

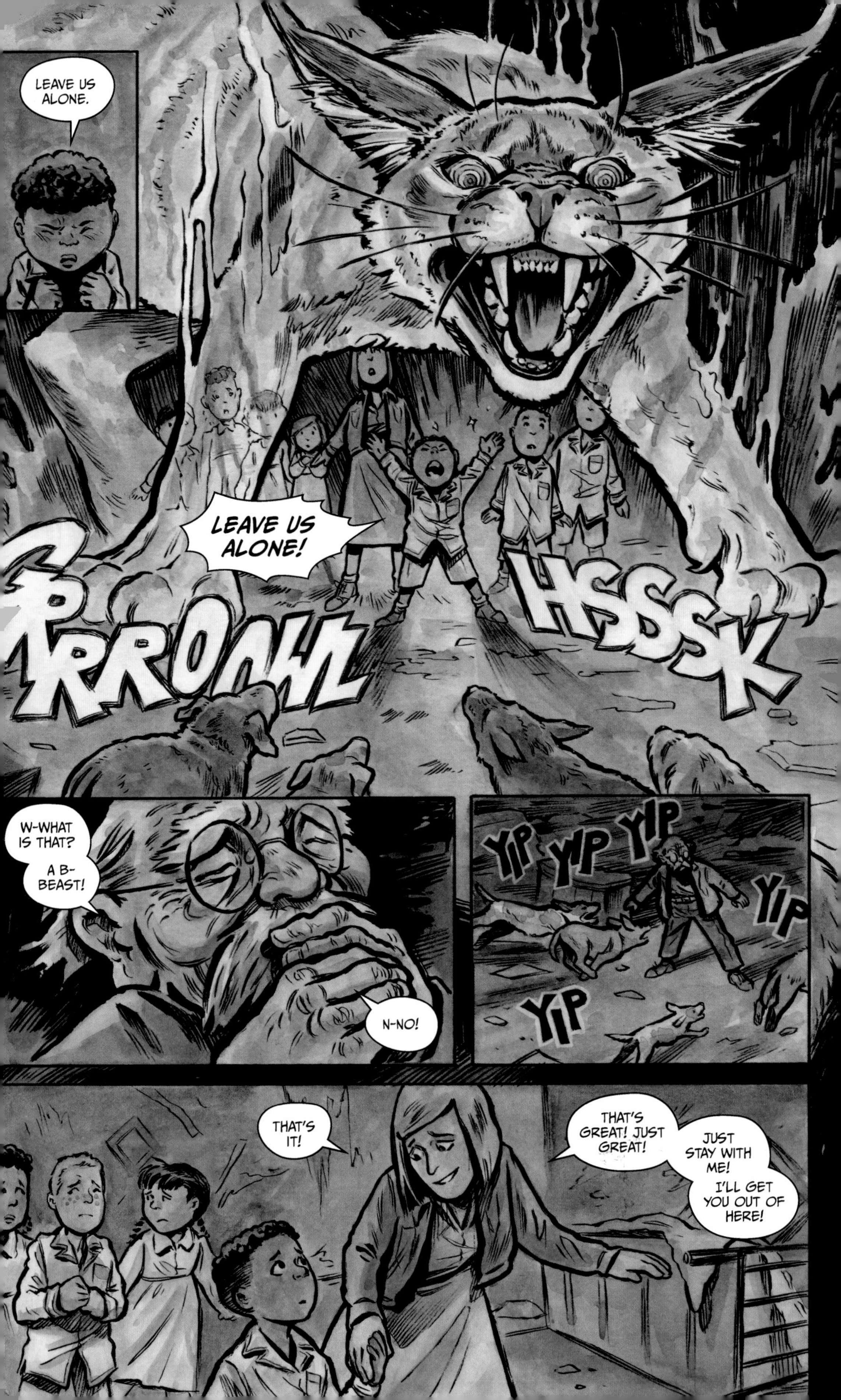
LEAVE US ALONE.
LEAVE US ALONE!
RRROOWL
HSSSK
W-WHAT IS THAT?
A B-BEAST!
N-NO!
YIP YIP YIP
YIP
YIP
THAT'S IT!
THAT'S GREAT! JUST GREAT!
JUST STAY WITH ME!
I'LL GET YOU OUT OF HERE!

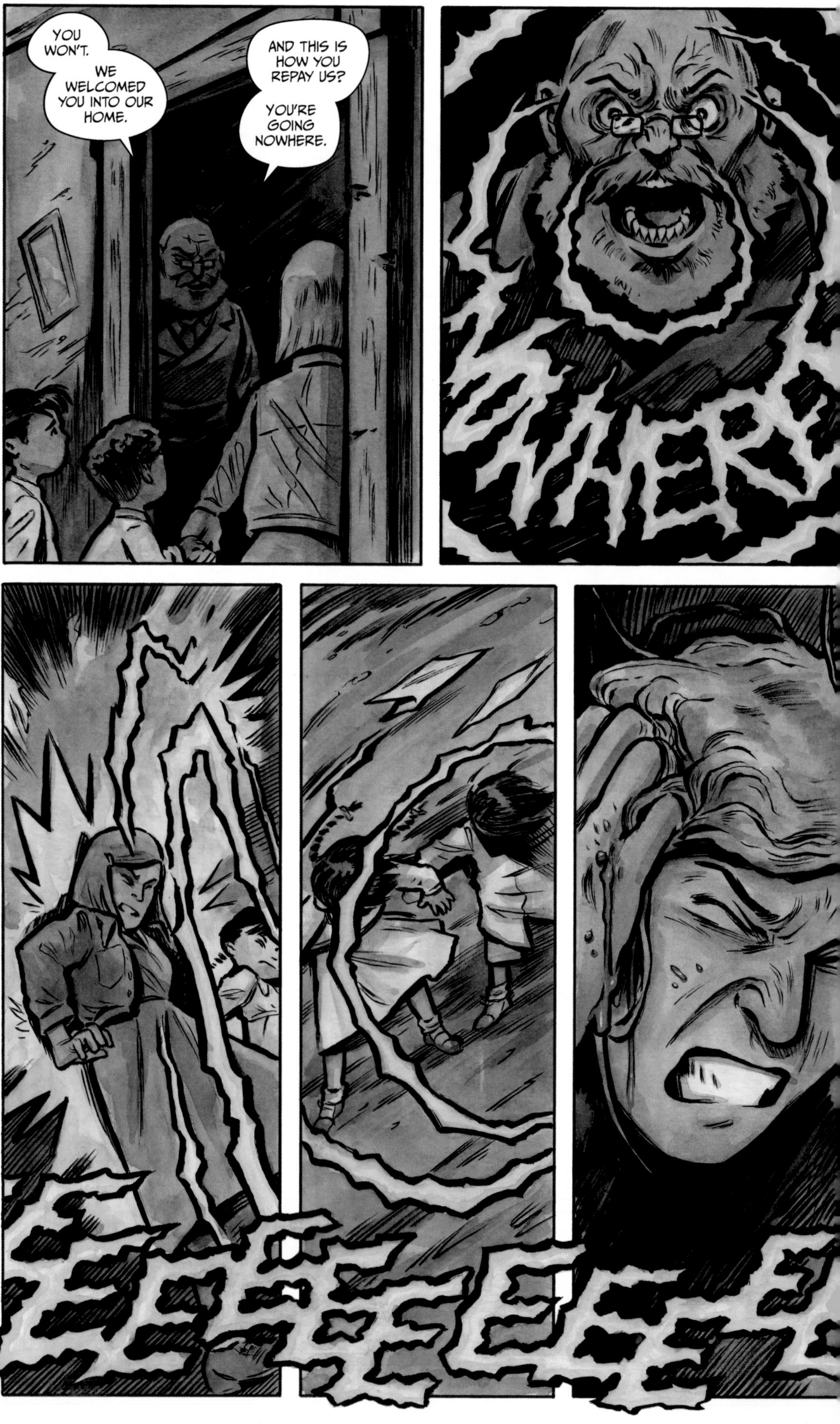
YOU WON'T.
WE WELCOMED YOU INTO OUR HOME.
AND THIS IS HOW YOU REPAY US?
YOU'RE GOING NOWHERE.

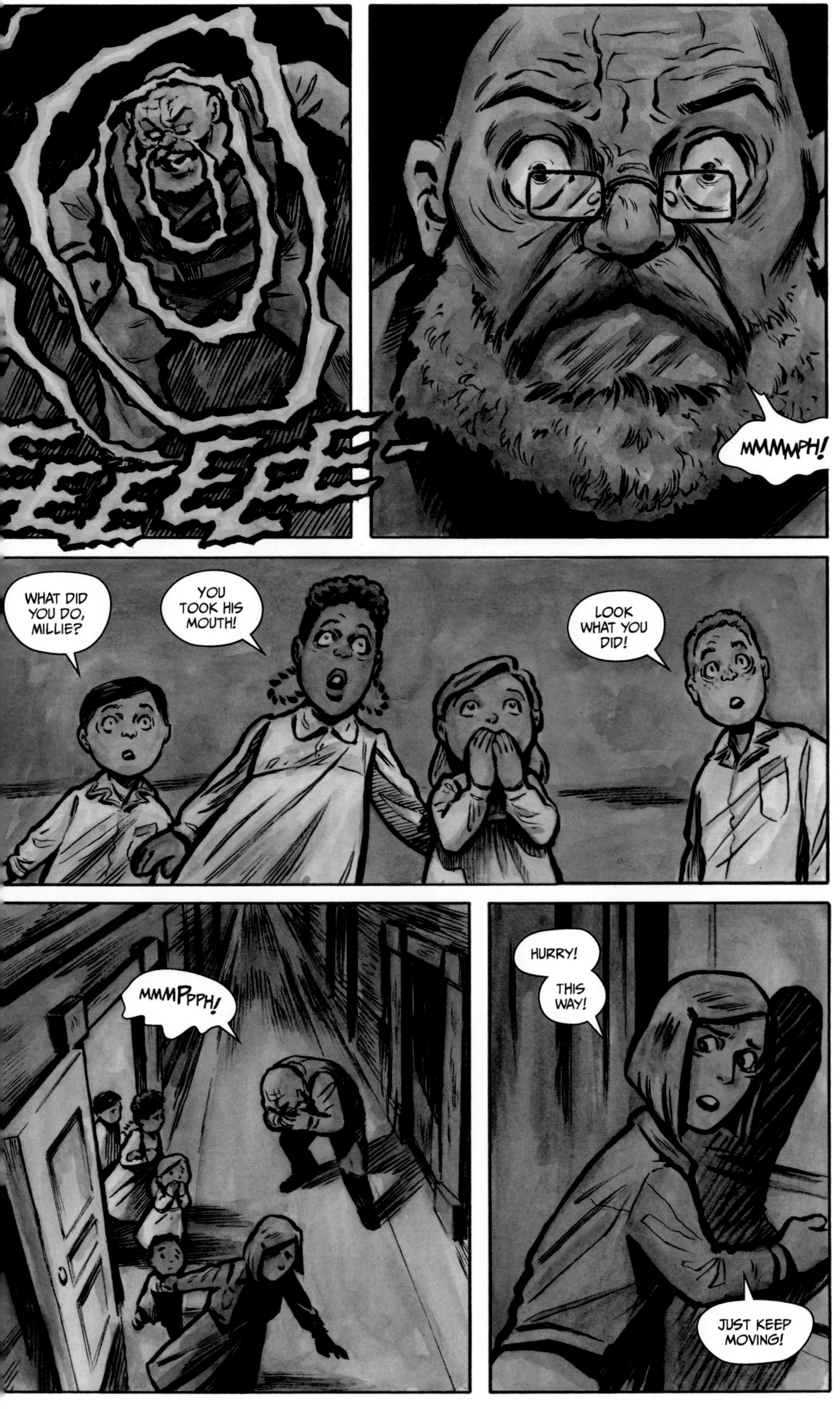
MMMMPH!
WHAT DID YOU DO, MILLIE?
YOU TOOK HIS MOUTH!
LOOK WHAT YOU DID!
MMMPPPH!
HURRY!
THIS WAY!
JUST KEEP MOVING!

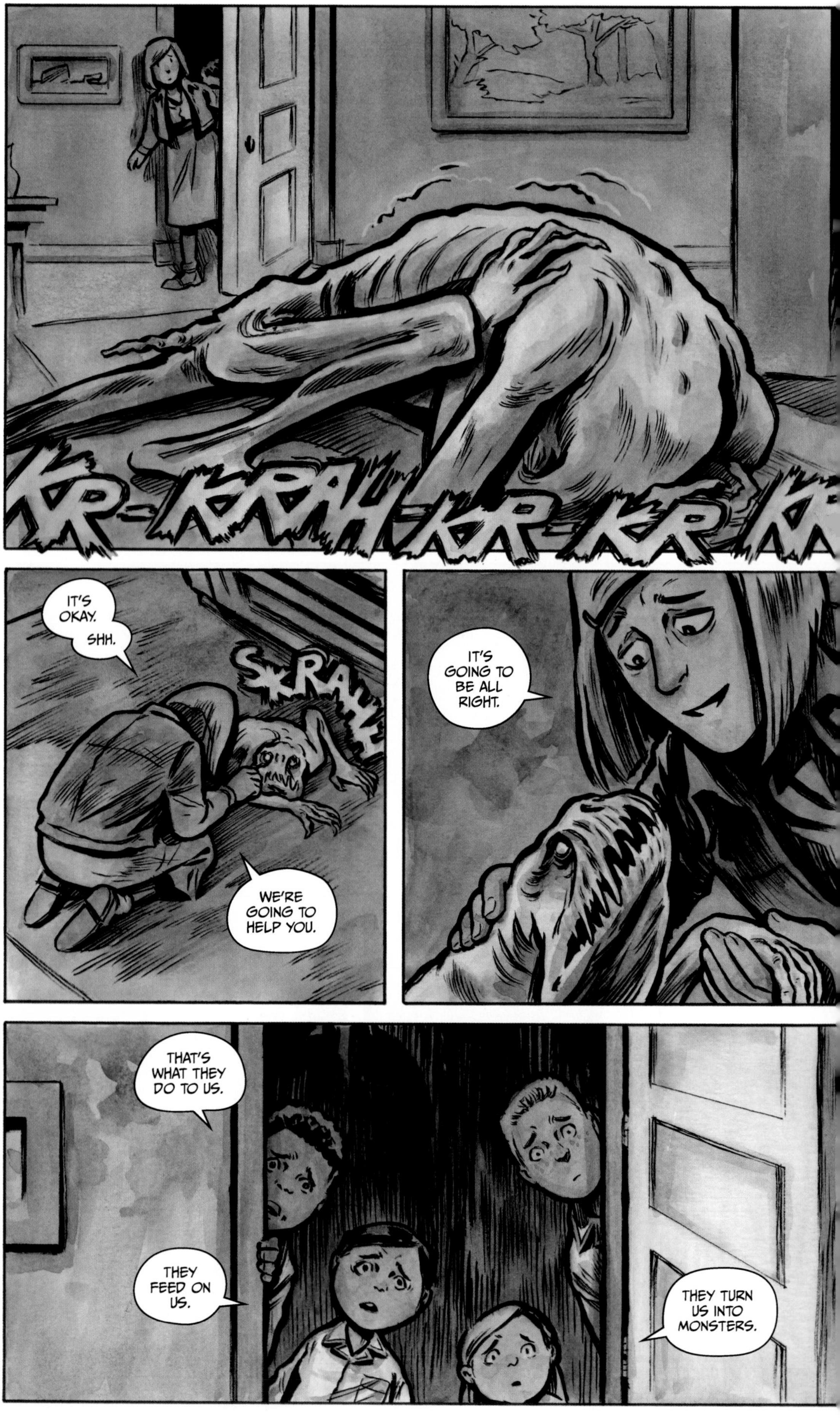
KR-KRAH KR-KR-KR
IT'S OKAY.
SHH.
SKRAW
WE'RE GOING TO HELP YOU.
IT'S GOING TO BE ALL RIGHT.
THAT'S WHAT THEY DO TO US.
THEY FEED ON US.
THEY TURN US INTO MONSTERS.

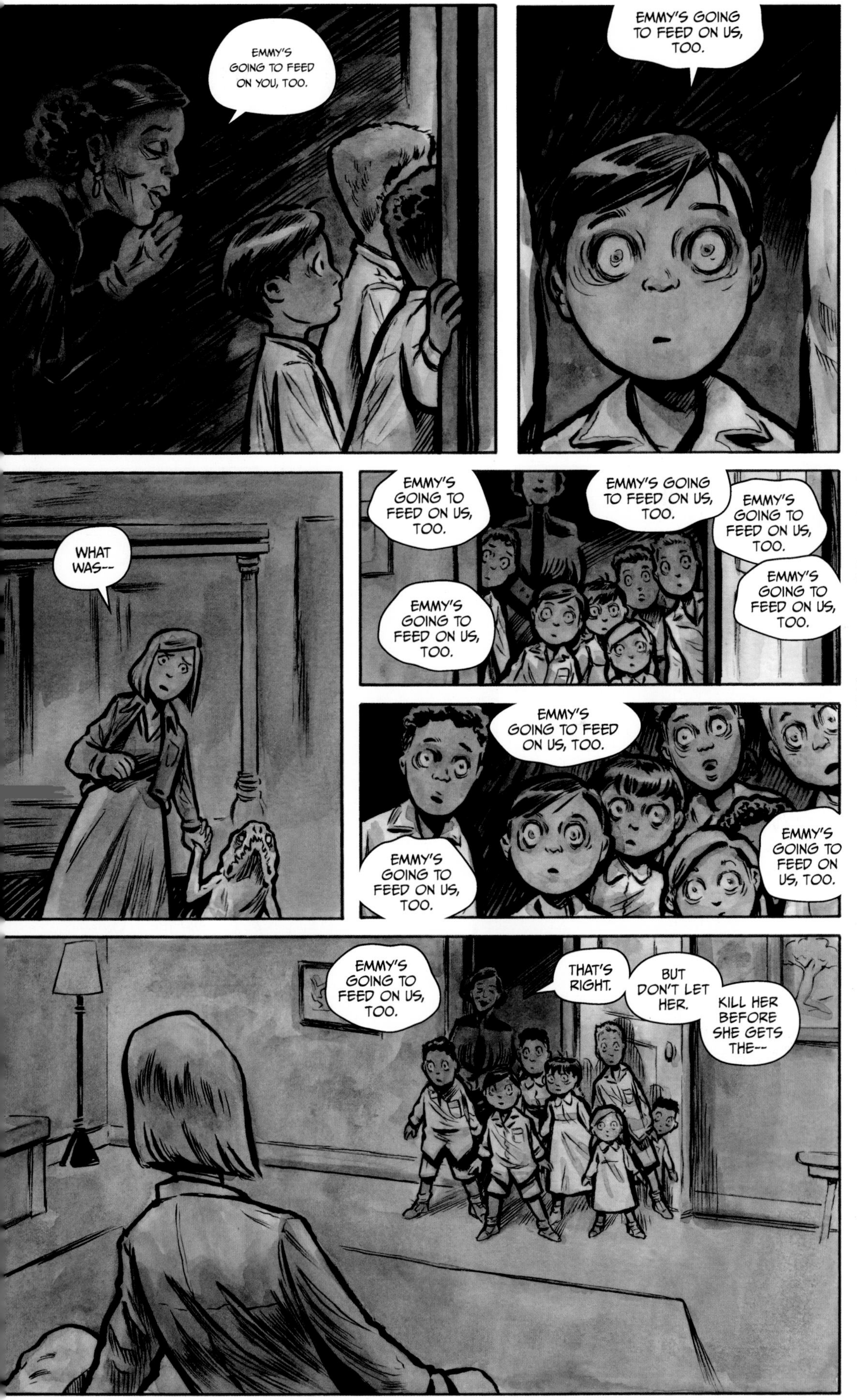
EMMY'S GOING TO FEED ON YOU, TOO.
EMMY'S GOING TO FEED ON US, TOO.
WHAT WAS--
EMMY'S GOING TO FEED ON US, TOO.
EMMY'S GOING TO FEED ON US, TOO.
EMMY'S GOING TO FEED ON US, TOO.
EMMY'S GOING TO FEED ON US, TOO.
EMMY'S GOING TO FEED ON US, TOO.
EMMY'S GOING TO FEED ON US, TOO.
EMMY'S GOING TO FEED ON US, TOO.
EMMY'S GOING TO FEED ON US, TOO.
EMMY'S GOING TO FEED ON US, TOO.
THAT'S RIGHT.
BUT DON'T LET HER.
KILL HER BEFORE SHE GETS THE--

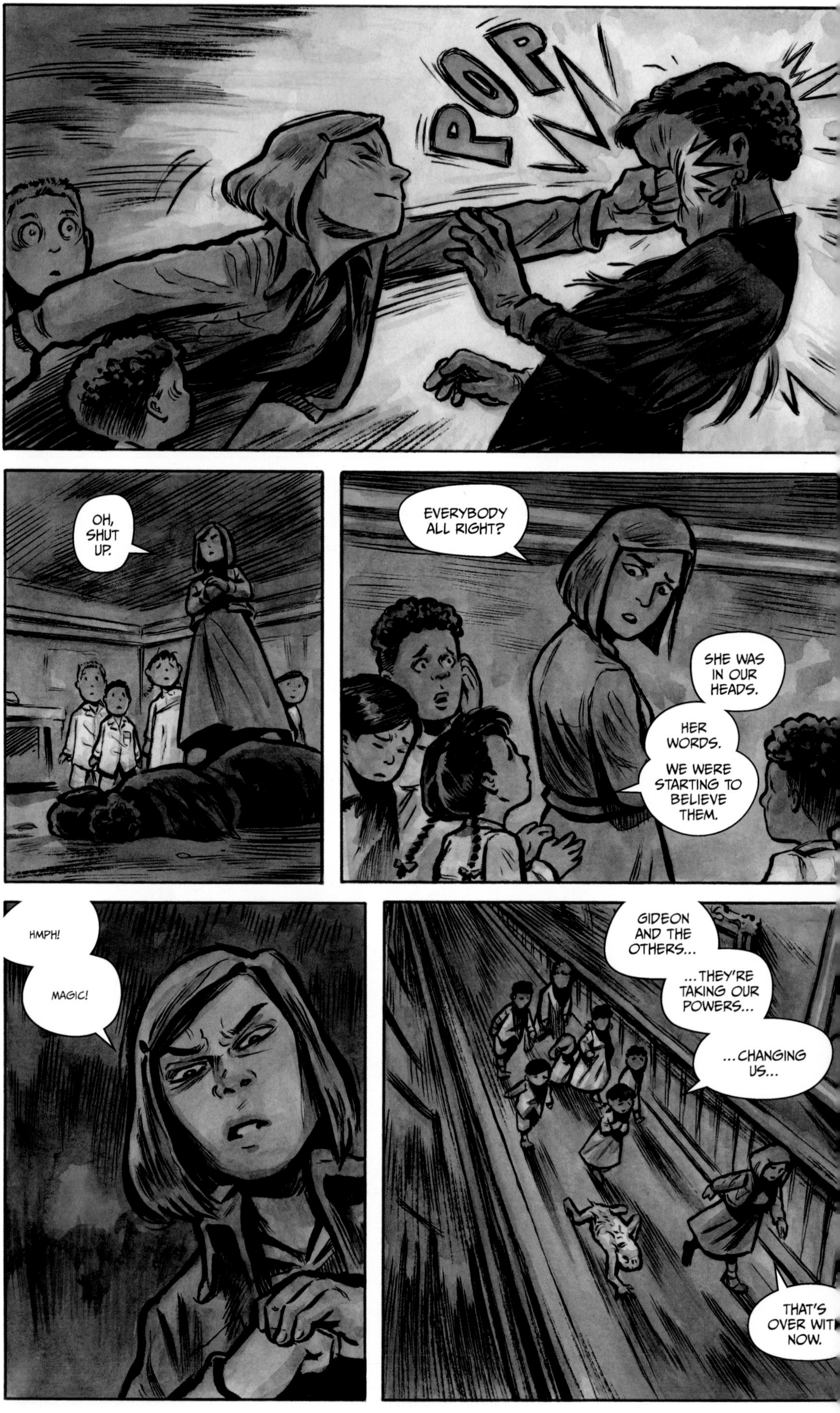
POP
OH, SHUT UP.
EVERYBODY ALL RIGHT?
SHE WAS IN OUR HEADS.
HER WORDS.
WE WERE STARTING TO BELIEVE THEM.
HMPH!
MAGIC!
GIDEON AND THE OTHERS...
...THEY'RE TAKING OUR POWERS...
...CHANGING US...
THAT'S OVER WITH NOW.

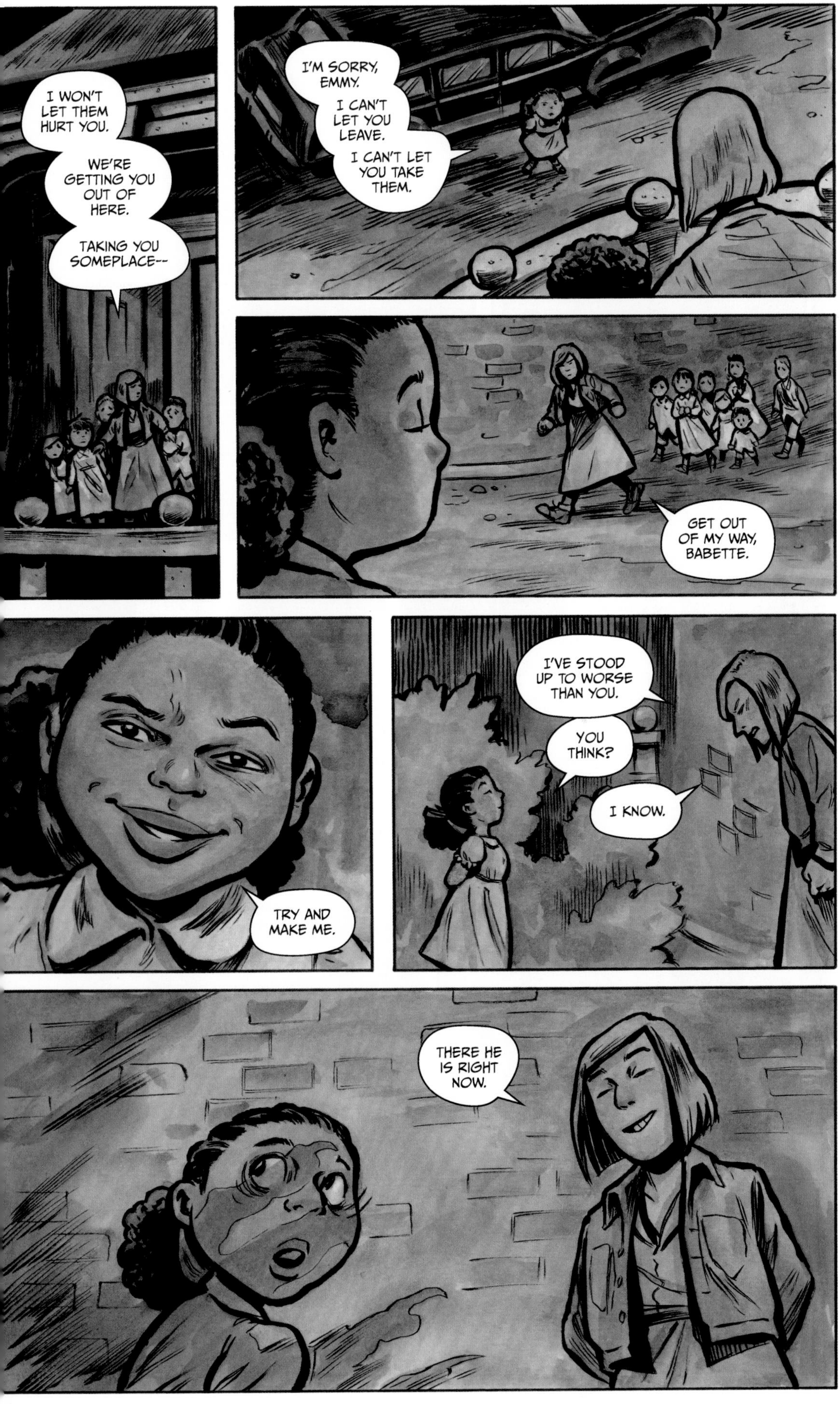

I WON'T LET THEM HURT YOU.
WE'RE GETTING YOU OUT OF HERE.
TAKING YOU SOMEPLACE--
I'M SORRY, EMMY.
I CAN'T LET YOU LEAVE.
I CAN'T LET YOU TAKE THEM.
GET OUT OF MY WAY, BABETTE.
TRY AND MAKE ME.
I'VE STOOD UP TO WORSE THAN YOU.
YOU THINK?
I KNOW.
THERE HE IS RIGHT NOW.

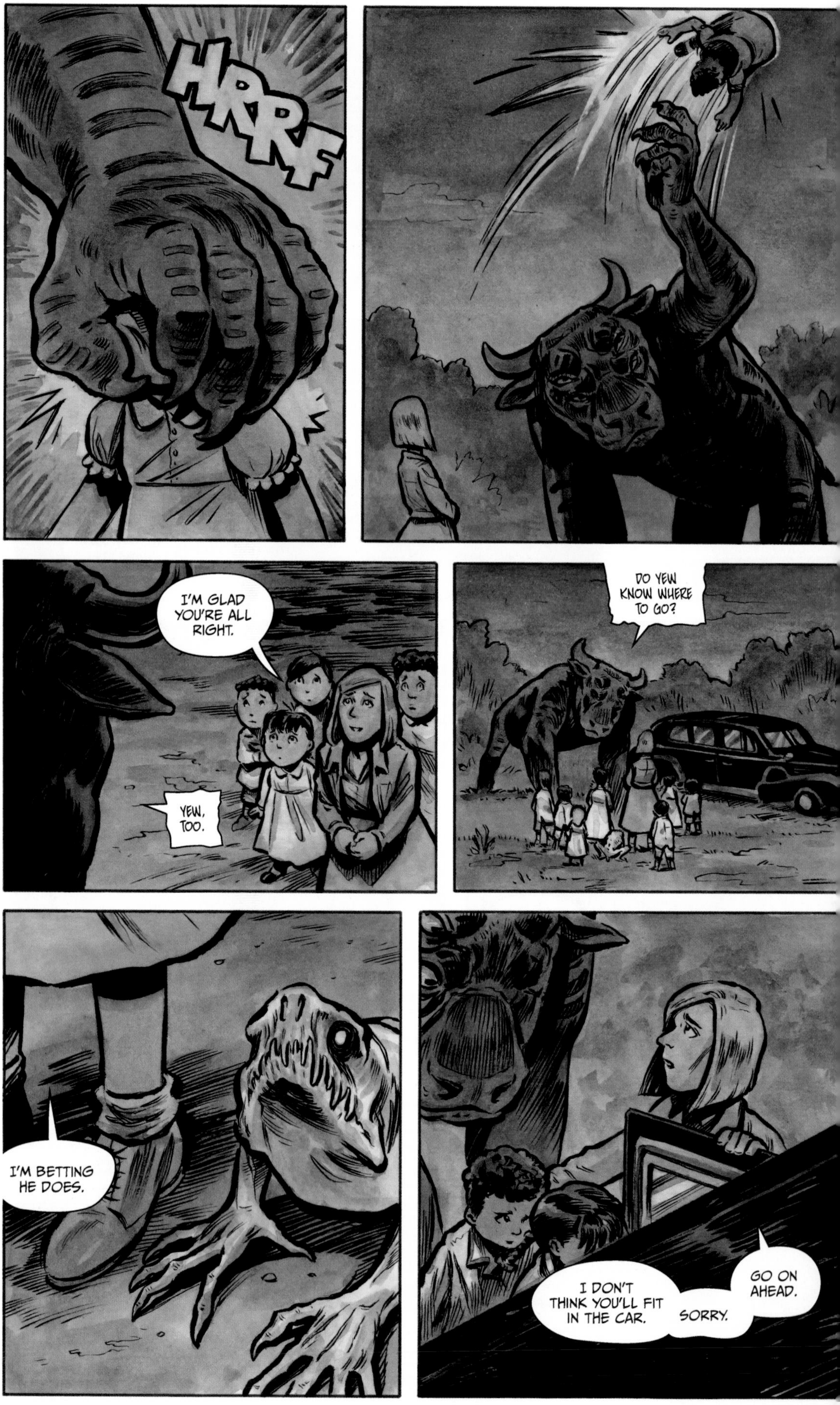
HRRF
I'M GLAD YOU'RE ALL RIGHT.
YEW, TOO.
DO YEW KNOW WHERE TO GO?
I'M BETTING HE DOES.
GO ON AHEAD.
I DON'T THINK YOU'LL FIT IN THE CAR.
SORRY.

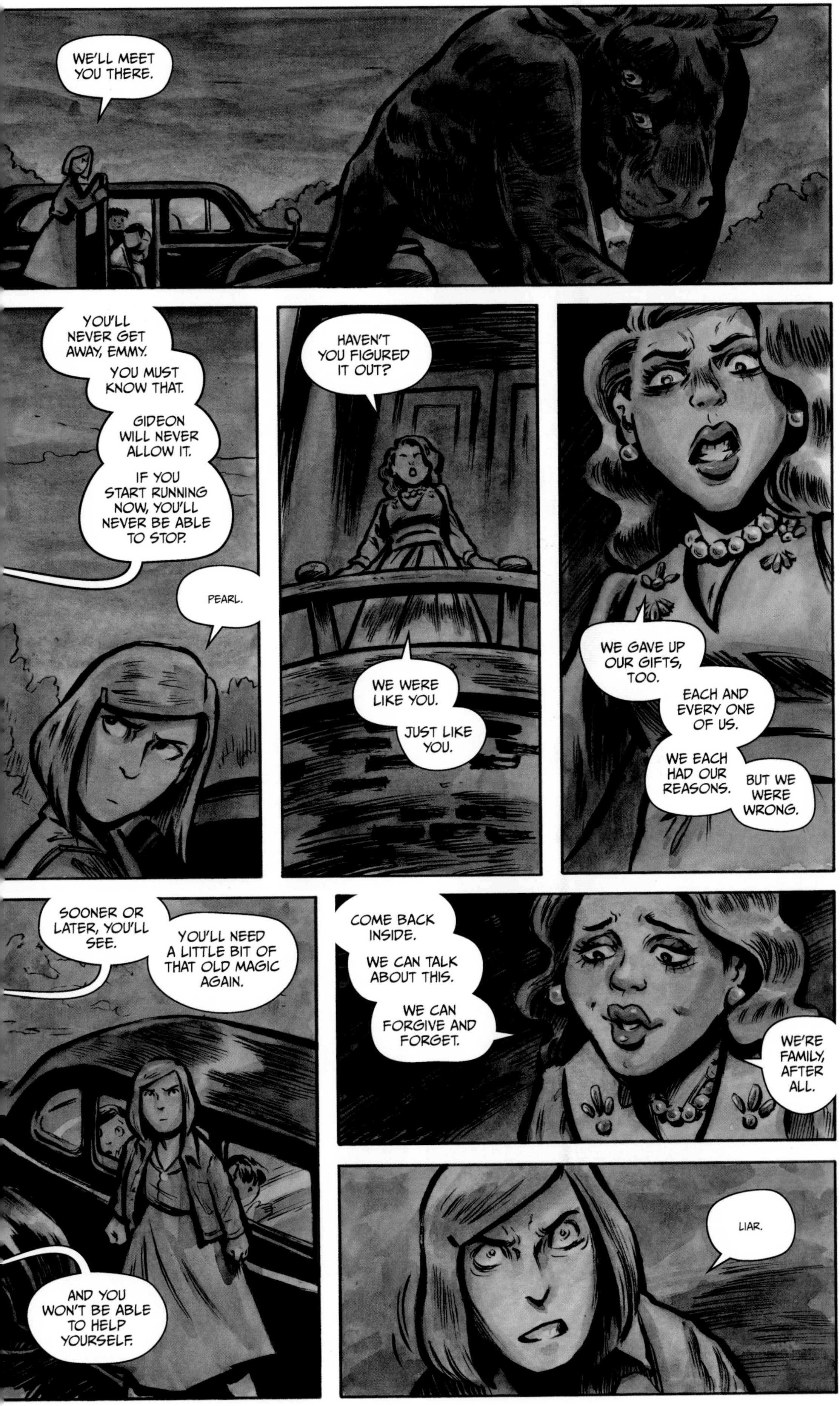
WE'LL MEET YOU THERE.
YOU'LL NEVER GET AWAY, EMMY.
YOU MUST KNOW THAT.
GIDEON WILL NEVER ALLOW IT.
IF YOU START RUNNING NOW, YOU'LL NEVER BE ABLE TO STOP.
PEARL.
HAVEN'T YOU FIGURED IT OUT?
WE WERE LIKE YOU.
JUST LIKE YOU.
WE GAVE UP OUR GIFTS, TOO.
EACH AND EVERY ONE OF US.
WE EACH HAD OUR REASONS.
BUT WE WERE WRONG.
SOONER OR LATER, YOU'LL SEE.
YOU'LL NEED A LITTLE BIT OF THAT OLD MAGIC AGAIN.
AND YOU WON'T BE ABLE TO HELP YOURSELF.
COME BACK INSIDE.
WE CAN TALK ABOUT THIS.
WE CAN FORGIVE AND FORGET.
WE'RE FAMILY, AFTER ALL.
LIAR.

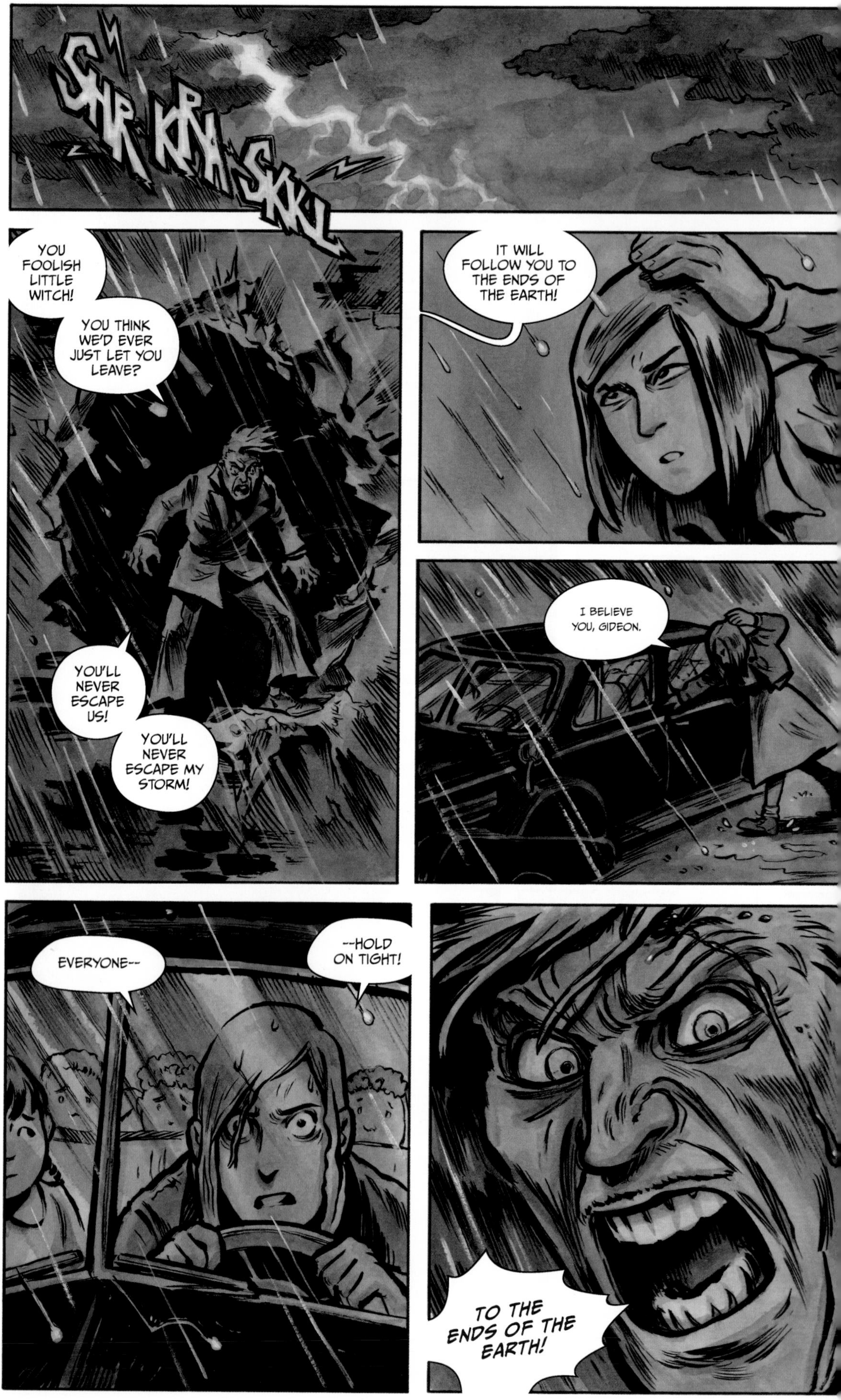
SHR-KRA-SKKL
YOU FOOLISH LITTLE WITCH!
YOU THINK WE'D EVER JUST LET YOU LEAVE?
YOU'LL NEVER ESCAPE US!
YOU'LL NEVER ESCAPE MY STORM!
IT WILL FOLLOW YOU TO THE ENDS OF THE EARTH!
I BELIEVE YOU, GIDEON.
EVERYONE--
--HOLD ON TIGHT!
TO THE ENDS OF THE EARTH!

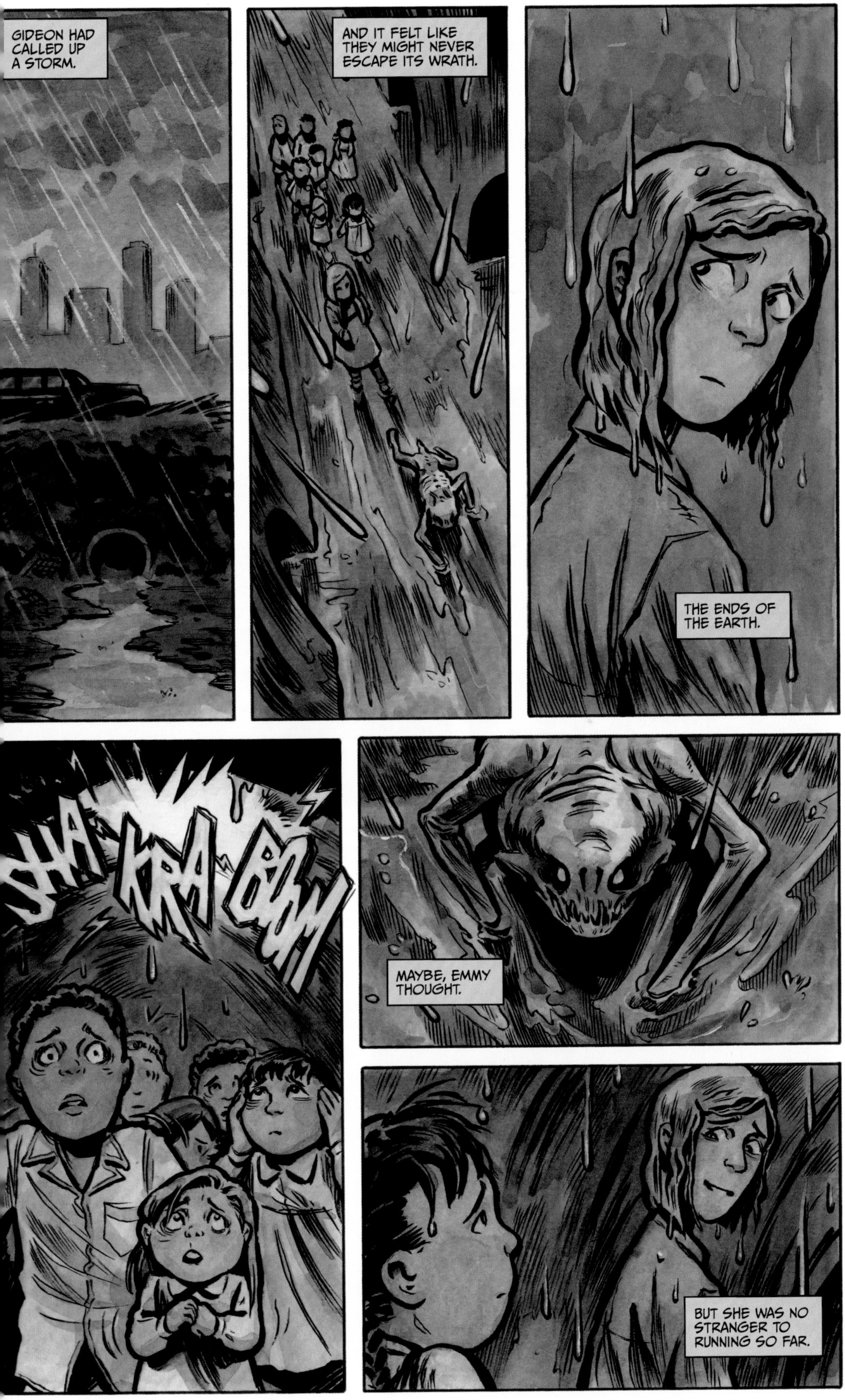
GIDEON HAD CALLED UP A STORM.
AND IT FELT LIKE THEY MIGHT NEVER ESCAPE ITS WRATH.
THE ENDS OF THE EARTH.
SHA KRA BOOM
MAYBE, EMMY THOUGHT.
BUT SHE WAS NO STRANGER TO RUNNING SO FAR.

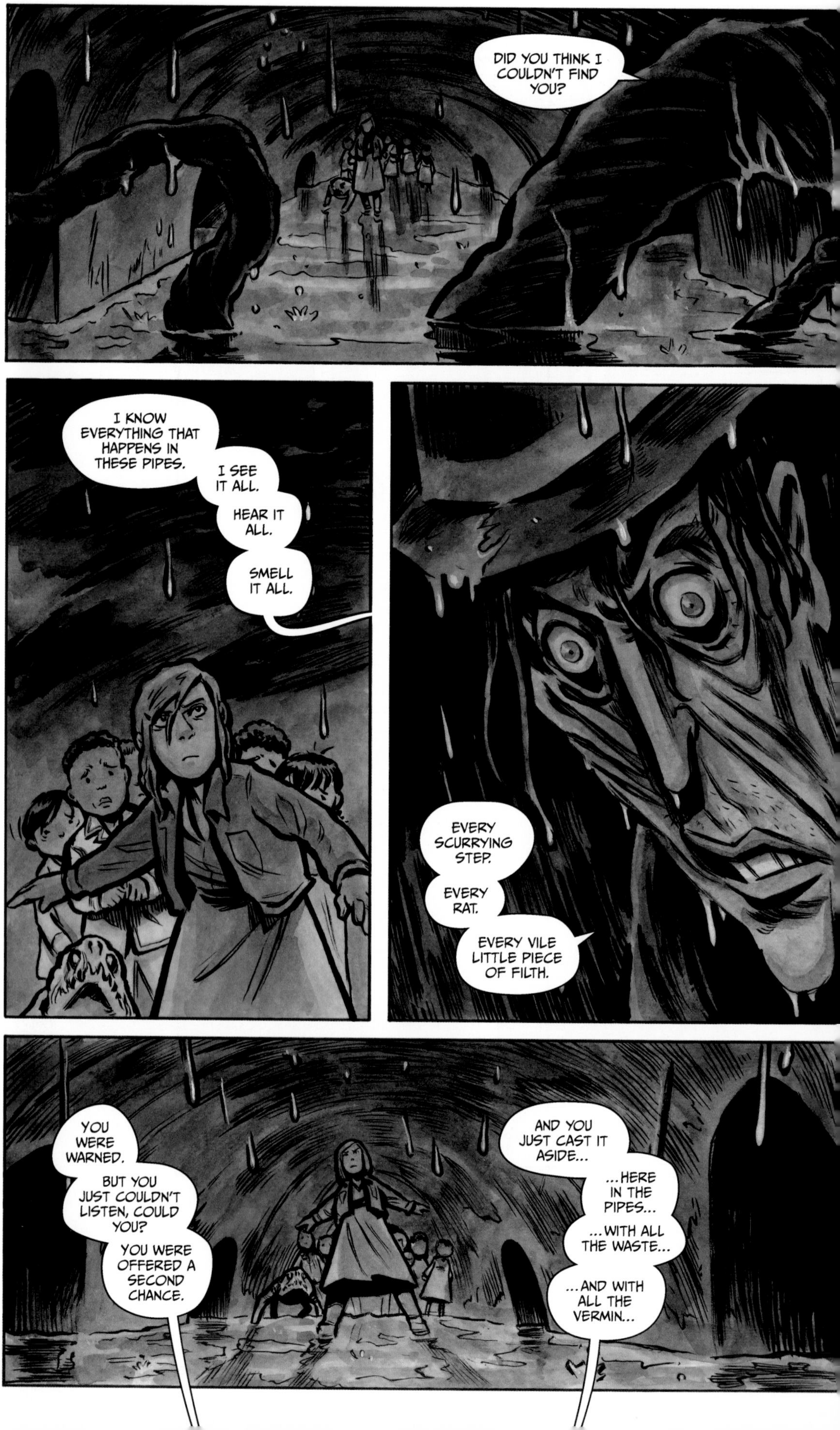
DID YOU THINK I COULDN'T FIND YOU?
I KNOW EVERYTHING THAT HAPPENS IN THESE PIPES.
I SEE IT ALL.
HEAR IT ALL.
SMELL IT ALL.
EVERY SCURRYING STEP.
EVERY RAT.
EVERY VILE LITTLE PIECE OF FILTH.
YOU WERE WARNED.
BUT YOU JUST COULDN'T LISTEN, COULD YOU?
YOU WERE OFFERED A SECOND CHANCE.
AND YOU JUST CAST IT ASIDE...
...HERE IN THE PIPES...
...WITH ALL THE WASTE...
...AND WITH ALL THE VERMIN...

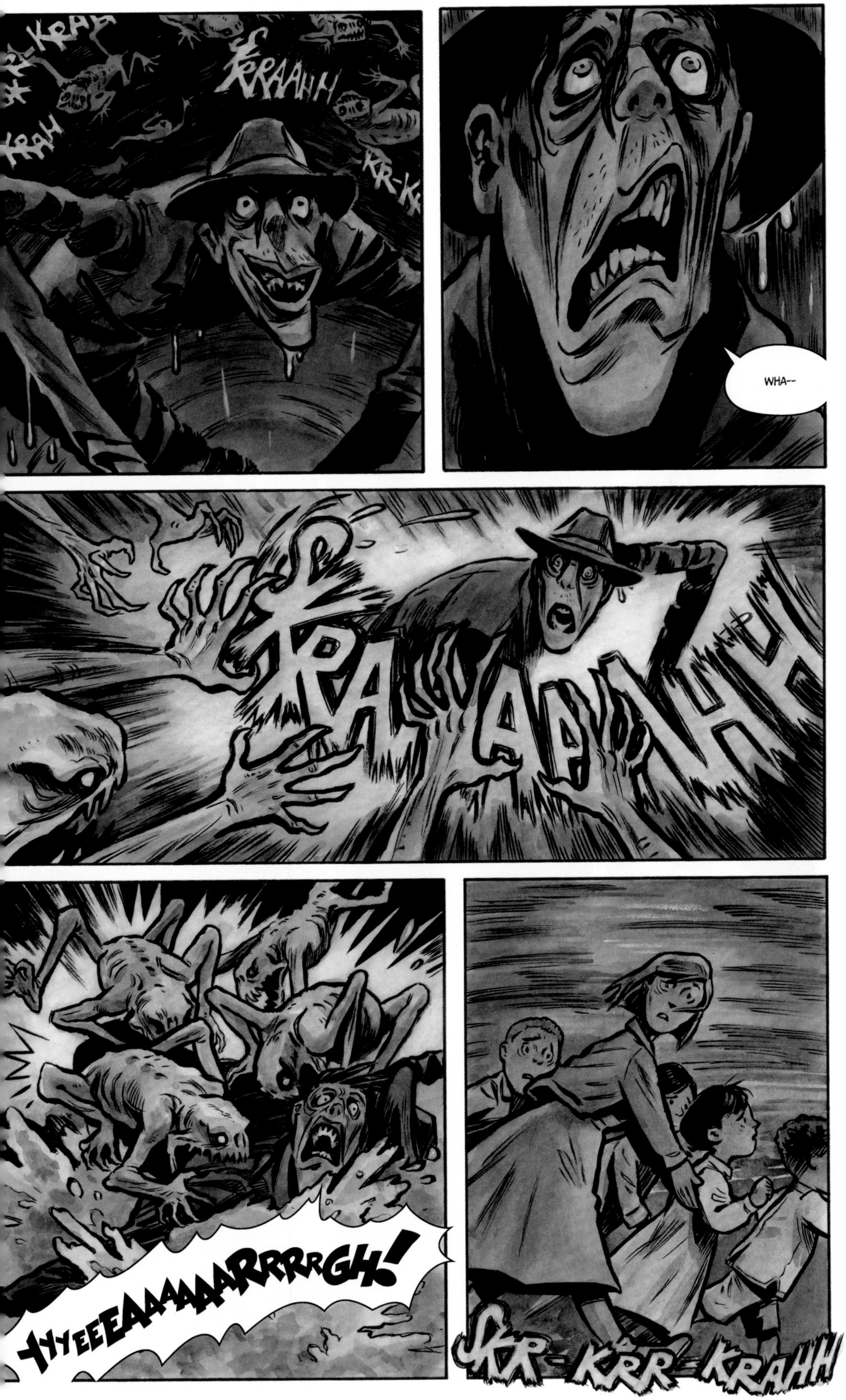
KRAAHH
KRAH
KR-K
WHA--
KRAAAAHH
YYYEEEAAAAAARRRRRGH!
SKR-KRR-KRAHH

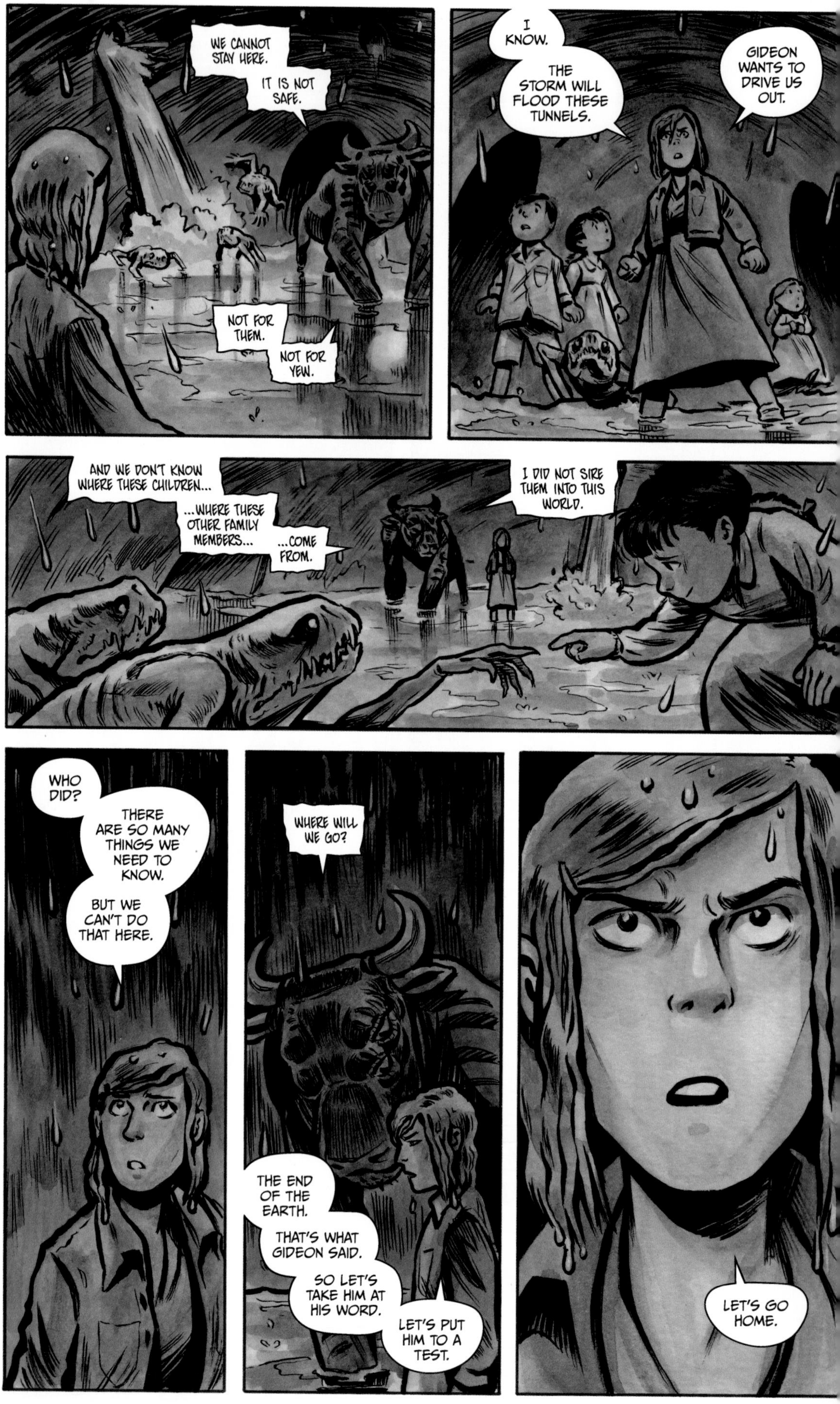
WE CANNOT STAY HERE.
IT IS NOT SAFE.
NOT FOR THEM.
NOT FOR YEW.
I KNOW.
THE STORM WILL FLOOD THESE TUNNELS.
GIDEON WANTS TO DRIVE US OUT.
AND WE DON'T KNOW WHERE THESE CHILDREN...
...WHERE THESE OTHER FAMILY MEMBERS...
...COME FROM.
I DID NOT SIRE THEM INTO THIS WORLD.
WHO DID?
THERE ARE SO MANY THINGS WE NEED TO KNOW.
BUT WE CAN'T DO THAT HERE.
WHERE WILL WE GO?
THE END OF THE EARTH.
THAT'S WHAT GIDEON SAID.
SO LET'S TAKE HIM AT HIS WORD.
LET'S PUT HIM TO A TEST.
LET'S GO HOME.

TALES FROM
HARROW
◄ SKETCHBOOK ►
COUNTY

DINER

FANCY
CLOTHES

**NOTES BY
EMILY SCHNALL**

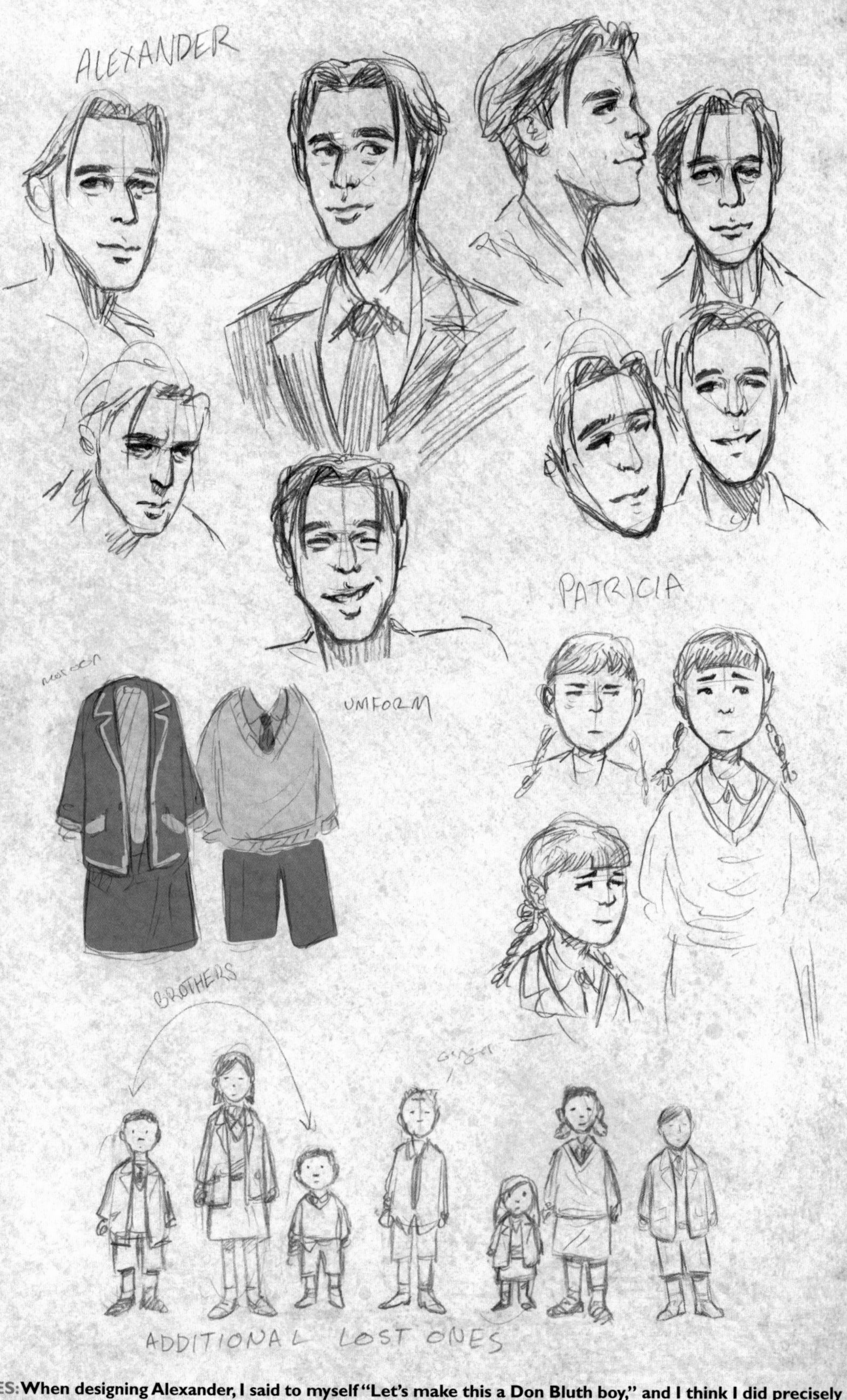
ALEXANDER
PATRICIA
UNIFORM
BROTHERS
ADDITIONAL LOST ONES

ES: When designing Alexander, I said to myself "Let's make this a Don Bluth boy," and I think I did precisely that. The Lost Ones took a bit more trial and error. It's so important to make each character feel unique enough when designing an ensemble group like this, but obviously they still have to feel cohesive. It was helpful using a uniform style that had a few optional layers to it; that gave me some leeway to differentiate them by their clothes.

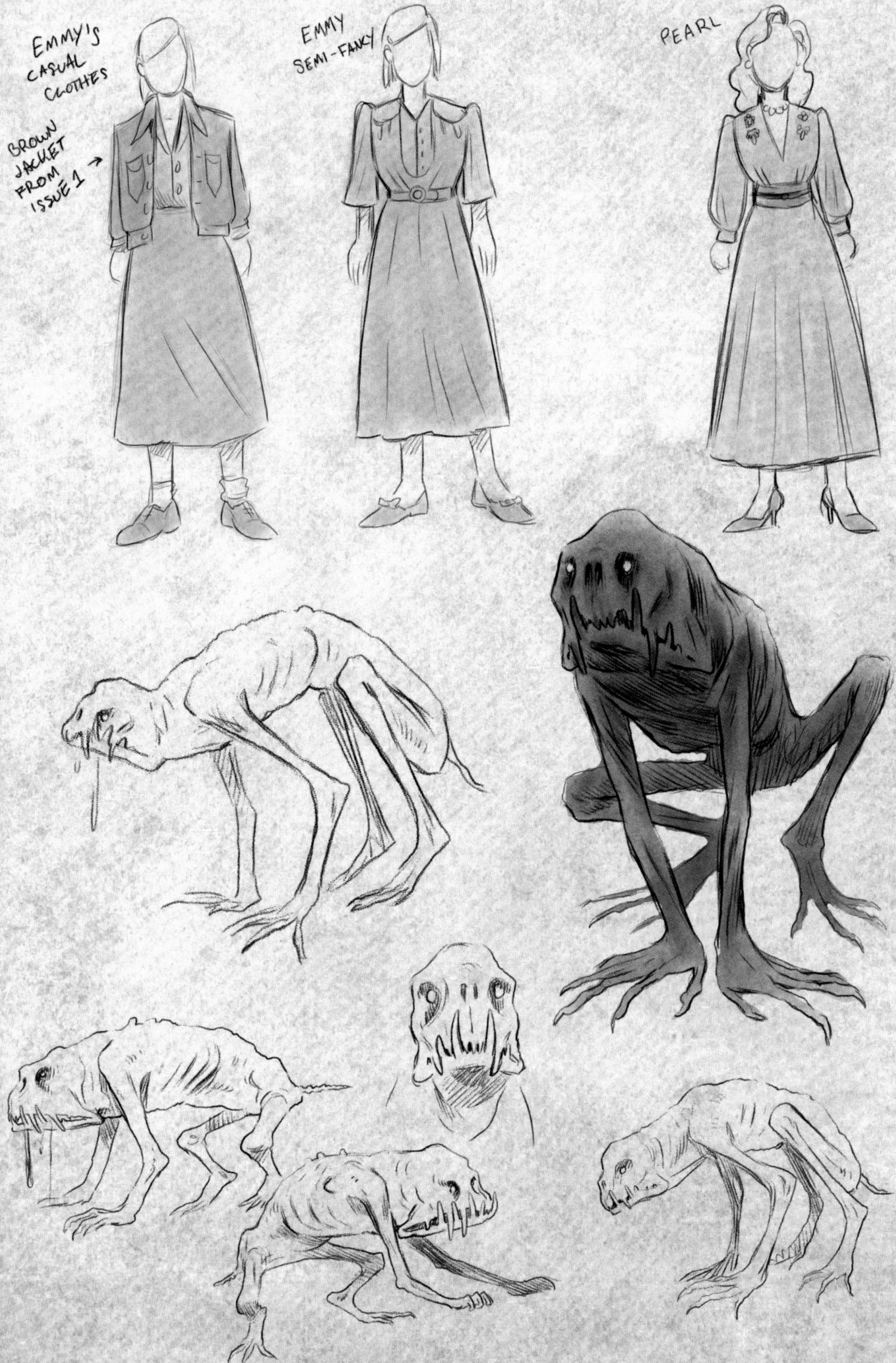
EMMY'S CASUAL CLOTHES
BROWN JACKET FROM ISSUE 1
EMMY SEMI-FANCY
PEARL

ES: **It's tough to design a goblinish little quadruped that doesn't look like a thousand other monsters we've seen before! For these guys I keyed in on having a big ol' head with just about no neck to give them a more unique silhouette. I used a viperfish as a starting point when thinking about their head shape—that led me to their lumpy, vaulted skull and wide mouth.**

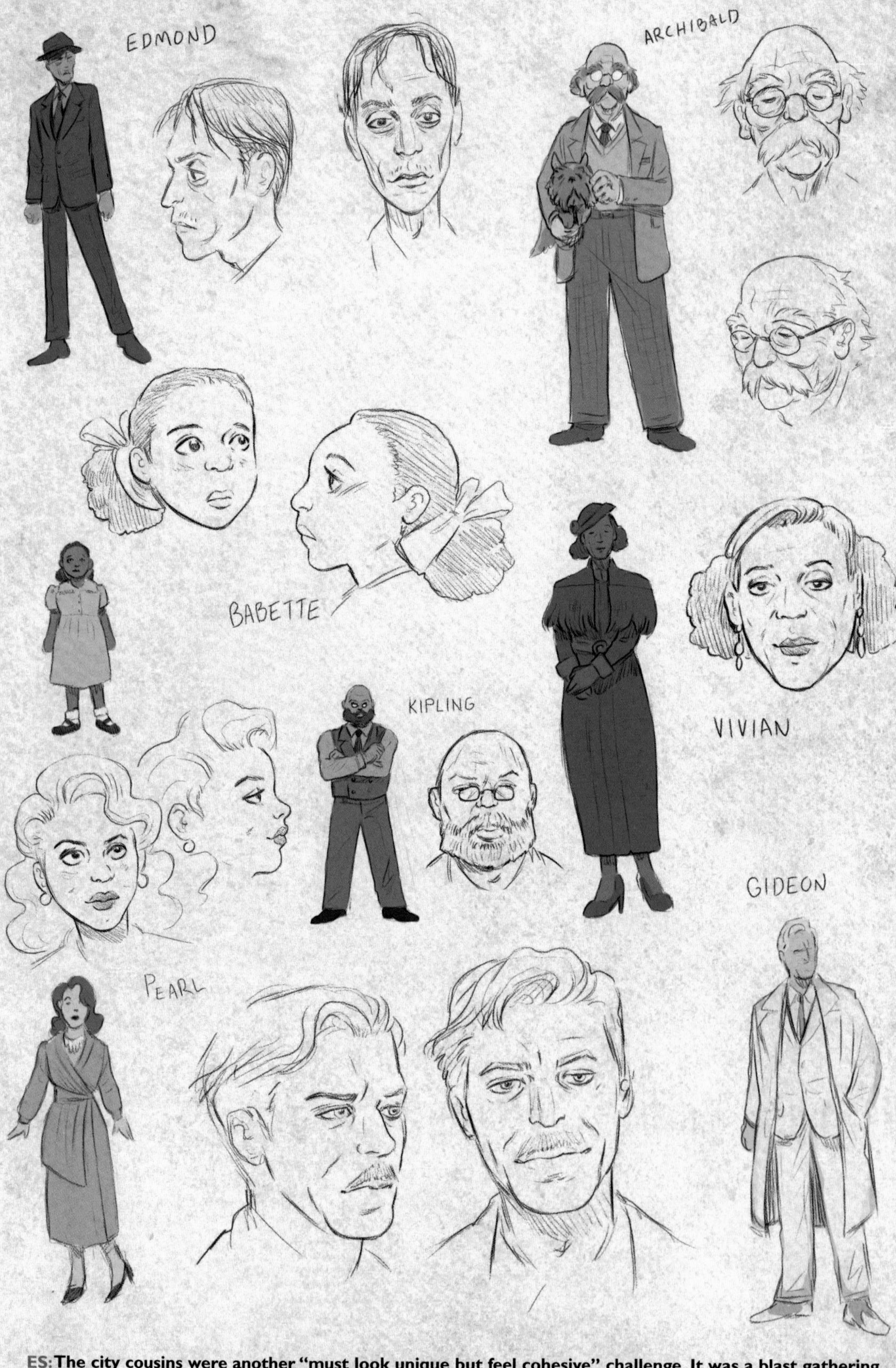
EDMOND
ARCHIBALD
BABETTE
KIPLING
VIVIAN
GIDEON
PEARL

ES: **The city cousins were another "must look unique but feel cohesive" challenge. It was a blast gathering reference for high-end 1940s fashion—I LOVE the real life inspiration for Vivian's dress, some insane hair thing. Edmund's design probably took me the longest; I needed to nail the right level of creepiness. Archibald was definitely the fastest; I knew immediately he had to carry around a miniature schnauzer and sport matching facial hair.**

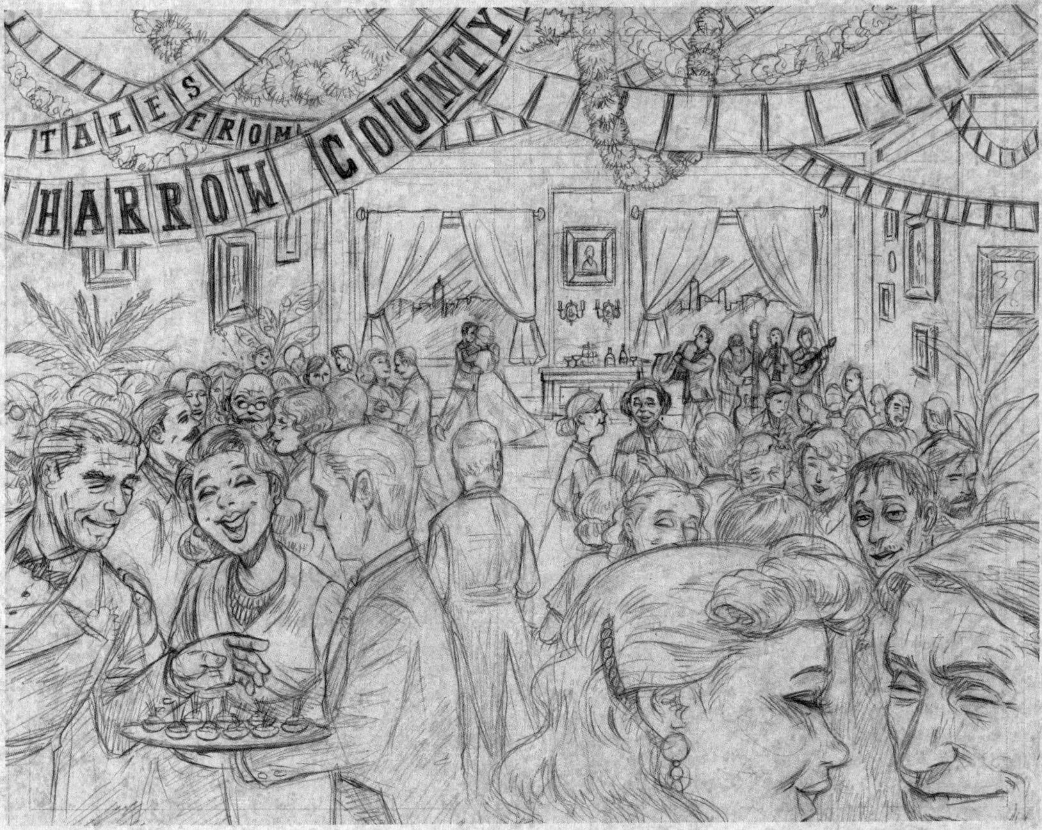
TALES FROM
HARROW COUNTY

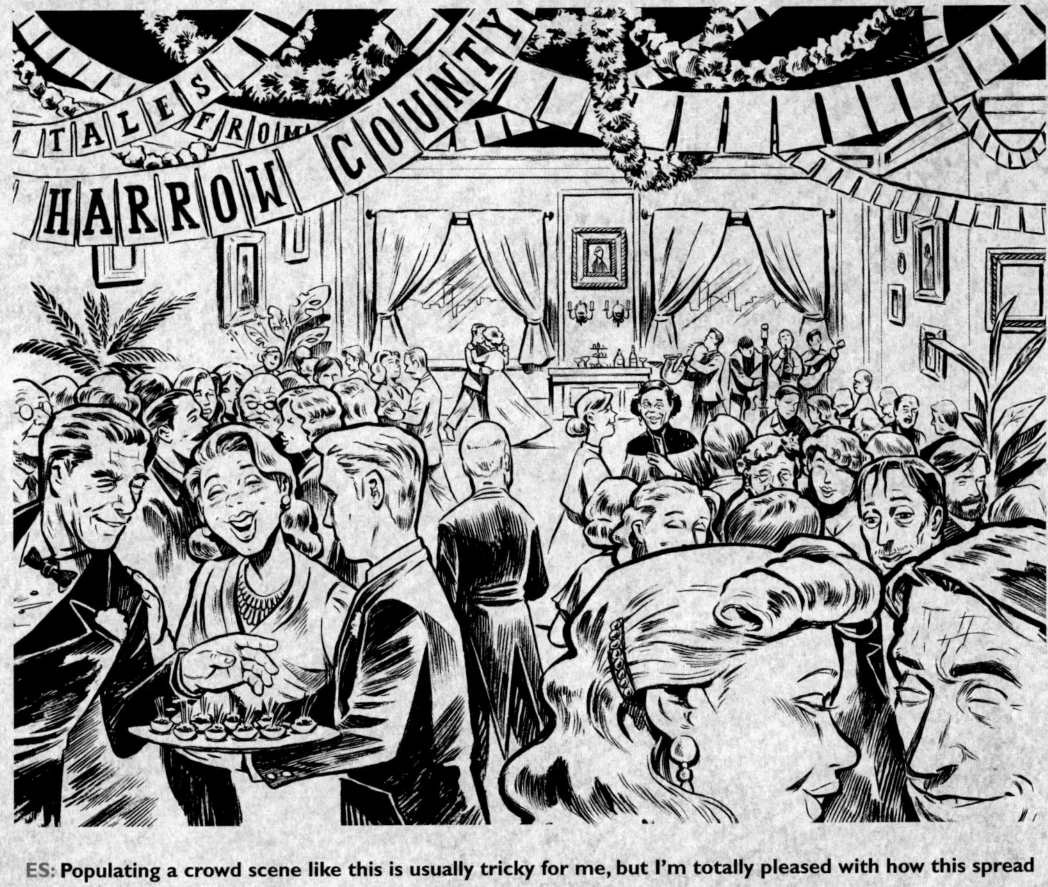
TALES FROM
HARROW COUNTY

ES: **Populating a crowd scene like this is usually tricky for me, but I'm totally pleased with how this spread turned out. I like that you can play Where's Waldo with the city cousins here!**

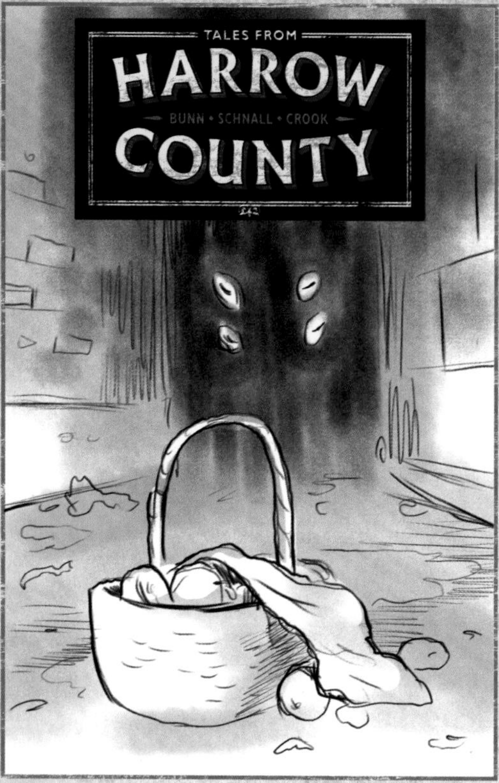
TALES FROM
HARROW
BUNN • SCHNALL • CROOK
COUNTY

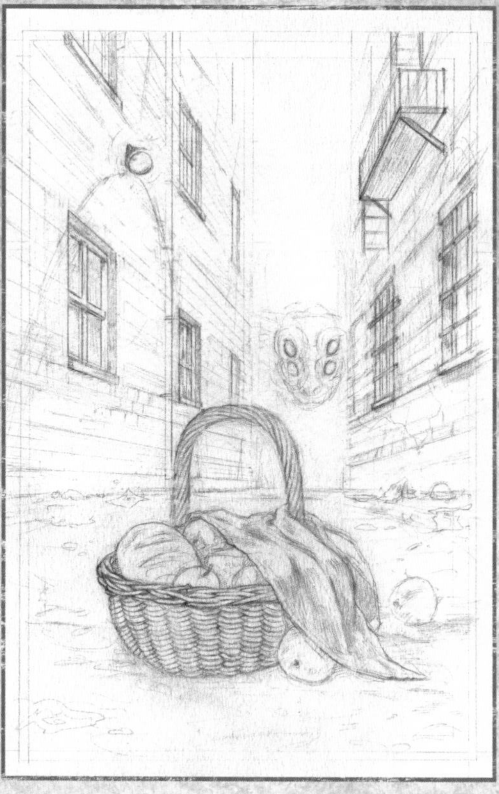

ES: In this cover I wanted to come right out of the gate screaming "CITY!!" because that's somewhere Harrow hasn't gone before. I thought I'd be a little coy about Emmy's return in this arc, but wanted to hint at another familiar face!

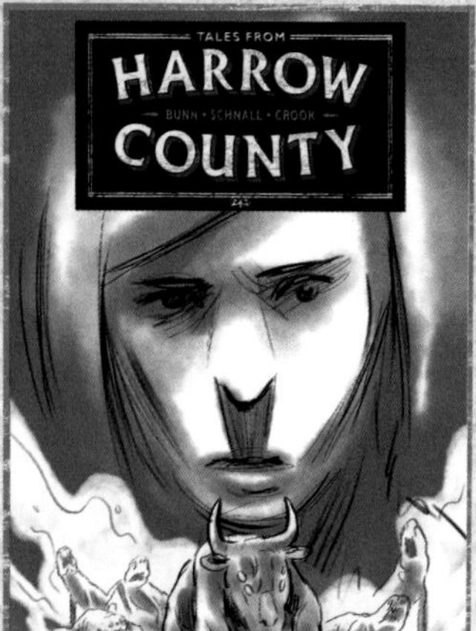
TALES FROM
HARROW
BUNN • SCHNALL • CROOK
COUNTY

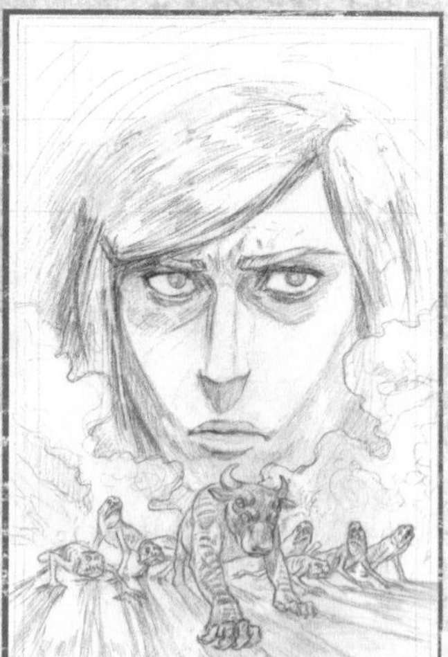

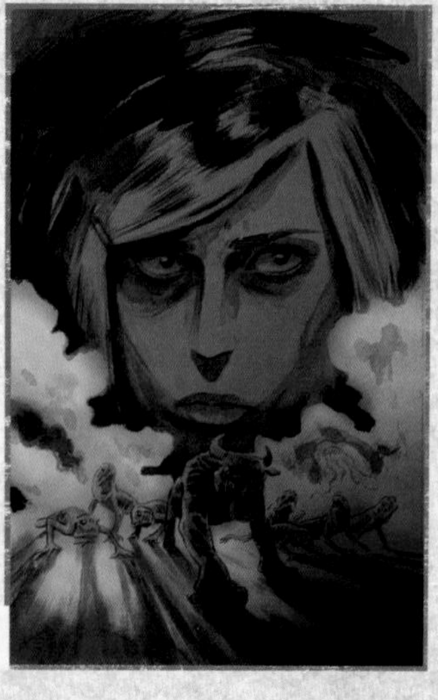

ES: I swear I made dozens of color palette mockups for this one and finally landed on this murky, night-time feel. I had some pretty loud pinks and purples I was experimenting with, but I think this one better reflected the quiet, brooding feeling I was going for here.

For the all covers in this arc, I followed a process of slowly building up ink washes and layers of watercolor and gouache. I find I can get a nice variety of textures with a combo of waterproof ink plus those paints, because the ink layers stay crisp and the colors can get continually worked and pushed around as the art is built up.

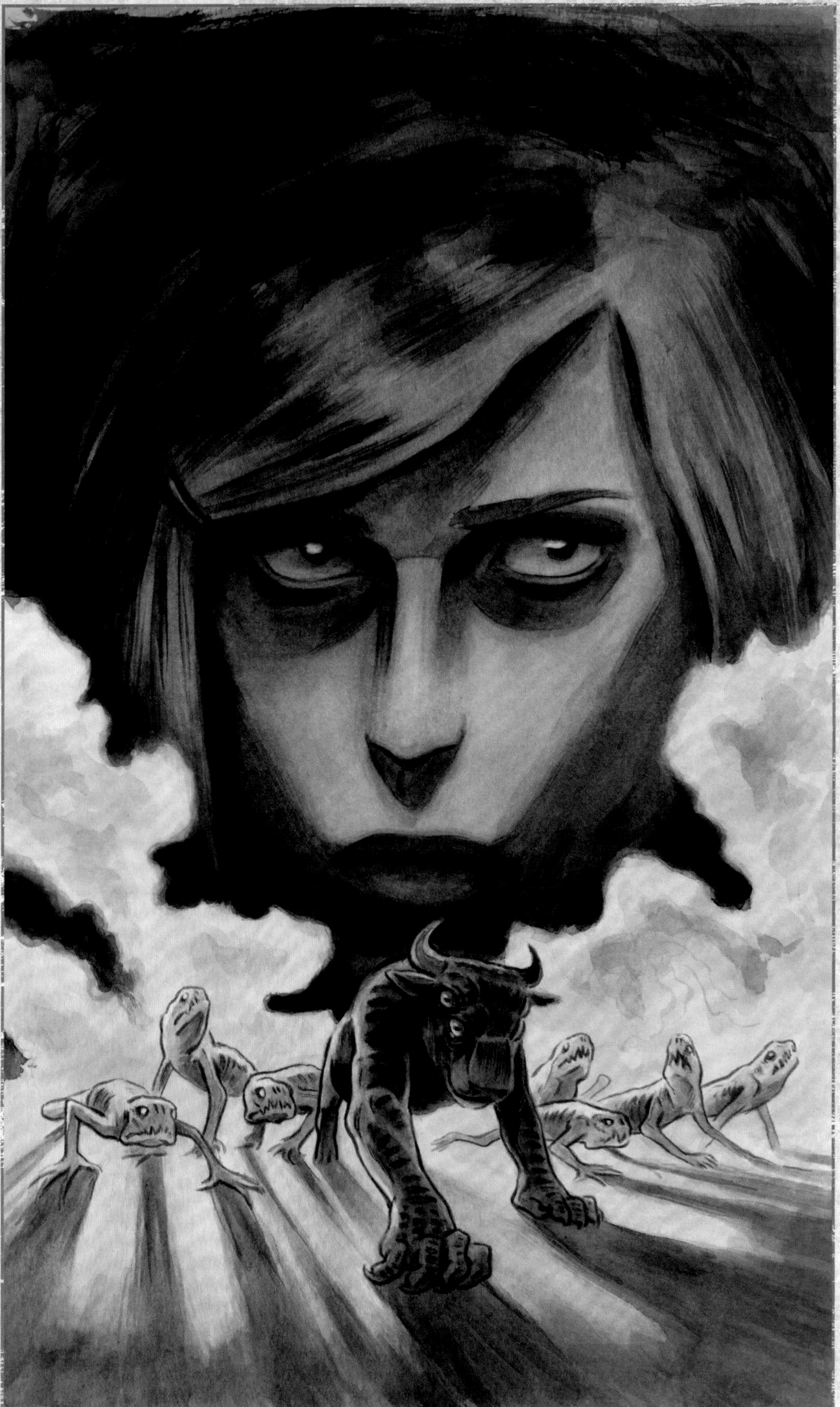

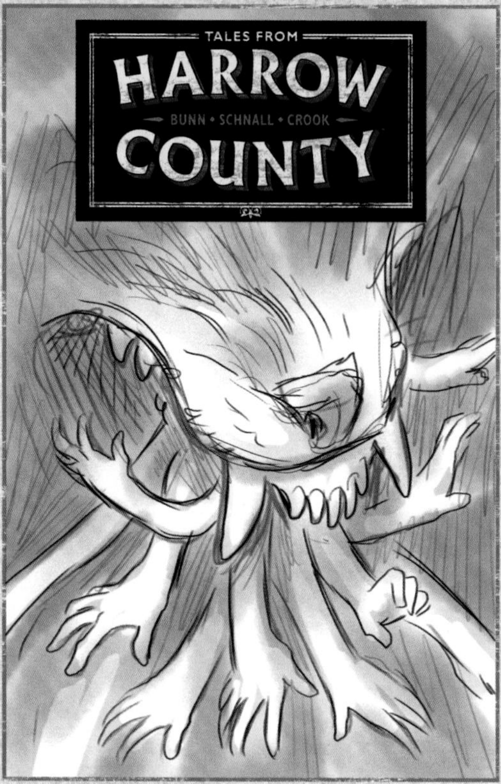
TALES FROM
HARROW
BUNN • SCHNALL • CROOK
COUNTY

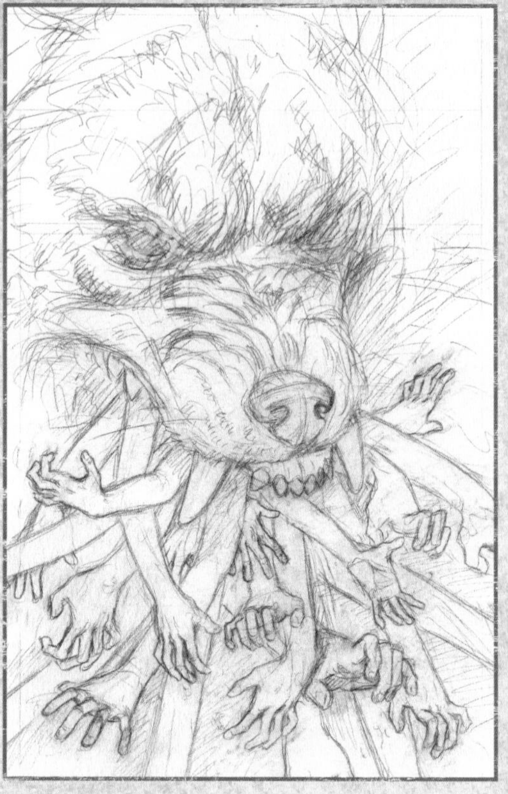

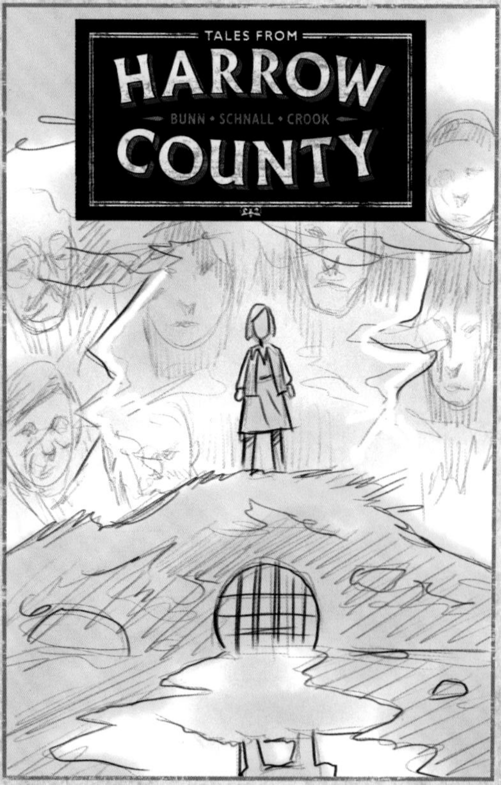
TALES FROM
HARROW
BUNN • SCHNALL • CROOK
COUNTY

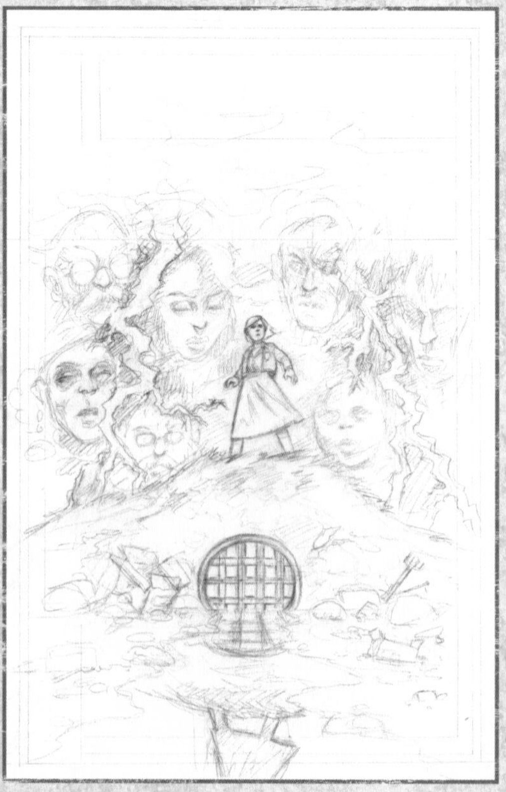

ES: **In my heart of hearts, I always want to be making weird stuff like the issue #3 cover—I should really unleash the beast and do more! The issue #4 cover was a fun one to work on, painting all those loose cloud faces. I think it was Tyler who suggested giving a bit more motion to Emmy's stance after the thumbnail, that really made all the difference!**

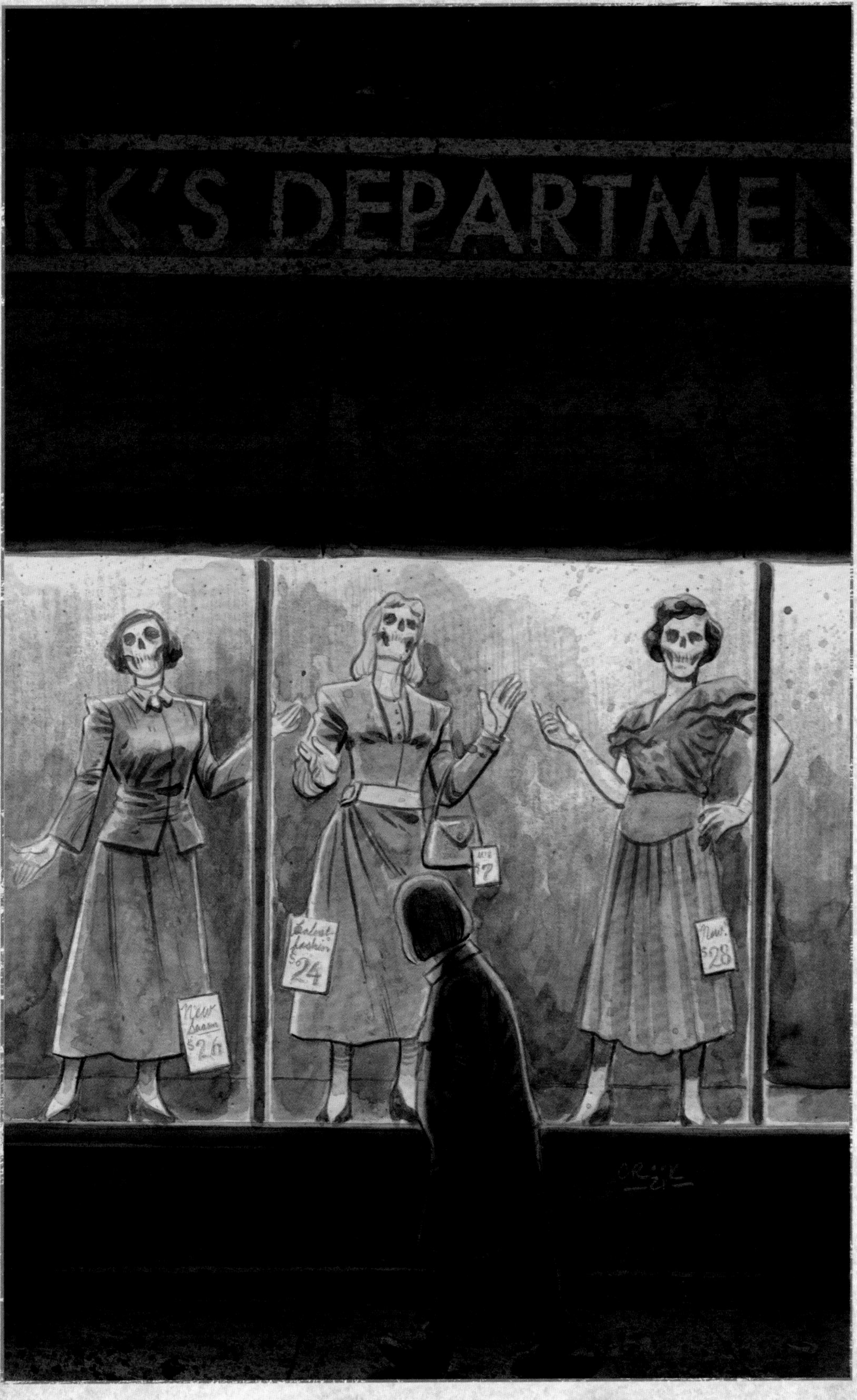
RK'S DEPARTMEN
New Season $26
Latest fashion $24
$7
New $28

ISSUE #1 COVER VARIANT ARTWORK BY
TYLER CROOK

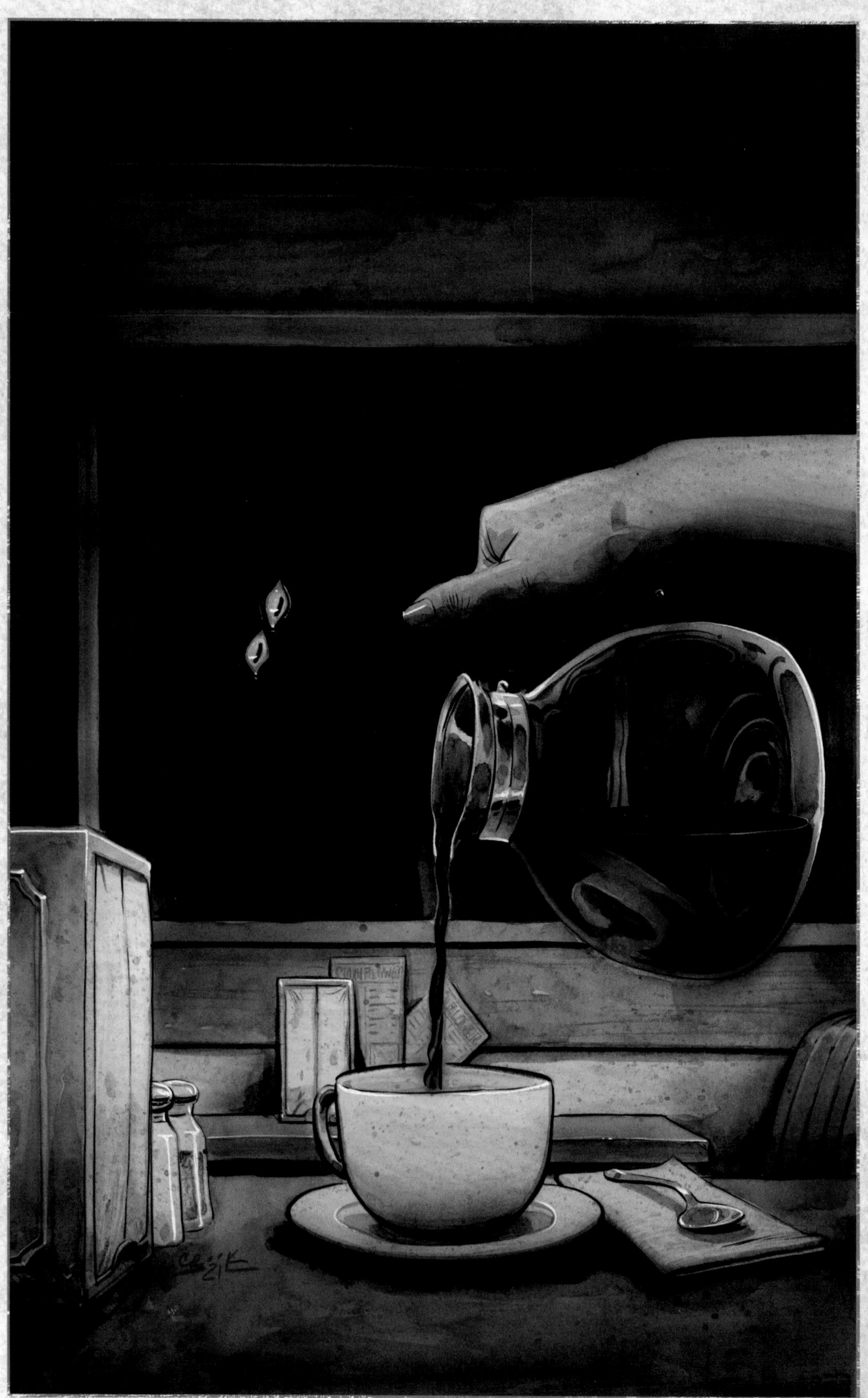

ISSUE #2 COVER VARIANT ARTWORK BY

TYLER CROOK

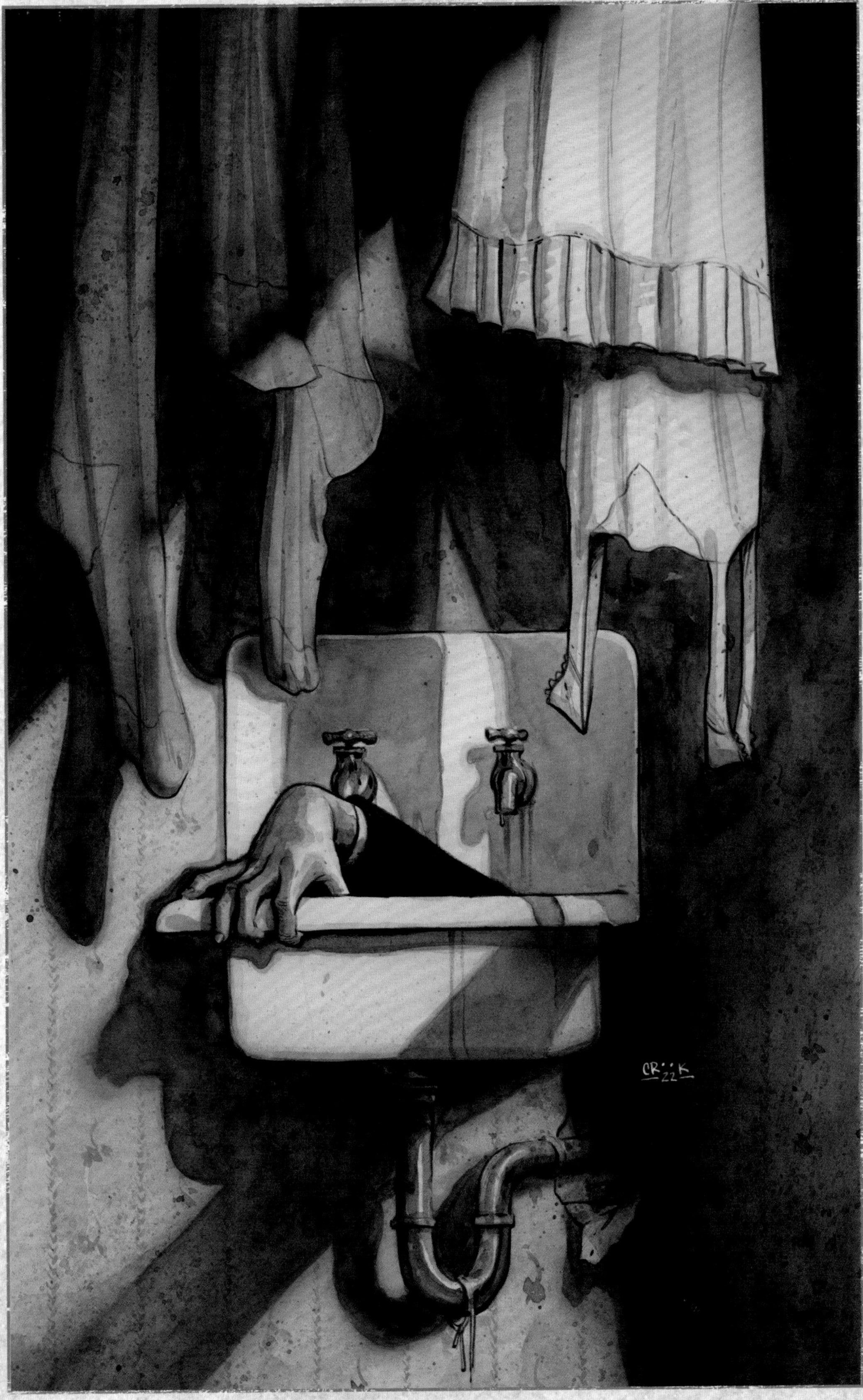
CR'22K

ISSUE #3 COVER VARIANT ARTWORK BY
TYLER CROOK

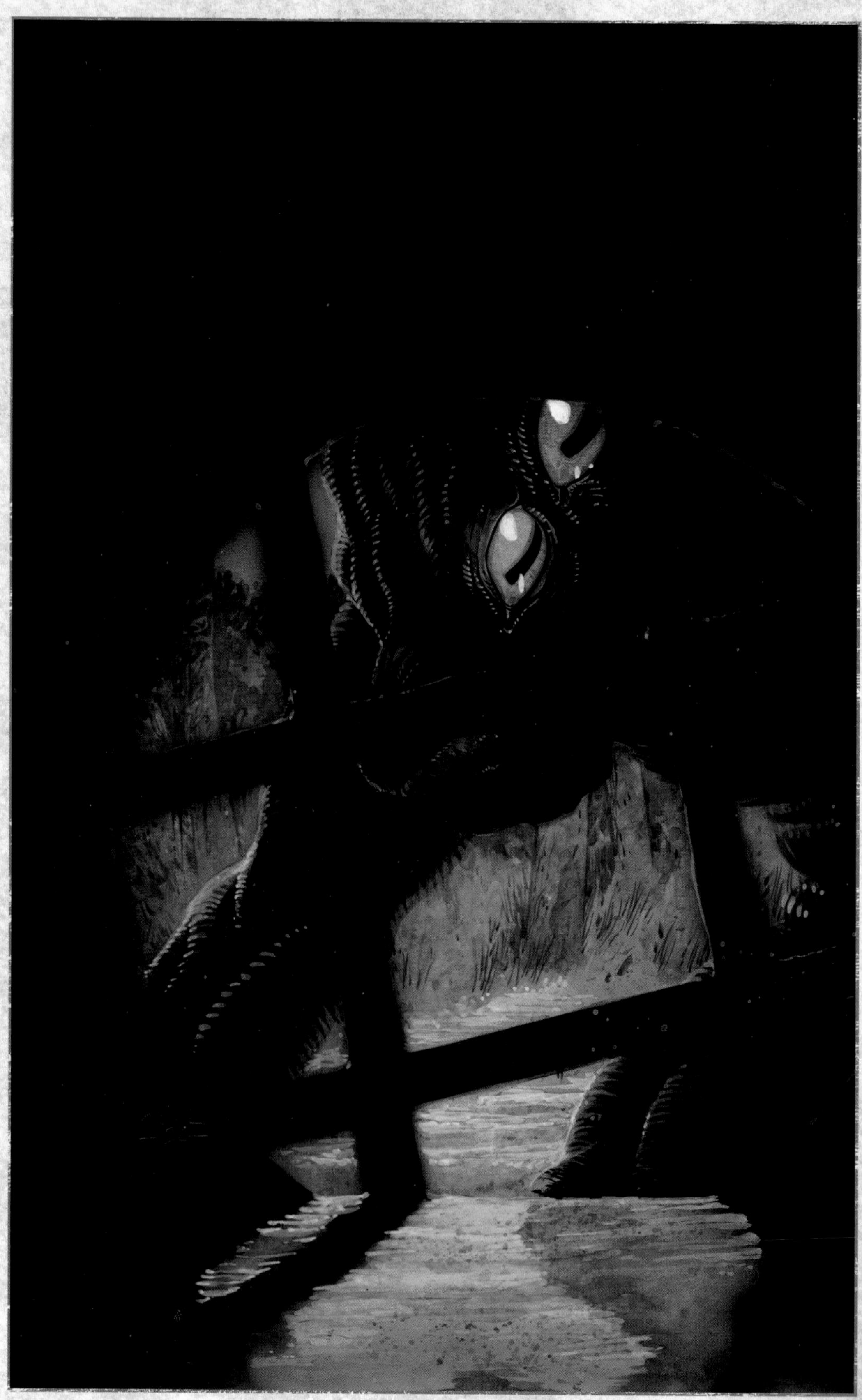

ISSUE #4 COVER VARIANT ARTWORK BY
TYLER CROOK

"CROOK FINDS BEAUTY IN SQUALOR AND MISERY; HIS PANELS ARE BRILLIANTLY COMPOSED . . . HIS ARTWORK REMAINS RADIANT EVEN WHEN COVERING THE DARKER SIDE OF LIFE."

—BIG COMIC PAGE

MORE TITLES FROM

TYLER CROOK, CULLEN BUNN,

AND DARK HORSE

HARROW COUNTY

VOLUME 1: COUNTLESS HAINTS
Tyler Crook and Cullen Bunn
ISBN 978-1-61655-780-5 | $14.99

VOLUME 2: TWICE TOLD
Tyler Crook and Cullen Bunn
ISBN 978-1-61655-900-7 | $17.99

VOLUME 3: SNAKE DOCTOR
Tyler Crook and Cullen Bunn with Carla Speed McNeil and Hannah Christenson
ISBN 978-1-50670-071-7 | $17.99

VOLUME 4: FAMILY TREE
Tyler Crook and Cullen Bunn
ISBN 978-1-50670-141-7 | $17.99

VOLUME 5: ABANDONED
Tyler Crook and Cullen Bunn with Carla Speed McNeil
ISBN 978-1-50670-190-5 | $17.99

VOLUME 6: HEDGE MAGIC
Tyler Crook and Cullen Bunn

VOLUME 7: DARK TIMES A'COMING
Tyler Crook and Cullen Bunn
ISBN 978-1-50670-397-8 | $17.99

VOLUME 8: DONE COME BACK
Tyler Crook and Cullen Bunn
ISBN 978-1-50670-663-4 | $17.99

HARROW COUNTY OMNIBUS

VOLUME 1
ISBN 978-1-50671-991-7 | $29.99

VOLUME 2
ISBN 978-1-50671-992-4 | $29.99

HARROW COUNTY LIBRARY EDITION

Tyler Crook, Cullen Bunn, Carla Speed McNeil, and Jenn Manley Lee

VOLUME 1
ISBN 978-1-50671-064-8 | $39.99

VOLUME 2
ISBN 978-1-50671-065-5 | $39.99

VOLUME 3
ISBN 978-1-50671-066-2 | $39.99

VOLUME 4
ISBN 978-1-50671-067-9 | $39.99

TALES FROM HARROW COUNTY

VOLUME 1: DEATH'S CHOIR
Tyler Crook, Cullen Bunn, and Naomi Franquiz
ISBN 978-1-50671-681-7 | $17.99

VOLUME 2: FAIR FOLK
Tyler Crook, Cullen Bunn, and Emily Schnall
ISBN 978-1-50672-261-0 | $19.99

VOLUME 3: LOST ONES
Cullen Bunn, Tyler Crook, and Emily Schnall
ISBN 978-1-50672-995-4 | $19.99

B.P.R.D. HELL ON EARTH

THE RETURN OF THE MASTER
Tyler Crook with Mignola and Arcudi
ISBN 978-1-61655-193-3 | $19.99

THE DEVIL'S ENGINE AND THE LONG DEATH
Tyler Crook with James Harren, Mignola, and Arcudi
ISBN 978-1-59582-981-8 | $19.99

RUSSIA
Tyler Crook with Duncan Fegredo, Mignola, and Arcudi
ISBN 978-1-59582-946-7 | $19.99

GODS AND MONSTERS
Tyler Crook with Guy Davis, Mignola, and Arcudi
ISBN 978-1-59582-822-4 | $19.99

THE DEVIL'S WINGS
Tyler Crook with Laurence Campbell, Joe Querio, Mignola, and Arcudi
ISBN 978-1-61655-617-4 | $19.99

LAKE OF FIRE
Tyler Crook with Mignola and Arcudi
ISBN 978-1-61655-402-6 | $19.99

DEATH FOLLOWS

Cullen Bunn with A. C. Zamudio and Carlos Nicolas Zamudio
ISBN 978-1-61655-951-9 | $17.99

BAD BLOOD

Tyler Crook with Jonathan Maberry
ISBN 978-1-61655-496-5 | $17.99

WITCHFINDER: THE MYSTERIES OF UNLAND

Tyler Crook with Kim Newman, Maura McHugh, and Mike Mignola
ISBN 978-1-61655-630-3 | $19.99

THE STONE KING

Kel McDonald and Tyler Crook
ISBN 978-1-50672-448-5 | $19.99

MANOR BLACK

VOLUME 1
Tyler Crook, Cullen Bunn, and Brian Hurtt
ISBN 978-1-50671-201-7 | $19.99

VOLUME 2: FIRE IN THE BLOOD
Cullen Bunn, Tyler Crook, and Brian Hurtt
ISBN 978-1-50671-973-3 | $19.99

DARK HORSE BOOKS

AVAILABLE AT YOUR LOCAL COMICS SHOP OR BOOKSTORE! To find a comics shop in your area, visit comicshoplocator.com
For more information or to order direct, visit DarkHorse.com